RADICALS

MEREDITH BURGMANN is a former academic who also served as a (Labor) president of the NSW Upper House. She is the co-author, with Verity Burgmann, of *Green Bans, Red Union: The saving of a city*, which was reissued twenty years after its original 1998 publication. Meredith has also authored books on ASIO and misogyny. She is the founder of the Ernie Awards for Sexism. On retirement from parliament, she was elected president of the Australian Council for International Development. Meredith is a Sydney Swans ambassador.

NADIA WHEATLEY is an Australian writer whose published works include picture books, novels, biography, memoir and history. *Five Times Dizzy* (1982) was hailed as Australia's first multicultural book for children. Other social and political issues explored in her work include conservation, unemployment, refugees and learning from Country. Among her numerous awards is the NSW Premier's History Award (2002) for *The Life and Myth of Charmian Clift*. Nadia's most recent book is the memoir *Her Mother's Daughter* (2018).

Just like the Sixties, this book is a mesmerising kaleidoscope of unforgettable characters doing brave things, inventing new ways to talk and act and express themselves and, above all, reinventing politics as their radicalised generation went to work to banish injustices like racism, sexism, conscription and, looming over everything else, the Vietnam War.
We also are treated to their diverse personal stories, the family ties many of them needed to rebel against, and the inventing of new ways of living that still guide them today.

Anne Summers – author of Australian feminist bible
Damned Whores and God's Police

The old saying, if you remember the Sixties you weren't there — *Not True*! An exciting time of change that shaped Australia and the world for decades to come, perhaps forever. Vietnam, women's rights, land rights, Springboks, Gove, Bjelke-Petersen, Black Power, flower power, Freedom Riders, abortion rights and socialism – the list goes on.
Thank you, Radicals – you made a better place for us.

Linda Burney – First Nations trailblazer

During the Sixties we were tired of suppressing our discontent as we lived in our inward-looking society. We wanted a forward-thinking, dynamic world, one that cared about ALL its people. Then along came our magnificent RADICALS, and of course, GOUGH!
Aah, the memories. What a buzz!

Patricia Amphlett (Little Patty) –
epitomises the 'It's Time' excitement

To achieve the change we desperately need now, it is crucial to look back on how we got the change we take for granted.

Craig Reucassel – saving the planet today

*To all our comrades who were part of the radical Sixties.
Despite our differences, we all fought for a better world.
Particularly we remember those who have died
– some of them far too early.*

RADICALS
REMEMBERING THE SIXTIES

Meredith Burgmann
& Nadia Wheatley

NEWSOUTH

A NewSouth book

Published by
NewSouth Publishing
University of New South Wales Press Ltd
University of New South Wales
Sydney NSW 2052
AUSTRALIA
newsouthpublishing.com

© Meredith Burgmann and Nadia Wheatley 2021
First published 2021

10 9 8 7 6 5 4 3 2 1

This book is copyright. Apart from any fair dealing for the purpose of private study, research, criticism or review, as permitted under the *Copyright Act*, no part of this book may be reproduced by any process without written permission. Inquiries should be addressed to the publisher.

ISBN   9781742235899 (paperback)
          9781742245133 (ebook)
          9781742249650 (ePDF)

A catalogue record for this book is available from the National Library of Australia

Internal design Josephine Pajor-Markus
Cover design Debra Bilson
Cover image Spiro Agnew visit to Australia. Protest against the Vietnam War, 1970. National Archives of Australia

All reasonable efforts were taken to obtain permission to use copyright material reproduced in this book, but in some cases copyright could not be traced. The authors welcome information in this regard.

The Woodstock generation will go to its grave with a sense that it is special. And indeed, even those of us who weren't invited to the party must concede that there was something unique about the Sixties.

Timothy Noah, 'The Big Massage',
Washington Monthly, February 1984

Contents

Introduction	xi
Meredith Burgmann: That glorious time to be alive	1
Nadia Wheatley: The girl who threw the tomato	16
Gary Foley: Fighting for truth, justice and the Aboriginal way	33
Geoffrey Robertson: The right side of history	52
Margret RoadKnight: Troubadour	70
Albert Langer (Arthur Dent): Hardened apparatchik	83
David Marr: Taking on the rich and powerful	102
Margaret Reynolds: Born feminist	118
Brian Laver: Fighting fascism	138
Bronwyn Penrith: Miracle child	156
Ellis D Fogg (Roger Foley): I hate being bored	171
Peter Duncan: Activism works ... and it works in parliament	187
Vivienne Binns: Searching for Truth	205
Gary Williams: A lot of stuff just happens ...	223
Peter Batchelor: Don't mourn but organise	242
Helen Voysey: The kid from the sticks	258
John Derum: We were mad 'Milligan anarchic'	275
Robbie Swan: Fun along the way	290
Jozefa Sobski: Opening doors to other worlds	306
Peter Manning: Taking a stand	324

Conclusion	340
Biographies	353
References	379
Acknowledgments	384
Index	386

Introduction

Meredith Burgmann and Nadia Wheatley

Saturday 6 June 2020. 1.30 pm.

We stand in Sydney's Town Hall Square, two women in our seventies, holding handwritten placards. Meredith's says, '*Remember John Pat. 1966–1984*'. Nadia's says, '*Solidarity! Black Lives Matter*'.

We have stood here before, many a time, for a variety of campaigns and causes. But this time is a bit different. Mindful of the pandemic, we are both wearing face masks, and we are doing our best to stand a metre-and-a-half from other protestors. After weeks of lockdown, it feels surreal to be outdoors and in a crowd, but the oddest thing is that, as we look at the faces (also mostly masked) around us, we see no one whom we know. Indeed, there seems to be no one else here over the age of forty. We find it a cause for optimism that our generation of Sixties radicals is not irreplaceable.

From the microphone at the top of the steps, speeches crackle, interspersed by periodic bouts of chanting. Around us, a sea of red, black and yellow surges and swirls.

The recent death in the United States of George Floyd and the subsequent protests by the Black Lives Matter movement have given a new edge to the Aboriginal campaign against deaths in custody, which has been running since the 1980s. Signs around us bear the number 432: the tally of Indigenous Australians who have died in custody since the 1991 Royal Commission into Aboriginal Deaths in Custody. None of those deaths has led to a single conviction of any officer of the law.

'*Too many coppers, not enough justice!*' the chant rises.

The Law is out in force today, and it looks as if violence (not to mention a public health problem) could well result from the way police are acting. Barricades are preventing social distancing by squashing people close together.

'Just like the old days', we agree, as we survey the ranks of uniforms.

But what was it that originally took the two of us onto the streets?

ONE OF THE BEST-KNOWN SLOGANS OF THE SIXTIES IS THE claim that '*The personal is political*'. Although no one is sure who first said this, nevertheless it expresses the spirit of the time.

Of course, in any era, people bring their personal history to their political life, but in this book we relate the personal stories of a number of people from our generation who – either in reaction to a particular Sixties issue or simply in response to the *zeitgeist* – rejected the political views and values of their family, school, church and class. These radical about-turns were often accompanied by epiphanies, awakenings, revelations and other such 'aha' moments.

Five decades on, our society seems to have moved so far from that hopeful and innocent era that even using the

Introduction

word 'radical' may need a bit of explanation. In the current political climate, the term has come to be associated with the kind of people who go off to fight for ISIS or who occasionally run amok in their homeland. It is also used for members of the alt-Right.

To describe such racists and warmongers as radicals is an affront to those of us who became radicals in the Sixties and who continue to see ourselves as radicals to this day. For us, radicalism means openness and freedom. It means the particular kind of grassroots organisation and New Left ideology that arose in opposition to the hierarchical structures and dogmatism of the Old Left. And it means fun, not fundamentalism.

It was this that the two of us were discussing a few years ago over dinner, when we came up with the idea of a book about the Sixties. After all, both our lives had been transformed over a short period in 1968, initially through our involvement in the anti-Vietnam movement, but soon through taking part in other campaigns.

To outsiders, witnessing our sudden donning of National Liberation Front badges and our increasingly frequent appearances at the Central Court in Liverpool Street, we probably seemed surprising radicals. Both of us were from middle-class and politically conservative backgrounds. Both of us had been educated at single-sex private schools. Both of us were raised in the dreary puritanism of Sydney Anglicanism. But – as we relate in our own accounts in this book – there was a great difference, too, in our respective backstories.

Apart from any personal issues we might have brought to our activism, for both of us – as for all the comrades whose stories we tell here – the catalyst for our radicalisation was the shared experience of growing up in the political circumstances of Australia in the 1950s. Certainly, the ferment of the Sixties was an international phenomenon, and for young radicals from Berlin to Berkeley it represented some sort of reaction to a Cold War childhood. But in this country, there was something in particular to drive us wild.

This was a person known to his supporters as 'Ming' and to his class enemies as 'Pig Iron Bob'. Elected in 1949 to head the first Coalition government of the Liberal and Country parties, Prime Minister Robert Gordon Menzies cast a long shadow over the childhood and adolescence of our post-war generation.

For a twenty-year-old Australian today, who has lived through seven prime ministers, it would be impossible to imagine how stultifying it was to grow up under a single one – and a patriarchal, conservative one at that. For many of our contemporaries, the snowy-haired father of the nation was conflated with the father who was forever telling them to turn that flaming rock-and-roll music down, and get a haircut while they were at it!

It is easy to point to the Menzies government's support for policies such as White Australia and Assimilation, not to mention the military commitment in Vietnam, but just as bad was the cultural repression. Growing up behind the white picket fence of Menzies' Australia was *deadly boring*.

To our parents, however, this social and political stasis seemed wonderfully safe. They had suffered the double-whammy of coming of age through the Great Depression and the Second World War. Unlike their generation, we had shoes on our feet, food on our plates, fillings in our teeth, peace in our time (kind of), and most of all – we had education! What did we have to grumble about?

Introduction

Nothing – and everything!

Often unable even to say what was wrong, we knew we had to make our escape, using whatever resources we had.

Whereas Millennials can express their views by way of Twitter, TikTok and Instagram, most of us did not even have what we called 'a telephone' (now known as a landline) in our cockroach-infested share houses and bed-sits. If we had a message too long to graffiti onto a wall, we had to type it onto a wax stencil, and then crank out inky copies on a duplicating machine.

Or we could go onto the streets and seize front-page headlines by getting bashed and arrested by police. That was social media, in the Sixties.

BUT *WHEN* WERE THE SIXTIES?

A mood and a movement, more than a specific slice of time, the decade is defined in this book as roughly spanning the years between 1965 and 1975.

In accordance with this chronology, the start of our Sixties is marked by a change that occurred within the anti-Vietnam movement after the introduction of conscription in November 1964 – a change that over the next few years brought both a broadening of support and an intensification of activism. The year of 1965 saw the Freedom Ride for Aboriginal civil rights, and in 1967 a whopping 90 per cent of Australians voted YES in the referendum that was widely seen at the time as some sort of guarantee of social justice for Aboriginal people. (A promise still not delivered.)

In January 1966, Menzies finally retired, but the Coalition landslide in the federal election later that year was a terrible blow both to the Labor Party and to opponents of the Vietnam War. It did, however, result in Gough Whitlam being elected to the leadership of the ALP.

For our generation, there was still no relief from growing up under a Coalition government. Over the next six years, the highest office in the land was successively held by a man who disappeared at sea, a man who drank too much, and a man whose main distinction seemed to be his overly large ears. Their policy initiatives remained effectively the same as those of Menzies.

Meanwhile, the anti-war movement received a boost to its profile in response to police bashings of protestors during visits by American President Lyndon B Johnson (October 1966) and South Vietnam's Prime Minister Air Vice-Marshall Ky (January 1967). By 1968, the explosion of what seemed to be revolution in Paris and Prague was mirrored on the streets of Australian cities, even if we didn't have any cobblestones to throw at the constabulary.

With the first Moratorium (1970), this decade reached midpoint, before moving into the anti-apartheid campaign of 1971 and the Aboriginal Embassy (founded under a beach umbrella outside Parliament House on 26 January 1972), and on to the optimism of the November 1972 *It's Time* election. True to his promise, Gough and his government ended conscription, brought the troops home from Vietnam and replaced the White Australia Policy with something new, called 'multiculturalism'. All of this was a victory for radicalism.

Our 'Sixties' concludes with the Dismissal of the Labor government in 1975, and the return of a Liberal/Country Party Coalition under a wealthy squatter who told the unemployed that 'Life wasn't meant to be easy'.

But if that is a rapid recap of some of the political

Introduction

campaigns of the decade, politics alone did not make us radicals. As the various stories related here make clear, every radical brought a personal narrative to the struggle.

CHOOSING PARTICIPANTS FOR A BOOK SUCH AS THIS IS A BIT like inviting people to a party. You need enough diversity to provoke interesting conversations, but you want the guests to have enough in common to avoid too many fights afterwards in the car park. As well, any guest list has constraints of availability and geography.

In this case, the geographical challenge was our own. Coming from Sydney, we knew more people from here, but our 'guests' also include people who grew up or came of age in Melbourne, Adelaide, Canberra, Rockhampton, Townsville, Nambucca Heads, Hobart and Brungle, in the Snowy Mountains.

While Australian radicalism of the Sixties was a diverse phenomenon, the stories included here give a sense of its range. And these accounts do all fulfil the brief of being about awakenings and conversions. Most of our participants had parents who voted for Menzies – if they didn't vote for the DLP! There is only one person who was what Americans call 'a red diaper baby', and she found her own pathway to a part of the Left that was anathema to her parents.

In this eclectic mix, there is a Maoist, an Anarchist and a Trotskyist, as well as a number of people who (like us) were lower-case socialists, communists and anarchists, or a mix of all three. Others were not aligned with any particular ideology. There are two lesbians and a gay man, and a plethora of feminists. Australia in the Sixties was by and large an Anglo monoculture and this is reflected in the backgrounds of our guests, but there are three people whose families had recently arrived from Europe, and there are three First Australians.

As far as occupations go, there is a folk singer (of course!). There is a union organiser. There is a historian. There is a mathematician. There is an actor. There is a schoolteacher, and a doctor. There are two journalists, and two lawyers. Perhaps more surprisingly, there is a tennis professional. There is also a professional marijuana grower. One person is an avant-garde artist; another is a sculptor of light.

For all of these individuals, the crucial thing that would shape their lives was the spirit of the Sixties.

That spirit was a powerful and heady mix of street marches and sit-ins, of sexual liberation, of music (folk and rock), combined with alcohol and/or drugs (which, in those halcyon days, were mostly fairly gentle). This was reinforced by a particular type of comradeship shaped by the experience of living in crowded share houses together, handing out leaflets together, getting arrested together, boozing together or getting stoned together, and singing Spanish Civil War songs together. Although there were schisms and divisions between followers of different ideologies and factions, we all believed we could change the world.

And it was this same belief that caused the two of us, at the age of seventy-plus, to stand in Town Hall Square on 6 June 2020, in defiance of the premier's ban on public gatherings and in support of Aboriginal people campaigning against deaths in custody. Under our face masks, we were silently singing 'We Shall Not Be Moved'.

Introduction

FINALLY, A PROVISO: THIS BOOK DOES NOT SET OUT TO BE a comprehensive history of the era. Think of it, rather, as a bunch of people talking to the two of us and – through us – to each other, and to you. This conversation is a collective reminiscence composed of individual awakenings that turned twenty people into radicals. While we have done our best to check facts, ultimately the meaning of these 'aha' moments is in the eye of the beholder. You may know different versions of some of these stories, but always bear in mind:

If you remember the Sixties, you weren't there.

MEREDITH BURGMANN
That glorious time to be alive

I was born and bred in the north-western Sydney suburb of Beecroft, which I've always described as the second most boring place in Australia. When I was seven, we moved to the next-door suburb of Cheltenham, which is THE MOST boring place in Australia. Happily white, Protestant, middle-class, public-servant families lived in leafy surrounds and world ignorance. Unlike the racy residents of the North Shore, we were too upright and boring to have classy sex scandals, or casual embezzlement incidents. Even our railway connection, the 'main line', was considered so unstylish that 'main line' residents were to be pitied.

I was the third of four children, which totally suited me. I was ignored my entire childhood, being neither the son, the first daughter, or even the baby. I was left to my own devices and never felt any pressure to be anything. My mother was the daughter of a fierce Country Party misogynist grazier from the Southern Tablelands and my father was the oldest child of the 'Red Bishop' of Canberra and Goulburn – Ernest Henry Burgmann – about whom I was to learn a lot in later life. But growing up in Beecroft and Cheltenham, all I knew about him was that he had baptised or confirmed most of my friends – and most of New South Wales, it sometimes seemed.

Meredith Burgmann

The reason I didn't know about my grandfather's very radical activity was simply because my mother hid it from us, and my father, who was a very reserved person, never thought to talk about it. I'm sure he would never have thought it was in any way an issue, but I think my mother, who at this stage was a card-carrying member of the Liberal Party, would have found it a bit disturbing. She much preferred to think of him as the holy man rather than the political man. For us children, he was the warm, all-embracing grandad who liked to tell us of his years as a bullocky and timbercutter. 'Always have a sharp axe' was his astute advice.

However, having a grandfather who was a bishop always made me feel slightly special, which I think I carried with me through most of my childhood.

I grew up with my mother's conservative politics. Although my father – head of the textiles division, and later chairman, of CSIRO – had been a quiet Labor voter all his life, he never really talked about his political views. On the other hand, my mother, who was very outspoken, convinced me that Sir Robert Menzies was a great man and that Arthur Calwell was a bit … 'common' was the word that was used.

It's important to point out here that both my parents were very committed Christians, and we were brought up believing in Christian concepts of equality and justice. There was no racism, apart from the unthinking 1950s racism of expressions like 'nigger in the woodpile'. But there was no belief that any person was better than anyone else. And certainly, there was a view that women were equal. In fact, I think my mother always basically believed that women were better. She was determined that my two sisters and I have an education, because her father had pretty well refused to let her have one – even though he had encouraged her brothers, who really weren't as academically inclined as the girls in the family.

DESPITE HAVING BEEN BROUGHT UP ATTENDING SUNDAY School and church (I came top of Divinity in the Sydney diocese when I was ten), I had never been a very committed Christian. I found it difficult to sit in church and listen to the fire and brimstone sermons of our very low church Anglican minister, with whom my mother had constant disagreements – my parents coming from the more intellectual and progressive high church tradition of Canberra and Goulburn. And although I was very influenced by my Christian upbringing, in that strictures such as 'do unto others' and 'look after those who cannot look after themselves' were very ingrained in me, I'm not sure I ever really believed. The only time in my life I felt I was having a religious experience was when I was 'saved' by evangelist and English cricketer the Reverend David Sheppard, in 1963. I went forward to the altar in St Andrew's Cathedral in Sydney in an emotional moment, but looking back I have never been quite sure whether it was the fluency of his sermon or his batting strokes that swept me along.

After the local primary school at Beecroft and 'Opportunity Class' at West Ryde, I arrived at my secondary school, Abbotsleigh, in second year. I had spent my first year with my parents in England and Europe, where my father was working. At the time, my parents thought I was doing correspondence school work, whereas I was actually roaming the halls of the Imperial War Museum, which was free; or soaking up the Constables and Hogarths in the National Gallery; or watching Alec Guinness and Brian Rix in Drury

Lane farces (for the incredibly cheap price of a shilling in the bleachers during the matinee sessions). In short, I had done no school work in the entire year, so was at a bit of a loss when I arrived in high school.

Abbotsleigh was a typical posh Anglican girls' school on Sydney's upper North Shore, except for one thing. The headmistress was Betty Archdale, famous as the captain of the English women's cricket team and purported to be the first woman to hit a century at the Sydney Cricket Ground. Although her cricketing triumphs were always foremost in my mind, more important in terms of our schooling was her mother's suffragette background and her own reputation as a radical educationist. 'Archie' gave us current affairs lessons, lectured us on the importance of self-discipline and refused to call us a 'ladies' college'. We were a 'girls' school' and that was that.

During my time there, I also had a history teacher who, looking back, was obviously quite a radical. But regardless of what we were being taught in the classrooms, something else was going on in our heads. We knew we were expected to grow up to be North Shore matrons. We were meant to marry a King's boy or, second best, a Barker boy, and become a grazier's wife; or to teach for a while before marrying a North Shore doctor.

I never really fitted that paradigm, because I just didn't look like a North Shore girl. Not only had I committed the worst social faux pas, which was to live on the 'main line', I had bad skin and very, very unruly hair, which I have struggled with all my life. I didn't understand fashion or style, because my mother had no interest in clothes or fashion at all. I lived almost entirely in the mind, and obsessively played cricket, hockey and tennis without being a proper part of the

Abbotsleigh circus. Although I was made Head Girl in my final year (1964), I never really felt that I fitted in.

Long story, but most of the 'academic' stream of my year failed both maths exams in the Leaving Certificate. Although I matriculated, I did not get into Sydney University, so I decided to do the Leaving again. As I'd been Head Girl, I couldn't possibly go back to Abbotsleigh, so I enrolled at Sydney Tech in Ultimo, and that was one of the best decisions I ever made in my life.

At tech, I came across good teaching in all my subjects, even maths, in which I got an A (something I still boast about to this day). And this also gave me a year to think about the world. I suppose it was almost like having a gap year, which was not a common thing in those days. During my time at tech, I met friends of my older sister, Bev, who had already arrived at Sydney Uni. My sister's friends were all from either the SCM – the Student Christian Movement – or from the Newman Society, which was the progressive Catholic organisation at university. I found the guys – and it was mostly guys – from the Newman Society very interesting and compelling characters. This was a weird development. I'd never really known a Catholic until then. I'd certainly never talked to one. I remember coming home from a day with my sister's friends and saying to my mother, 'Mum, there are all these Catholics at university'. And she said, 'Yes, dear, there are lots in the world'.

SO I ARRIVED AS A FIRST-YEAR STUDENT AT SYDNEY University in 1966, still with quite conservative views about party politics, but feeling increasingly concerned about the issue of Vietnam because of my … I would like to say conversations, but really it was me sitting around listening while the Catholic intellectuals from the Newman Society – such as Father Ted Kennedy, Bob Scribner, John Iremonger and Peter Manning – held forth about politics. These children of Rome and a few token Protestants, including my friend David Garrett and my sister Beverley, would sit round campfires late at night either at 'Scribby's' shack at Bundeena or at Father Ted's lodge on Parramatta Road (yes ... yes ... we had campfires at the lodge).

Apart from the faux glamour of being with big boys talking about important stuff (Scribby was my first-year history tutor), my growing unease about our presence in Vietnam was both an intellectual concern and an emotional response to the increasingly brutal images on our tiny boxy television screens every night. I was much more concerned about the issue of the war than I ever was about conscription. I was opposed to conscription, but to me the issue seemed to be that we were sending people overseas to kill other people in our name. By the end of 1966, I had decided that the war was wrong. What was probably more devastating at a personal level was that the ongoing revelations of the falsehoods surrounding the Tonkin Gulf incident – the pretext for America's escalation of the war – had also convinced me that my government was lying to me. They were not telling the truth about Vietnam ... so what else were they lying about?

University was a huge liberation for me in many ways. I became involved with the Students' Representative Council (SRC), standing to be the Arts Women's Rep in my first year at uni. There, I met Sydney identities Michael Kirby, Richie Walsh, Bob Ellis, Geoff Robertson, Alan Cameron, Jim Spigelman, Percy Allan, Beth Cameron and Dany Torsh – all of whom are still my friends. Of these new friends, Geoff Robertson probably had the greatest influence on me; we became quite close, and he acted almost as the Svengali in many of my escapades at university.

By the time I got to university, whatever religious belief I'd ever held had just slipped away. So what was to take its place? A wonderful teacher at Sydney Tech, Henri Strakosh, had given me the classic English history book *The Common People* (by GDH Cole and Raymond Postgate) to read. This had a huge effect on me. Reading about the vicissitudes of working-class English people resonated much more deeply with me than any political tome could have. My Anglophile mother and my aversion to reading difficult theory combined to make *The Common People* my perfect little 'aha' moment.

The influence of that book and my strengthening opposition to the Vietnam War led to me waking up one day and deciding I was a socialist. It was as simple as that. It sort of came to me overnight, and I remember going into the SRC offices in the old MacCallum building the next day, meeting Geoff Robertson in the corridor and saying, 'Geoff, Geoff, I think I'm a socialist'. And he said, 'Don't be silly, Meredith. We're all socialists'.

During this first year at university I got involved in the sit-ins in the Fisher Library protesting about the increase in library fines. Dany Torsh's then husband, Max Humphreys, had organised the protests, and when Humphreys was expelled for this little example of participatory democracy Geoff Robertson decided to take his case before the Proctorial Board, an ancient and previously unknown appeal tribunal of university grandees. To my astonishment, I was chosen as his witness. Geoff explained to a reasonably anxious fresher – me – that he wanted a really respectable student participant to be the star turn. This was the last time that I was to be described as respectable. Appearing before the Proctorial Board was quite terrifying, but there was also a sense of excitement – and being put through my paces by Geoff was a real thrill. Perhaps it was a portent of things to come, and my endless court cases of the next few years. However, at that stage I had still never taken part in any protest outside the university.

IN 1967, MY SECOND YEAR AT UNI, I STARTED LIVING AT Women's College. As I had barely scraped through first year, my parents reasoned that this would give me more time to apply myself to my books. I of course reasoned that it would give me more time for my extracurricular activities: I was playing table tennis for the university, I was secretary of SUDS (Sydney University Dramatic Society), and I was still very involved with the SRC – and of course I was having a fantastic social life. I had discovered the Forest Lodge Hotel and the delights of alcohol. I had also discovered how to iron my hair, which improved my social life immeasurably.

Throughout my time at Women's College, I found myself more and more alienated from the North Shore lifestyle. Although I had never really felt I fitted in, I became even more convinced of this as I saw my college friends demeaned and put upon by the rugger bugger boys from the male colleges. The difference between my male friends on campus – the cheery, whiskery, slightly nerdy boys of the tacky Left – and the boys from the surrounding colleges, was huge. I couldn't understand how college girls could put up with it.

My only close friend in this environment was Nadia

Wheatley. Very late one night when I was sitting in my room, struggling with John Donne and his obsession with roses and death and other stuff, I heard a clump clump clump coming along the corridor. Opening my door, I discovered Nadia – wearing a red flannel nightie and gumboots – on her nightly mission to salvage the last of the toast from the kitchenette in our wing. Once we had introduced ourselves she took pity on my obvious lack of 'Eng Lit' aptitude and thus began my regular late-night poetry instruction. This was to last for the two years I was in college and certainly helped me through the torture of English honours. We might have bonded over my problems with the English romantics but our friendship was forged over our protest activity and ensuing arrests. (The only other girl in college who openly opposed the war was an American exchange student, Shelley Hack, who ended up in Hollywood as the fourth *Charlie's Angel* – but that's another story.)

IT WASN'T UNTIL JUNE 1968 THAT I TOOK PART IN MY FIRST demonstration against the war. I'm not sure what led me to actually take to the streets. I suspect that it was just inevitable. The assassinations of Martin Luther King in April of that momentous year and Bobby Kennedy in June had rocked our world. Especially Bobby … He had promised to stop the war, and we believed him. I remember walking back to Women's College crying after hearing of his death, because now the war would continue and Vietnam would be bombed forever. I think we all believed that the electoral road had been taken away from us by violence, so maybe it was our turn to throw some bombs.

Meredith Burgmann

Hey hey LBJ, how many kids have you killed today?
Ho Ho Ho Chi Minh, dare to struggle, dare to win!

In one tumultuous fortnight, I took part in a sit-in at the Commonwealth offices in Martin Place; protested against Prime Minister John Gorton, also in Martin Place; celebrated Independence from America Day by occupying Liberal Party Headquarters in Ash Street; and demonstrated outside the Young Liberals Conference at Anzac House.

The demonstration against John Gorton turned out to be my first arrest. We had sat down in Martin Place outside Gorton's Sydney office, and we decided to stay there until we were all removed. It was mortifying to eventually find on my charge sheet that I was charged with obstructing access to the men's toilet in Martin Place. We had absolutely no idea that that was where we were sitting. The arrest seemed almost anticlimactic. It wasn't frightening; it wasn't even particularly exhilarating. But I had a certain satisfaction that I was doing my bit towards stopping the war. And my major concern was that my knickers didn't show as I was dragged away.

Another ironic moment, which I didn't really savour until much later, was that I shared the paddy wagon with John Fisher, the shy, gangly grandson of Andrew Fisher: the Labor prime minister who had dragged us into the First World War, promising Britain our colonial support 'to the last man and the last shilling'.

Finding myself locked up, I realised for the first time the incredible boredom that hits you when you are held on your own in a room with no reading matter and no one to talk to. This was often my problem, as in many of my arrests I was the only girl detained. I could always hear the male arrestees down the hallway all having wonderful arguments and singsongs. There would be, say, thirty in a cell, whereas I'd be down the other end of the corridor on my own, or perhaps with a nice lady pickpocket or shoplifter. Bliss it was indeed when other girl protesters like Nadia Wheatley and Helen Randerson joined me in those smelly cells.

The media fell upon the image of the fallen North Shore schoolgirl with the clerical pedigree. 'Bishop's Granddaughter Rides into Battle' and other embarrassing headlines became the order of the day.

Exactly a month after my first arrest, one of the more bizarre episodes of my increasingly weird life occurred. The leader of Students for a Democratic Society, Mike Jones, had decided that we should picket the Regent Theatre in George Street because it was showing a 'shoot 'em up' pro-Vietnam War movie, *The Green Berets*, starring John Wayne. Mike was considered to be charismatic and was certainly a powerful orator. I was not entirely sold on his charismatic qualities, but I was continually astounded by his confidence and his absolute certainty about the correctness of all our actions. Self-doubt was not in Mike's DNA. It was the first time I had ever encountered such certainty, and it was remarkably comforting.

So, a small group of us gathered outside the beautiful old Regent Theatre and started handing out leaflets to the uninterested theatregoers. Suddenly the police appeared and arrested every one of us. Talk about over-reaction! A lovely photo exists of me being gripped in a huge bear hug by Chief Inspector (later Assistant Commissioner) Stackpool of Sydney City Area Command. They had even sent in the heavies.

The explanation for this blanket clean-up was only revealed years later. A fellow student (later a very senior public servant) had rung the local police as a prank and told them that we had planned to rush down the aisle and cut off John Wayne's head with a machete. What a great idea! If only we'd actually thought of it first! Once again, I was charged with obstruction, and months of hanging around Central Court in Liverpool Street ensued.

One of the strange results of this continual 'waiting around at court' routine was that we all knew each other's middle names. '*Jeremy Glynn Fisher Gilling*' would be bellowed out by the court attendant. '*Michael Cornelius Hetherington Jones* ... [he never lived that one down] *Michael Cornelius Hetherington Jones* ...' until eventually someone found him, and then another name would echo through the beautiful old corridors of Central Court.

How did my lovely, staid, middle-class parents react to my high-profile life outside the law? They were both wonderful. My mother had become increasingly distressed by the war in Vietnam. She totally accepted the force of my beliefs and only begged me never to get arrested for 'language', a promise that I readily agreed to; and kept. She did not tell me at the time, but later I discovered that she had received poison-pen letters about me and was sometimes snubbed at Pennant Hills Golf Club because of my activities. Although the attacks I myself endured from engineering students and college boys were like water off a duck's back, I know she was hurt by these petty nastinesses. My father, who no doubt quietly agreed with my views, simply asked me not to get arrested for a brief period while he was being appointed to the Executive of CSIRO, which was a Cabinet appointment. Once again, I readily agreed. Although the media was always keen to play up the 'youth rebelling against their parents' angle on our mass civil disobedience, it was never so in my case.

THE UNIVERSITY WAS ON FIRE. NOT ONLY WERE THERE Front Lawn meetings at least three times a week, but students from the other tertiary institutions started arriving at our meetings – enthusiastic newbies from Macquarie and impossibly trendy types from 'Kenso Tech' (the University of New South Wales).

Our Front Lawn meetings were legendary. It was where Wayne Haylen and Barry Robinson burnt their draft cards; where we discovered the head of the NSW Police Special Branch, Fred Longbottom, sitting in his police Mini, tape-recording our meeting; where we liberated draft resister Mike Matteson from police custody and cut off his handcuffs with bolt cutters. It was real *Boys' Own Annual* stuff.

By this stage, Vietnam had taken over our lives. The demonstrations, and consequently the arrests, seemed to multiply. I had always been a busy girl and this was my chance to be busy writ large. We were organising demonstrations, going on demonstrations, being arrested, being in court for our arrests, turning up in court to be witnesses in other people's court cases and generally making nuisances of ourselves. I remember SRC heavy Percy Allan making a speech where he argued that we must rip up the daffodils of the bourgeoisie until they agreed to bring the troops home from Vietnam. It made total sense to me at the time. For the entirety of 1968 I really don't think any hard academic work took place. Certainly not for me, and probably not for most of my friends.

Down Broadway to central Sydney we would march, in a flurry of Liberty prints, slingbacks (ugh), desert boots and duffle coats.

Meredith Burgmann

One, two, three, four, we don't want your fucking war!
Five, six, seven, eight, stop the war, negotiate!

Not a message T-shirt in sight. That didn't happen until the *It's Time* election of 1972. The Left at that time was remarkably united. It was easy to be united about something as stark as the war and conscription. Yes, we had battles about whether our slogan should be 'Bring the Troops Home' or 'Victory to the Vietcong' but we all still turned up the next day at the demonstration.

It is hard to comprehend how overwhelming the Vietnam War was in our young lives. Daily our friends and boyfriends were dealing with court cases or conscientious objector cases ... or they were in hiding. Each night we would see tragedy and lifeless bodies on our TV screens. The 1960s was the first time that newspapers or films ever really showed dead bodies, and it was cataclysmic for a nice little ex-Anglican from Beecroft.

IT IS NOT AN EXAGGERATION TO SAY THAT VIETNAM changed my life. I was originally enrolled in English honours and was about to embark on a life as a famous novelist (I thought), but as a result of my Vietnam activities I gradually found myself pulled towards the study of politics, ending up doing my postgraduate work in it and being a political science academic for twenty years – not to mention ending up in parliament.

However, it was not just my academic life that changed course. My political views were changed forever. I came out of the Sixties with a belief in internationalism, direct action, participatory democracy, and the unending struggle against racism and sexism. The overarching slogan of the day, '*The personal is political*', is still part of my everyday mantra.

The Sixties was 'that glorious time to be alive'. I remember one particular demonstration where someone actually took a photo. We forget how rare it was for students to take photos in those days. None of us had cameras, and we were too busy to stand still and pose anyway. This photograph shows me standing on top of a truck in front of the university's Great Hall, waving a Vietcong flag, wearing a red headband, a floral mini dress and my beloved ankle-length white boots, all of which were the height of fashion. In more ways than one, the revolution had certainly arrived for me.

NADIA WHEATLEY
The girl who threw the tomato

When I was growing up, I was a good girl; a very good girl.

As the only child of a mother whom I adored, I never had any cause to be naughty. And as the child of a father whom I feared, I was cowardly and compliant.

'Be a good girl', my mother would say as she delivered me to a friend's place, or to the home of one of my relatives; then as she kissed me goodbye, she would add: 'As you always are'.

As a good girl in someone else's house, I offered to set the table and do the wiping up, did not interrupt adults or answer back, kept my elbows tucked in at my sides at the dinner table, and ate everything on my plate.

Perhaps this reputation I had for goodness was the reason why my relatives were so surprised when – overnight, it seemed – at the age of nineteen I became very publicly very bad. Looking back, I can see how this apparently new Nadia, who exploded out of me in the winter of 1968, had been building up a head of steam for twelve years.

The girl who threw the tomato

ALTHOUGH GOODNESS WAS THE DEFAULT MODE OF MY early childhood, in 1956 it became something that I began consciously to strive towards. One Saturday in the July of that year, I went to a friend's seventh birthday party. I returned home to find that my mother had disappeared. When my father told me that she would be gone for a long time, I thought this meant that she was dead. Summarily deposited into the home of an aunt and uncle, I believed that I could bring her back to life by being good. Amazingly, it worked. Reunited after five months, my mother and I had two years together (and without my father: bliss!) before I was pulled out of class one afternoon and told that Jesus could not bear to live in heaven without her. I said nothing, did nothing. Words, actions, even tears: all seemed inadequate.

Now nine years old, and dumped into the family of a classmate, I continued to offer to set the table and do the wiping up, ate everything on my plate, and never, never answered back. Naturally, this did nothing to endear me to the three children who were the rightful members of the family. Nor did it cut any ice with my foster mother, whose rules would have tested the goodness of a saint.

I can hear her voice now: 'I've got a bone to pick with you, Nadia ...'. Those words would make my stomach cramp with fear, as I realised I had broken some unknown law of the household, for which I would have earned myself a Bad Mark.

Recorded against our names on the Bad Mark Chart attached to the kitchen wall, these were awarded for accidental infringements as well as for wilful wickedness. I think what fuelled my particular sense of injustice was the fact that there was no proportion to the system. A pair of socks left accidentally under the bed warranted two

Bad Marks; two homicides would have brought the same outcome. Nor was there any time off for Good Behaviour.

Although I was polite, obedient and helpful, I regularly committed the crimes of forgetfulness, untidiness, and reading when the sun was shining. Every week I collected as many Bad Marks as the other children in the family. Yet while their offences were simply punished with deductions from their pocket money, my criminal record carried a very real danger: from time to time, my foster mother would threaten to send me to live with my father, who continued to terrify me.

Of my foster father, I have written elsewhere. His long-term sexual abuse was ultimately far more damaging than the mind-games played by my birth father. Yet as the only person who gave me praise and affection, he won my devotion and my loyalty. At night, when he came to my bedside, he smelled of rum and power. Although at the time I knew he was the Australian head of a multinational company, it wasn't until a few years ago when I read his obituary that I realised he was one of the Faceless Men of the Liberal Party. Politics was never mentioned in the house.

My main escape from all of this was the world of books. To avoid getting a Bad Mark, I would retreat to one of my hiding places – behind the couch in the lounge room; inside the clump of oleanders near the garage – and read. Sometimes, too, I would write.

When I was fourteen, books began to offer an escape of a different kind. A chance remark from one of my teachers alerted me to the fact that there was a place at Sydney University called Women's College, where students could live. I didn't care about getting a degree – since the age of four, my plan had been to write books when I grew up, and I didn't need a degree for that – but I saw this as a possible refuge from both the foster family and my father. Over my last two years at school, I read my way to freedom. I was sixteen years old in January 1966 when my Leaving Certificate results gained me a place at Women's College.

THROUGH MY FIRST YEAR AT UNIVERSITY, I WAS LIKE a creature let out of a cage: running wild, and yet lacking any knowledge about how to survive outside captivity. Thanks to my foster mother, I did not know how to talk to boys. Thanks to my foster father, I confused sexual contact with love.

As I entered my second year, the impact of my mother's death – delayed for so long – overwhelmed me. During that year, I spent a lot of time in my room with a DO NOT DISTURB sign on the door. I was doing honours in English, but I had read most of the set books while I was at school. *Is this all there is to university?* I used to wonder. In seminars, I sat with my arms clasped across my chest, in a passive aggressive lump. And when I say 'lump', I mean it: my body had inflated like a barrage balloon.

On a perpetual diet, I never went to college dinner. Hours later, finding myself to be starving, I would roam the corridors looking for the loaf of bread that was provided in the pantry of every wing. That was what I was doing in the early hours of one morning in the winter of 1967, as – clad in my red viyella nightshirt and the gumboots I wore over thick socks to keep my feet warm – I galumphed along the corridor of one of the college wings.

Suddenly, a door flew open.

I can still see Meredith Burgmann in front of me at that

moment, with her silver hair seeming to fizz with electricity. And I can still hear her squeak of relief as she realised that the sound she'd heard outside her door was not some marauding college boy but just a fat girl in gumboots. Within moments, we were eating Vegemite on toast together, as we would do on many nights over the coming months. Although Meredith was not in some sort of self-imposed retreat from the world (far from it), she shared my habit of staying up late and sleeping until lunchtime. At first, this seemed to be the only thing we had in common.

As I look back, however, I can see that neither of us fitted in at Women's College. The difference was that Meredith – who came from a loving and supportive family – could afford to come across as an eccentric, whereas I thought I wanted to be the same as the other girls, but I didn't know how to do it. Anyway, while insomnia and a shared status as misfits brought Meredith and me together in 1967, it was not until the next year that we really made ourselves outcasts in college society.

FROM THIS POINT, I CAN START DATING THINGS FROM THE box of newspaper clippings and pamphlets that I have dragged around with me over the years. So I know it was on Wednesday 19 June 1968 that my road-to-Damascus experience occurred.

College lunch was already in progress that day when Meredith arrived in the refectory. As she joined the table of girls with whom I was sitting as I nibbled on a lettuce leaf, the topic of discussion was the usual Women's College fare: who had been invited to the Paul's Formal (not me!), and what they planned to wear. Out of the blue, Meredith suddenly asked, 'Does anyone want to go on a demonstration this afternoon?'

I heard my lone voice piping up: 'I'll come'.

As I now read newspaper articles from that day, I learn that a 'large but unsensational' Front Lawn meeting, convened by the Students' Representative Council, had resolved to send a deputation of five students to wait on the minister for Labour and National Service that afternoon. The aim was to present a list of objections to certain new amendments to the National Service Act, whereby the university Administration could be obliged to pass on to the government the birth dates of twenty-year-old male students. This was rightly characterised as dobbing. At the lunchtime meeting on campus, some students had decided to support the deputation by simultaneously holding a peaceful protest outside the minister's office in Martin Place. As Meredith and I made our way to the bus stop on City Road, I did not know any of this. Nor was I aware that this was the first time that Meredith herself would go downtown for a demonstration.

'What's it about?' I asked.

'Conscription.'

Had I even heard of it? Possibly not. I never read the newspaper or watched television. Despite my disillusionment with the English department, my world was limited to the territory between *Beowulf* and *The Waste Land*.

Meredith, on the other hand, was enrolled in the subject called 'Government'; primarily taught by left-wing academics, the course included a series of lectures on Vietnam. As we travelled into the city, she began by describing to me the Australian system of conscription via a lottery barrel and went on to outline the history of the war in which my country was engaged.

Indochina was still in the hands of the French when the bus arrived at Martin Place, but that didn't matter. This demonstration was against conscription, which even a political simpleton like me could see was wrong. Proud of the fact that my mother had volunteered to serve in the Second World War, I believed it was immoral to force people to fight.

It was mid-afternoon when we joined about a hundred other students (nearly all male) on the footpath in front of the building that housed the Commonwealth Offices. Accustomed to the college boy uniform of tweed coats and old school ties, I was instantly taken by the colourfulness of these young men with their patched jeans and badge-bedecked shirts, and their long flowing locks caught back in red headbands. As the deputation of student representatives prepared to go into the building to see the minister, there was a groundswell of feeling that we should accompany them in support.

Making my way with the others through a tiled vestibule and into a lift, I had no sense of doing anything illegal. This was a public building, after all. On the seventh floor, a corridor took us directly into a large open-plan office, where everyone started milling around among the secretaries and clerks sitting at their desks. Although the minister wasn't in, nobody seemed deterred. Over the next few minutes, more and more demonstrators came up from the street. At the same time, groups of office workers were catching the lift back down; they seemed happy to be getting an early mark. By four o'clock (according to the report in the next day's *Australian*) there were ninety-two of us in the office.

Once the occupation was in progress, the atmosphere continued to be relaxed. Some of the students amused themselves by stacking some desks and chairs across the doorway, but to use the word 'barricade' would be stretching things. A certain level of tedium set in. Finally, a lookout stationed at the window shouted that a couple of paddy wagons had arrived in Martin Place.

'Remember, no violence ...' counselled a young man who was holding a megaphone.

'Sit down!' voices shouted when about a dozen policemen began to approach along the corridor. 'Everybody sit down!'

I joined all the other people who were flopping onto the carpet. It was a bit like an impromptu game of musical chairs. Except that there wasn't any music. Or chairs.

A silver-haired policeman introduced himself before telling us that he was going to read the Crimes Act. 'After that', he said, 'I will ask everyone to leave the building. Anyone who remains will be liable to two years gaol'.

When he said that, I truly believed that, if I remained there, I could be put in prison for two years. Yet I had no sense of fear. Instantly put in mind of my foster mother's system of Bad Marks, I felt that getting two years gaol for sitting cross-legged on the floor of a public office was even more ridiculous than getting two Bad Marks for accidentally leaving a pair of socks under my bed. And so I stayed.

'*We shall not be moved*', people started singing. I had never heard the song before, but within moments my voice was joining in.

'Link arms!' someone shouted.

We all did.

Working in pairs, the police began to drag demonstrators down the corridor to the lift.

'When they pick you up, let your body go limp', the pencil-thin boy sitting beside me recommended. 'You're heavier that way', he explained.

I had never before thought of being heavy as an asset.

'*We shall overcome …*' we all sang.

Time fell into a warp as I waited for my turn. I had no idea what was happening to the other demonstrators when they arrived on the ground floor. Were they indeed being carted off to gaol for two years? The question was of no concern to me.

'*Deep in my heart, I do believe that we shall overcome, some day …*' I sat and I sang until it was my turn.

As two policemen grabbed my arms and began to haul, I became aware of a logistical problem. Because of a Women's College prohibition against wearing trousers on campus, I was in a dress – which rode up my thighs as I was dragged. Yet being – literally – in the hands of the law, I could not pull my dress back down to a reasonable level of decency. So preoccupied was I with the issue that I forgot about going limp in order to make myself heavier.

Obviously it didn't matter: 'We've got a baby whale this time', one of my policemen observed as we entered the lift. I was mortified.

After the short descent to the ground floor, I was dragged across the tiled vestibule and then I was tossed down the steps, more like a minnow than a whale. All I could think about was not revealing my Bonds Cottontails. As I landed on my bottom in Martin Place, some of the other demonstrators cheered. It was only at that point that I realised I was not under arrest; and nor was anyone else.

Struggling to my feet, I felt as if an enormous burden had been lifted from me. This was not as simple as relief at the fact that I wasn't about to go to gaol for two years. It was an unaccustomed feeling, which I can only describe as happiness.

Over the coming heady days of my political awakening, my endemic depression disappeared. I no longer hid behind my door, but went freely onto campus. While the worst of my despair had been caused by my sense of disempowerment, joy came when I felt that – small and pathetic as I was – even I could act to try to make the world a better place.

WHEN I THINK OF THAT CRUCIAL (INDEED, CRUCIBLE) YEAR of 1968, there always springs into my mind a couplet from Wordsworth's poem on the French Revolution:

Bliss was it in that dawn to be alive,
But to be young was very heaven!

The poet might have been writing about me.

As I ran around the streets at night, sticking posters onto telegraph poles (DON'T REGISTER FOR NATIONAL SERVICE!) and painting graffiti onto walls (STOP THE VIETNAM BLOODBATH!), I did not simply feel alive in a new way, but for the first time in many years it actually seemed as if I was *young*. Having missed out on being a teenager, I was having fun.

'*One, two, three, four –*' I shouted as I marched through the city. '*We don't want your fucking war!*' I had been silenced for so long that to use my voice was in itself a form of liberation: to open my mouth and let years of frustration and anger come out.

'Link arms!' After being accustomed for so long to being alone, I loved the physical contact of demonstrations, the sense of being held in an embrace that went beyond the sexual. Feeling other people in solidarity with me, and myself in solidarity with other people: this made me feel safe.

'*Pig today – bacon tomorrow!*' And while I did not seek out violence, nor did I mind the push and shove that occurred as a flying wedge of male authority-figures knocked me to the ground. Physical pain was so much better than the other kind. But soon the other kind was to hit me, full force.

ON THE AFTERNOON OF FRIDAY 2 AUGUST 1968, DRAFT resisters Mike Jones and Jeremy Gilling were arrested in a tiny, non-violent protest outside the George Street cinema that was showing the Pentagon's propaganda movie, *The Green Berets*. As they were hustled into a paddy wagon, Meredith and I and our good friend, Marie Ely, sat down in front of the vehicle and were promptly arrested for obstruction. In the photograph that appeared on the front page of that evening's edition of the *Sun*, I looked as if I was kneeling demurely at prayer. (Shades of the good girl of my recent past.)

It was after I was bailed out and got back to my college room that the sky fell in. Hearing the fresher on duty shouting that there was a phone call for me, I hurried to the booth in the entrance lobby of my wing. Just as I can remember all the physical details of the afternoon at the end of 1958 when I was pulled out of class and told of my mother's death, in the same way I can still see and smell and hear every aspect of this particular moment, when I stood in that phone booth and picked up the receiver and heard the voice of one of my aunts saying in my ear: 'When Jesus took your mother to live with Him in Heaven, I couldn't understand how He could do such a thing. But now I know that it was to save her from ever knowing she had a Commie for a daughter. Oh, how she would have hated you!'

This was the beginning of a second death of my mother, far worse than the first. Initially, my new-found joy turned to grief, a grief that seemed to have no limits. Within a short time, however, grief was transformed into anger.

Now that the final tie with my mother was cut, I had nothing to lose. If indeed she would have hated me, then I might as well be as bad as bad could be.

It was less than a year later that I did something so terrible that it brought down upon me not just the wrath of an aunt but also the blood-lust of the premier of New South Wales, the minister for Education, the leader of the RSL, the proprietor of the *Daily Telegraph*, and the combined authorities of Sydney University. Somewhere in this mix of angry old men there was also my foster father, now a member of the University Senate. If that first sit-in in the government office brought about my radical awakening, it was a humble tomato that took my radicalism to the next stage.

It all came about by accident.

ON 1 MAY 1969, A GRADUATION CEREMONY WAS TO BE addressed by the University Visitor; this was the one-legged Victoria-Cross-winning war veteran, Sir Roden Cutler, who was also the Governor of New South Wales.

Although this event had no military connection, the vice-chancellor provocatively invited the Sydney University Regiment (SUR) to come onto campus to form a ceremonial guard to mark Cutler's arrival. Many members of the SUR were engineering students and college boys, who on a number of occasions had attempted to break up left-wing meetings by throwing punches as well as over-ripe fruit and rotten eggs. Indeed, when the regiment had marched onto campus in Orientation Week that year, they had mercilessly kicked a set of Quaker triplets who had lain down on the road in front of them, and one of the cadets had even bayoneted a member of Students for a Democratic Society (SDS). For the Left, it was a matter of principle that the regiment, like the police, had no place on the university campus.

When news of the proposed ceremonial guard got out, SDS leader, Mike Jones, announced that there would be a non-violent sit-down in front of it. On the other side of the divide, the head of the regiment wrote to all SUR members *not* called up for guard duty at the event, asking them to come along in *civilian* clothes to defend the guard. On Wednesday 30 April, notices went up around the engineering faculty, urging students to come along the next day and 'stir' against SDS and the Labor Club.

Meanwhile, I was at the pub: it was my twentieth birthday.

I was still in a celebratory mood when I went back to the Forest Lodge Hotel at about eleven o'clock the next morning in the company of a mischievous gay comrade and the SDS member who had been bayoneted during Orientation Week. By 1 pm, when the Front Lawn meeting was due to start, we were reluctant to leave the beer garden, but duty called.

As we passed the corner shop opposite the pub, my gay friend observed that cooking tomatoes – displayed in a box out the front – were on special. He had the bright idea of buying half a kilo, so that he and the SDS member could retaliate when the engineers started throwing *their* fruit, as we knew they would do. Naturally, neither of the boys had a bag, so I reluctantly agreed that the four over-ripe tomatoes could be put into my cloth shoulder-bag. Within minutes, I could feel them becoming soggy.

By the time we arrived at the Front Lawn, there were 2000 people in attendance. Labor Club and SDS speakers were taking turns at the microphone, under a constant barrage of fruit, bottle tops, banana skins and milk cartons. At one stage, two members of the Right filled a metal garbage bin with water and hurled it – bin and all – at Mike Jones.

After this had been going on for an hour, three buses drove up to the roadway between the Front Lawn and the Great Hall and deposited the rifle-bearing cadets into the already-contested area. As they formed ranks, some twenty members of SDS sat down between their lines, while other anti-war activists milled around, shouting slogans. According to the next day's *Australian*, the 'opposing group of students, aided by members of the regiment, punched, dragged and kicked the demonstrators'.

Not wanting to get hurt, I stayed well to the back of the crowd. At a height of five foot two, I couldn't see the guard over the crowd of brawling blokes. So I certainly did not see the governor, who – ten minutes after the appearance of the buses – 'arrived unnoticed under police escort to be greeted by the wild scene'. Rather than going straight into the Great Hall, where the graduation ceremony was to take place, he '"purposely went ahead with the inspection"', as he later told a journalist from the *Sydney Morning Herald*.

Meanwhile, at the back of the throng, I was alone among the engineers and college boys, some of whom were continuing to toss their missiles. My two drinking companions had long since disappeared, and so – realising that I would never be able to give the cooking tomatoes to their rightful owners – I lobbed one into the air; and then another.

Nadia Wheatley

Anyone who knows me could vouch for the fact that I loathe and avoid sport. Never once in my school career did anyone ever select me for any game involving throwing balls (or catching them, for that matter). And so, when I tossed the tomato with my pathetic underarm action, I could not deliberately have hit the Great Hall, let alone a moving target (and particularly one that I could not see).

Nevertheless, as fate decreed, a tomato (whether one of mine, or somebody else's) splattered some seeds upon the lapel of the morning suit worn by the one-legged VC.

Throwing a tomato was not what I did wrong.

My mistake occurred later that day when, during a follow-up session at the Forest Lodge, I gave a jokey interview to a journalist from *The Australian* who wrote a comical gossip column under the name of 'Martin Collins'.

By the next day, both the government and the media were in full cry over the alleged attack on the governor. Premier Bob ('Run over the bastards!') Askin declared that 'the onus lies heavily on the university to do a bit of expelling'. The account by 'Martin Collins' of his conversation with 'the girl who threw the tomato' inflamed this further.

> The girl doesn't look like the sort of person who'd go around tossing fruit at the Governor. In fact, she's an honours student with a good academic record.
>
> She isn't a member of any of the groups that our political leaders keep describing as un-Australian and out to destroy our way of life.
>
> It's just that she likes throwing tomatoes at governors.

While by this stage the four tomatoes in my bag were being described as 'four *kilos* of tomatoes', it was this depiction of me as a good middle-class girl that proved to be so threatening to the men in power. I could have been the daughter of somebody like them. And of course, although they did not know it, I was. (While my foster father's role in the University Senate triggered my nightmares, he too had reason to be afraid.)

Over the coming weeks, students were invited to come forward and tell their stories to a Committee of Inquiry set up by the university. A number from both the Left and the Right complied.

I, on the other hand, was summoned to afternoon tea and a 'personal talk', alone, with the deputy vice-chancellor. This man, who was a professor of psychology, began by talking to me of my mother's death. His manner was that of counsellor-cum-kindly-uncle. As this was the first time anyone had ever spoken to me about the death, I soon had a lump of tears welling in my throat.

Once he had done his best to break me down, Professor O'Neil suddenly switched topics.

'And now for the sixty-four thousand dollar question. Did you throw the tomato at the governor?'

'No', I replied without hesitation.

This was not a lie. I had not thrown the tomato *at* Sir Roden Cutler. I had not thrown it *at* anyone.

At this point, the deputy vice-chancellor's whole demeanour changed from kindly uncle into a *pater familias* who has had his personal authority challenged.

'*That's it!*' he shouted.

Within moments, I was in the corridor with the tea

trolley. But I was not the same person who had been there half an hour before.

It was a few weeks after this that the Yeoman Bedell (head of campus security) arrived one evening at my Glebe bed-sit with two Alsatian dogs and an envelope daubed with red sealing wax. The document inside charged me not just with the tomato, but also with lying to the deputy vice-chancellor. (Two Bad Marks!)

The saga that unfolded over the next few months is too convoluted to relate here, but it included two appearances before the university's disciplinary body, the Proctorial Board, which was composed of five professors robed in scarlet and gold. For these occasions, the Yeoman Bedell also wore his ceremonial costume, which appeared to be modelled on the uniform of the Beefeaters at the Tower of London. I wondered: would this Star Chamber order the chopping-off of my head?

No, but as the state government, together with various right-wing lobby groups, continued to bay for the blood of 'the girl who threw the tomato', I was threatened with the double jeopardy of being 'sent down' from university, as well as a civil prosecution for assault.

Eventually, and mysteriously, the charges were abruptly dropped; to this day, I don't know what happened. But that made no difference.

Up until this episode, my law-breaking had been of a fairly minor kind: a bit of Obstruction here, a Good Behaviour bond there … If I had wanted to, I could have gone back to my career as a Good Girl. But for me, the confrontation with those powerful old men was a baptism of fire.

After the tomato, there was no going back.

GARY FOLEY
Fighting for truth, justice and the Aboriginal way

Nadia Wheatley

When I first knew Gary Foley, he had a great exit line. Whenever I drove him to the pub in Redfern, as he was getting out of the car he would say, 'Give us $10 – I need to buy some dynamite!' It always cracked me up.

That was at the end of 1971. Gary was twenty. I was twenty-one. Although we didn't know it at the time, that summer was a kind of watershed between two campaigns that profoundly shaped both the Aboriginal land rights movement and the political consciousness of whitefellas such as myself. These campaigns were the nationwide anti-apartheid movement (which had just concluded) and the activism that was kicked off when the Aboriginal Embassy was established in Canberra on 26 January 1972.

Gary Foley was a leading proponent of both these protests. In the film footage of the struggles at the Tent

Embassy, he is always at the forefront of the crowd, shouting through a loudhailer and resisting the bashing he is getting from the police. By contrast, an iconic photograph from the anti-apartheid campaign shows him as a lone figure, sitting behind a symbolic-looking fence-chain and holding a placard that says:

>PARDON ME FOR
>BEING BORN INTO
>A NATION OF
>RACISTS

Gary has always been very funny, and this slogan reveals his particular style of satire. As one of the writers of the landmark 1973 Aboriginal television comedy show, *Basically Black*, he came up with the character of Super Boong, who (in a spoof of Superman) was 'fighting for truth, justice and the Aboriginal way'. It's a great tag line for Gary Foley himself.

BORN IN 1950 IN GRAFTON, AT THE AGE OF FOUR HE MOVED to Tenterfield (on the southern side of the border between New South Wales and Queensland) when his dad got a job there with the sewerage works. Like many Aboriginal men, Gary's father found sport to be the ticket to social mobility. A year after arriving in town, Bill Foley was invited to join the local rugby league club, where he was a star player. In the wake of this success, the sewerage company offered the family a shack at the pipe depot. Until 1962 this would be home for Gary, his parents, and his younger brother and sister.

Those formative years in Tenterfield were a good time. Gary explains that 'there wasn't many blackfellas there'; as a result, the level of racism was lower than in most country towns. Indeed, the town's picture theatre was one of the few in regional New South Wales that wasn't segregated. Overall, he feels, 'It gave me a lot of self-confidence, knowing that I was as good as these fucking whitefellas'.

Unlike most Aboriginal kids of that era, Gary Foley even found school a positive experience – so much so that he is now in touch with his former classmates by way of a Facebook group called Tenterfield Memories. Speaking of that time, he makes a point of mentioning 'a really good teacher', who encouraged him at the age of ten to join the local public library. Looking for stories with Aboriginal characters, he discovered Ion Idriess's portrayal of the Aboriginal resistance leader, Nemarluk. Idriess remains someone whom Gary admires.

Another early influence was *The Goon Show*, on ABC radio. Even at primary school, Gary was acknowledged as 'the class clown'. He suspects this might have been a form of self-protection.

So far, so good. But in the early part of 1962, when Gary was starting his second year at Tenterfield High, Bill Foley's job with the sewerage company took him to Queensland, where Aboriginal people still lived under the restrictions of the Protection Act. While accompanying his dad on football trips across the border, Gary had seen enough of the Sunshine State to know he didn't want to live there. He refused to move.

'For the family, this created a big dilemma', Gary remembers, 'and I'm surprised Dad didn't just belt me and say, "You're coming. That's it." But my father was an interesting guy.

'And so in the end, to solve the dilemma, he said, "Well, you can go and live with your grandmother in Nambucca."'

Nambucca Heads, in the Foley family's traditional Gumbaynggirr Country, is a beautiful seaside town on the North Coast of New South Wales. Gary's paternal grandmother owned her house on a headland overlooking the estuary of the Nambucca River and the island that was a place of special significance for the Gumbaynggirr, but which by the 1960s had been taken over by the town's golf club. This grandmother's father, who had left her the house and three other blocks of land in town, had played an important role in the Australian Aboriginal Progressive Association in the 1920s, and she herself was a respected figure in Nambucca – not least because she was an active member of a number of different church congregations, both Protestant and Catholic.

When her twelve-year-old grandson came to stay with her, she expected to take him along on Sundays to whatever church she was attending that week. This was the first of a number of shocks Gary had when he moved south. Raised as an atheist by his father, he had never until this time set foot in a church. On the third week, he managed to escape by getting up very early and heading to the beach. This became his regular Sunday morning observance.

It was not as easy to get around the other problem that his new life presented. Along with the nearby towns of Macksville and Bowraville, Nambucca Heads was a place of pervasive and systemic racism, such as Gary had never experienced in Tenterfield. At the Nambucca cinema, he encountered segregation for the first time, and at Macksville High School he was branded with the stereotype of the

Fighting for truth, justice and the Aboriginal way

Aboriginal student. Accustomed to being regarded by teachers as clever and conscientious, he was now pre-judged as a lazy troublemaker. It didn't help that he was pretty much alone. Although there were a lot of Aboriginal kids in the area, most of them (including Gary's cousin, Gary Williams) went to Catholic schools.

A sign of Gary's isolation in Nambucca is the fact that he tells me about the one white boy who invited him into his home. It was no coincidence that this boy's family had moved up from Victoria. 'And they weren't like the locals. They didn't seem to mind a blackfella walking into their house, which caught me a bit by surprise. And I become great friends with this kid as a result.'

There was no such tolerance, a year or two later, when Gary made friends with a white girl.

'So were you forbidden to see her?' I ask.

'Oh fuck yeah.'

'By her father?'

'By the *town*! She came from Bowraville. Bowraville was known as the Little Rock Arkansas of Australia. If I'd ever been seen with her in *Bowraville* I would have been fucking lynched!'

I feel a shiver running through me as Gary names the town. It was twenty-five years after the time we are talking about that Bowraville became notorious as the place where three Aboriginal youngsters were murdered. But these crimes, for which no one has yet been brought to justice, underline Gary's description of the redneck culture of the place, as he perceived it at the time.

But how did the racism at Macksville High affect him?

'It threw me a bit', he admits, 'but, you know, I was able to stand up for myself. Partly because I was probably one of the smarter students in the class but also because I was a good sportsman'.

Like his dad, Gary was a footballer, but he was also a sprinter, regularly winning the 100-yard and 220-yard races, which he ran barefoot. And so there was a level of acceptance from the other kids at the school.

Almost as an afterthought, Gary says, 'But the thing that really impacted me at Macksville was being expelled from fucking school'.

One of the 'pioneers' of the Wyndham Scheme of education, whereby secondary schooling in New South Wales changed from five to six years, Gary was the only Aboriginal student at Macksville High to go on after the School Certificate. By 1965, when he was in fifth form, he only had one more year to do before he matriculated. At the time, he felt he was 'going great guns. I was a fucking gun student'. But this wasn't enough. He remembers:

'At the end of fifth form the headmaster called me into his office and he expelled me with these words. He said, "Don't come back next year, Foley."

'I was a bit shocked, and I said, "Why not?"

'And he said – his exact words were: "*We – don't – want – your – kind – here!*"'

As Gary recounts this memory, he carefully enunciates every word, with a pause between each one. Hearing him, I feel as if they were stamped into his brain.

'When the headmaster did that', Gary continues, 'he effectively demolished my ...', he pauses, considers. 'Well, he done severe damage to my self-esteem, my self-confidence and, worst of all, he destroyed my belief in education.'

As a result of this blatantly racist rejection, Gary avoided formal education for thirty years and he advised other Aboriginal people to do so, too.

'And I'm really angry now that for all those years – for thirty fucking years – I used to say to other blackfellas, "Don't worry about education. Don't worry about going to university, you don't need to do that."

'And I'm really angry with myself that I did that. But it was because of what that fucking headmaster done to me that made me like that.

'And I'm still angry about that, you know', he concludes.

It was when someone else insulted him, thirty years later, by suggesting he was 'a lesser human being' because he 'didn't have formal academic qualifications' that he took the challenge. At the age of forty-eight, he got first class honours in history at the University of Melbourne; a few years later, his PhD won the chancellor's award for excellence. This experience 'restored [his] belief in education'.

Significantly, when Gary tells me the story of his expulsion from Macksville High School, he cites the evidence. One of his fellow students, who went on to become a member of federal parliament, told the story in the House of Representatives at the time of the 2008 Apology, as an example of discrimination. When Gary was researching his PhD, he was 'reading Hansard one day, as you do', and he discovered this testimony.

'So there was my proof!' he exclaims. 'I felt vindication by her making that speech, because I'd always told that story and I never had any proof.'

Now a professor of history at Victoria University in Melbourne, and the curator of a massive archive of documents about Aboriginal history, Gary Foley is a historian with every fibre of his being. Again and again, as he yarns, he cites documentary evidence, checks and corrects himself about dates, and – when something is a matter of opinion – makes it clear that others might tell the story differently. ('This is *my* version, as a historian', he says on more than one occasion.)

It is a crime that thirty years of historical research and writing that Gary Foley might have done was denied to Australian readers because of the racism of a small-town schoolteacher.

'*We – don't – want – your – kind – here!*'

At the time of this rejection from Macksville High School, Gary had a scholarship from the Aboriginal Education Council and he was being sponsored at school by the Gosford Apex Club. So, after his summary expulsion, he thought that his whitefella sponsors would 'go and argue' with the principal to get him reinstated. Instead, they seemed embarrassed by his expulsion.

'Don't worry', they told him. 'We'll get you a job in Sydney. What are you interested in?'

At sixteen, Gary didn't know, but he admitted to liking tech drawing. So his backers got him a position as an apprentice draughtsman with a company in Sydney, where he moved in 1966. With pride, he talks about the designs he did for the ducted air-conditioning that was installed in a number of public buildings. But what was much more important was simply the fact of moving to Sydney.

Although his sponsors had put him into a boarding house on the north side of the harbour, he soon found his way to the Foundation for Aboriginal Affairs, in the city centre. This 'really fantastic social centre' offered young people a safe place to meet, out of the gaze of police. On Friday and Saturday nights there was a dance (at which the band members included Gary Williams), and on Sunday nights anyone who could sing or strum a guitar could have a go in the talent quest.

The Foundation was officially a non-political organisation, but there was naturally a crossover of interests with the Federal Council for the Advancement of Aborigines and Torres Strait Islanders (FCAATSI), which was running the campaign for the YES vote in the upcoming 1967 Referendum. Gary remembers that Faith Bandler and some of the other FCAATSI leaders tried to recruit the younger Foundation participants into helping. But at this time, political action was only a sideline for Gary Foley.

A severe beating by police would change that.

Backing up his account with specific details, Gary explains that two detectives from the notorious 21 Division beat him up in the Regent Street Police Station, after apprehending him in Railway Square for allegedly 'behaving offensively'. His 'offence' was that the police had seen him speaking to a female friend, who happened to be white. The police followed the beating with a warning: 'Tomorrow morning, you plead guilty to this in fucking court or you'll get some more of this'.

Gary Foley did what the coppers told him to do. For what would be the last time.

How he felt after this experience of unprovoked police violence has a great deal in common with the kind of outrage that many people of our generation describe after their first encounter with police. But what is extraordinary about Gary Foley's account is that, despite the racism he had suffered in Nambucca, the bashing took him by surprise.

'It was a big shock for me!' he says. 'But also it made me fucking angry because I didn't do what they were bashing me for.'

Gary Foley

One evening soon afterwards, Gary went to the Wayside Chapel to listen to the soapbox orator known as 'Webster'. Run by a progressive Methodist minister, the 'chapel' – at that time just a room in a block of flats in the Kings Cross red light district – was a drop-in centre and coffee shop, where young people gathered. On this occasion, Gary met a young Wiradjuri man by the name of Paul Coe. From Cowra originally, Coe was enrolled as a law student at the University of New South Wales.

'Listen', Paul Coe said, 'we're thinking of setting up a group to try and do something about the coppers'.

Still reeling from the bashing, Gary didn't need to be asked twice if he was interested in joining the 'crew', which included Billy Craigie and his sister, Lyn Thompson, as well as Gary Williams and a couple of others. The members of this informal group got together in Redfern, the inner-city suburb that had for decades been the centre of the Aboriginal diaspora in Sydney.

While Gary credits Paul Coe with his recruitment into this group, he adds that the other thing Coe did for him at that same time was to hand him a book, and say, 'Read this!' The book was *The Autobiography of Malcolm X*.

'And that book changed my life', Gary recalls. 'So between the cop-bashing and reading Malcolm X pretty much straight after, that's what politicised me. That's what set me on the road.'

Gary's story is a classic trajectory of a radical awakening. An event impinges so personally on someone that it triggers a sense of outrage at injustice. And then there is a theoretical follow-up. But the theory didn't stop at Malcolm X.

'Part of our philosophy', Gary says, 'was educate yourself, then educate the people'. This 'whole process of self-education' led the group to the model of the American Black Panther Party, whose armed patrols monitored the behaviour of the Oakland Police Department and challenged police brutality in that city. 'It just seemed to us that Oakland, California, was very similar to Redfern in Sydney.'

By now, the 1967 Referendum had won a resounding YES vote, but to young urban Aboriginal people it was clear that this had made no difference to the daily lives of Black Australians. Gary explains:

'That was a key element of the reasoning of my generation in Redfern – rejecting the strategy and tactics of the older generation.

'I mean, people like Faith had said to us, "Help us out with trying to get this YES vote up, because if we get a YES vote, things will change."

'Now, things didn't change, and so we as the younger generation thought, "Fuck the older mob, we're going to develop our own tactics and our own strategy."'

This rift between young and old Aboriginal activists mirrored the generation gap that was part of the broader political paradigm of the Sixties. At the same time, the strategy developed by the Redfern crew reflected the kind of grassroots community approach that was common to the ideology of the New Left. Although some members of the group later became infamous for a comic publicity stunt in which they declared themselves to be Australia's answer to Black Power, their main interest in the Panthers was in the 'social programs they were developing, and their strategy and tactics to counter police harassment'.

'We still thought that the idea of monitoring the police and collecting information on what they were doing was a good idea', Gary says. 'And we believed that, if we got enough information, we might be able to do something about what they were doing.'

One of the sites of arbitrary police persecution in the centre of Redfern was the Empress Hotel, which operated as both a political meeting place and a social centre. Realising that – unlike the Panthers' Pig Patrol – they couldn't carry guns, members of the small group started going into the Empress on a Saturday night 'armed with notebooks and pencils' in order to gather evidence of police harassment. After a few months, they had recorded dozens of incidents. But what to do with this record of infamy?

Paul Coe was 'the blue-eyed boy' of the dean of the Faculty of Law, Hal Wootten, so they went to see him. And when Professor Wootten proved to be sceptical about their accounts, they invited him to come to the pub with them on a Saturday night, to see for himself. On the night the dean arrived, the police 'did their usual trick' of assembling in large numbers and then arbitrarily grabbing people and shoving them into paddy wagons. 'If we'd have paid the coppers to perform, they couldn't have done a better job', Gary observes.

Hal Wootten was so shocked that he was ready to leap into the fray, but the team told him they wanted a different sort of help. In further discussions, they asked him to see if he could recruit some of his young graduates to come to Redfern and do volunteer work on a roster basis.

And so, in 1970, the Aboriginal Legal Service opened in a shopfront on Redfern's main street. This 'showed people in Redfern that what we were talking about with our little group was actually fucking doing something that was going to help them'.

A longstanding member of the Redfern community was

Paul Coe's auntie, Shirley Smith (known to everyone as Mum Shirl). She turned up soon afterwards, and said, 'Listen, you young pups! There's a lot of health problems in this community. Why can't we set up some sort of free medical service, like you've set up the legal service?'

So they called a meeting ...

'And as luck would have it, this mad, left-wing, mountain-climbing, pipe-smoking lunatic New Zealand doctor by the name of Fred Hollows turned up.'

With the support of Fred Hollows, the idea took off. Within a matter of weeks, the doors of the Aboriginal Medical Service opened in Redfern.

THAT WAS 1971.

In the same year, this small nucleus of Aboriginal activists played a role on the international stage when they took a prominent part in the demonstrations against the visiting South African rugby team. While their commitment came from the fact that they could see 'clear parallels between the apartheid system and the system that had existed in New South Wales and Queensland under the old Protection Board', the extent of their involvement was helped by a happy coincidence. By mid-1971, the group had moved their 'little black commune' out of Redfern 'to get away from the coppers', and were renting an old house in Bondi Junction. As luck would have it, the visiting Springboks, whose whereabouts were shrouded in the strictest secrecy, were put into a motel nearby.

'All we had to do was walk 20 yards and we were involved in the demos', Gary laughs. Indeed, that was where the famous photo was taken, showing him sitting with his placard.

Gary Foley

Beyond the success of the campaign in bringing international media attention to the injustice of apartheid, Gary points to its significance for their own group. He mentions meeting Zimbabwean activist Sekai Holland as one of the highlights, along with the links made with activists from the broad base of the anti-apartheid movement, including Meredith, her sister Verity Burgmann, and Peter MacGregor.

This connection in turn changed the consciousness of white radicals. Gary remembers how, on one occasion, Paul Coe 'jumped up and challenged the anti-apartheid protestors, saying "You're fucking being hypocrites, challenging racism in that part of the world. What yous need to do is think about here, where you mob are part of the problem."'

In fact, this point was made many times, and not just by rhetoric. Simply by knowing Aboriginal activists such as the two Garys, Paul and Isobel Coe, and Billy Craigie and his sister, Lyn, we non-Indigenous radicals were alerted to the racism of our own country.

And so white radicals who had been through the anti-apartheid movement began to support the campaign for land rights. As these new supporters 'boosted the numbers' at Aboriginal marches and rallies, Gary credits 'the size of those demos and the intensity of that campaign' with leading Prime Minister Billy McMahon 'into making his big mistake'.

In his inimitable style, Gary elaborates. 'So we're on a roll and McMahon, being the nervous little Nellie that he was, figured that what he needed to do to diffuse all of this agitation was to make a statement on land rights. Unfortunately, he chose the wrong sort of statement, and it was inevitable that that statement was going to trigger something.'

Fighting for truth, justice and the Aboriginal way

When McMahon's speech, provocatively timed for release on Australia Day 1972, rejected any possibility of granting Aboriginal land rights, four young activists – Michael Anderson, Billy Craigie, Bert Williams and Tony Coorey – immediately headed from Sydney to the lawn outside Parliament House in Canberra. Sitting under a beach umbrella, they proclaimed themselves the Aboriginal Embassy. Soon afterwards, someone gave them a small tent. When police arrived to move them on, it turned out that there was no law against camping on that particular bit of Australia – as long as no more than eleven tents were erected.

That same weekend, Gary Foley and a number of other Aboriginal activists were at a big anti-racism conference in Brisbane. As he and Bruce McGuinness headed to Melbourne, they stopped off at the Embassy. Gary would be there until July, when the government introduced a new law and the camp was brutally pulled down.

As a historian, he is now able to reflect on the long-term meaning of that struggle. He points out that the legality of the campsite worked in their favour. 'You remember the mantra of many people in the media and politics at the time: "We don't mind you blackfellas protesting as long as you do it legal and peaceful." And here was your quintessential fucking legal and peaceful protest that was really effective.'

As well, by making 'the authorities look like fools', the protestors 'appealed to the broader Australian attitude of larrikinism'. There was also residual goodwill: 'This was only five years after the 1967 Referendum, where 90 per cent of the Australian people had voted in support of Aboriginal rights'.

Overall, Gary claims that the Embassy ended the official era of Assimilation, which had aimed 'to make Aboriginal people cease to exist by turning us into white people with brown skin'. By establishing their own embassy, Aboriginal Australians proclaimed their separate and distinctive national identity, as well as asserting their demand for their own land.

But the very success of the Embassy brought its own downside. Gary argues that the official Assimilation policy was followed by what he calls a 'project of assimilation'. This began with 'the dispersal of Redfern'.

'I think that what had happened with the Embassy made the state government in New South Wales realise what they had on their hands if they had a fucking community like that in Redfern.

'Almost immediately afterwards, the state government introduced new policies in terms of public housing, dispersing Aboriginal families from Redfern into the western suburbs.'

Gary describes this as 'an enforced form of assimilation which destroyed what had been a really dynamic and fucking extraordinary community'.

Indeed. And the destruction goes on. A few days after my June 2019 conversation with Gary, the front page of the *Sydney Morning Herald* carried a story about a new wave of exclusion of Aboriginal people from affordable housing in the suburb. This compared the 300 Aboriginal people living in Redfern today with the 35 000 that were there in 1968. Most of this new diaspora were scattered across Sydney's outer western suburbs.

Gary himself hasn't lived in Redfern since the early seventies, but his move – initially connected with his friendship with Bruce McGuinness – was to Melbourne. After nearly five decades he is so acclimatised that, when we meet on a mid-winter afternoon, he insists we sit outdoors at his local cafe, where my feet quickly turn to ice. In my memory, I always place Gary in Sydney or Nambucca, but as we talk I see how he fits into this city where people are more earnest and intellectual. As he speaks of his work at Victoria University, it is clear that he loves teaching, loves engaging with his students, who include young white kids as well as 'some of this WAR mob'.

These are the Warriors of the Aboriginal Resistance, whom he describes as a 'good young mob – they're the grandchildren of my generation'. Nevertheless, the future he sees for them is bleak. 'I believe that things are worse today than they were when I got the fire in *my* belly. I think the assimilation project is so fucking advanced now that it's almost unstoppable.'

While Gary maintains that 'the emergence of a black middle class has really fucked the political movement as we knew it back then', he describes Native Title legislation as 'one of the biggest frauds that have been perpetrated in my lifetime'.

He repeats what he calls his mantra: '"*Native Title is not land rights and Reconciliation is not justice.*"

'So I mean, *we* were up against fucking incredible odds in our time, but I think that this young mob today – I'm glad that they're there, I'm glad that they're fucking putting up a fight, but the power of what they're up against is such that –'. Uncharacteristically, he breaks off. I've never before known Gary Foley to be lost for words.

When I ask him what his advice is for today's young radicals, he returns to his customary articulacy:

'The important thing is that the situation that confronts them is a lot more complex and difficult than the situation that faced us. But then, also, they've got potential weaponry that we never had. And I'm talking about social media. That should give them the ability to reach a broader fucking audience, or be able to sort of do more extraordinary things than we ever did.

'I reckon if we'd had the internet and social media back in the day, you know, we'd have won by now. But who knows?'

Overall, his advice to the young mob today is: 'Fight on regardless! Don't compromise. Don't believe the fucking hype. Do what you think is right'.

MAYBE THE BLEAKNESS OF THE WEATHER IS AFFECTING US, as the afternoon becomes longer and colder. The cafe proprietor is politely moving chairs back inside, while assuring us that it's OK to stay. He tells us we're brave.

'I'm not brave', I say. 'I'm from Sydney. I'm freezing.'

As we go on to speculate about the meaning of the new age-category of 'emerging Elders' that has recently started to creep into Acknowledgments of Country, suddenly Gary lets out one of his trademark cackles of laughter.

'Probably the only fucking real hope is that, the more this sort of shit goes on, the better the possibilities of satire and ridicule.' He goes on to talk again of *The Goon Show*: 'That's where Super Boong came from in *Basically Black*. You know, satire and ridicule are the only weapons that I think we can really fucking hit everybody with'.

Satire and ridicule: they're a long way from dynamite. But as he puts on his bike helmet and prepares to rides off into the cold, dark Melbourne night, Gary shifts into a polemic that owes more to the influence of the soapbox orator Webster than it does to Spike Milligan.

'I refuse to let people call me "Elder" and I refuse to let people call me "Uncle"!', Gary announces to the footpath that is empty of everyone except me. 'The only people allowed to call me "Uncle" are little kids – I'm not going to have a go at them – and my genuine nieces and nephews.'

He is really getting going now: 'When people call me "Uncle", I say, "Fuck off, I'm not your fucking Uncle and I'm not a fucking Elder."

'I don't want to be a fucking Elder.

'I'm a conscientious objector to Eldership, you know.

'*Fuck it!*' he concludes.

All the old fire is back.

GEOFFREY ROBERTSON
The right side of history

Meredith Burgmann

Only Geoff could do this to me ... insist that the one available time on a flying visit that he can spare to be interviewed is during the intermissions of *La Traviata* – at the Sydney Opera House. So I agree, and we set out on our road to the Sixties as Violetta prepares to die for no apparent reason in the arms of Alfredo.

I get there early and have a quick champers. Geoff arrives, almost on time, in a salmon-coloured jacket, pink shirt and a fair bit of sweat. At the bar we argue over how to pronounce Moët and I manage to misplace/lose the expensive program even before the first aria. Nothing has changed in fifty years. In the spirit of full disclosure, I probably need to add that Geoff and I have been friends since we were teenagers, and that he features in my own radicalisation story.

I had a whole bunch of written questions to ask him, based on his recent memoir, *Rather His Own Man* – but the Opera House bar is not the place to bring out a bulky book, so I decide to wing it.

The right side of history

I ask him, 'During your life in politics in the Sixties, was there ever a light bulb moment for you, where something clicked and you thought: "*The world has got to change*"?'

Geoff ponders, before replying in that wonderful plummy voice (I am one of the few people who can verify that he was born with it), 'Yes, there was. There were several light bulb moments. One was when we were debating at school – we were big into debating. I would have been about fifteen or sixteen and we were debating the subject *That Melbourne Needs 50 000 Negroes*. This had been provocatively said by a visiting American sociologist – apropos of the White Australia Policy'. Geoff goes into some detail about this incident in his memoir, so it was obviously pivotal in the life of the spotty and precocious Epping High School student.

He elaborates about the debate. 'First we thought that all we could say was that Melbourne just needed jazzing up. It was only when we started our one-hour preparation that we began to think – we suddenly started to challenge the White Australia Policy – I mean in Eastwood, a Sydney suburb, you could never …' He fails to finish his sentence. I knew exactly what Geoff was struggling to explain, coming as I did from the neighbouring suburb of Beecroft.

In the aforementioned memoir Geoff described his childhood thus: 'The Robertsons were a middle-class family in a middle-class house in a middle-class suburb, with a Hills hoist in the backyard and a small car in the carport'. It was a happy, loving family, with Geoff the oldest of three boys. Father, Frank, was a Commonwealth Bank executive and mother, Joy, a homemaker. Certainly nothing exciting there.

Geoffrey Robertson

SITTING HERE IN COSMOPOLITAN SYDNEY, TWIRLING OUR Moëts at the bar as we wait for our Italian opera to begin, it is hard to describe or even contemplate suburban Eastwood of the 1950s. He takes a liberating gulp and continues. 'You never saw ANYONE there who was different ... there was no Chinese restaurant, nothing, so we never even saw an off-white face. I think when we got to the moment when we had to debate, we suddenly felt our arguments were right. Growing up in this utterly boring no-blacks-of-any-sort country, we'd lost something.'

I interrupt this important thought with the banal observation that Beecroft was even more boring than Eastwood.

Geoffrey ignores the comment and ploughs on like a good advocate. 'So that was one important moment.'

Then he moves on to the issue that was to consume much of his working life – censorship. As always, I am a little thrown by how censorship can become such a huge, sometimes all-consuming concern for my radical friends, particularly lawyers. I am about to discover that for Geoff, censorship became entwined with another radicalising issue – an incident that scarred his soul.

It happened in Geoff's final year at Epping Boys High, a state school. One day, as he was travelling to school on the train, along with some kids from nearby private schools, Geoff saw they had copies of *The Tempest* – the final-year set text – that were much thicker than his own edition. After a bit of digging, he discovered that the state school kids had been issued with an expurgated edition of the text, with some of the sexual narrative deleted. He became furious with the NSW Department of Education.

'And that actually made me so angry I wrote a piece

The right side of history

of investigative journalism for our school paper – I think I was only fifteen – saying how rotten it was, and how it disadvantaged us, and that's when I saw the counterproductive aspects of censorship and it made me angry because it was affecting our careers. Yes. We would get lower marks, because we wouldn't understand the play, because every state school was issued a bowdlerised copy of the play, which removed the whole motive of the Prospero and Caliban relationships.' Geoff is really grumpy by now.

I realise here that Geoff's anger is just as much about the shabby treatment of the public school boys as it is about the unwarranted attack on the Bard. He then launches into a complaint about the censorship of his own satirical writings at school – specifically, a piece he had written about teachers getting threatened with the cane. That intervention was quite shocking to him. I put it to him that this indignation was caused by his anti-authoritarianism, and he adds, with indignation, 'and the teachers not being able to take a joke'.

I say, 'Your passions are all to do with the law but they are also about unjust situations. When you describe it in your book, you never describe it emotionally. It's all quite logical and rational'.

I might have expected Geoff to be a bit miffed but instead he replies, 'Yeah, but many years of law have …'

I (irritatingly) finish his sentence. 'Made you into a bloodless soul?'

He readily agrees. 'Yeah. It has. When I was upset about losing my first client to prison, John Mortimer [of Rumpole fame] taught me that I must never get emotionally involved with clients – only with lovers.'

He continues along this vein. 'I felt it quite strongly,

but of course I was a state school kid coming from Epping. For a while I think – I was somewhat nervous about taking on authority. I think my saving grace was I had a sense of mischief. I was a bit mischievous.'

I suddenly remember the old Geoff, and mischievous is exactly the right word. However, his statement about being nervous of taking on authority astonishes me. I had never observed a young person so sure of their actions or so comfortable in adult situations. Could it all have been bluff? We never really know the internal lives of others.

GEOFF THEN RUMINATES ABOUT BEING ONE OF 'MING'S kids', and says he was not attracted to Labor. Its leader, Arthur Calwell, had his own demerits, and Gough Whitlam had not yet emerged to offer fresh hope. I agree that 'Calwell Labor' was very different from 'Whitlam Labor', and that you can see why we were attracted to Whitlam Labor. What would Geoff have done if Labor had not become 'Whitlam Labor'?

He concedes that he probably would have gravitated towards Labor even without Whitlam as leader. 'Long, long after our student life, I undertook some research on how the White Australia Policy changed to the slightly off-White Australia Policy, and that of course was Calwell's doing – bringing in a lot of Bulgarians, Romanians, Greeks and swarthy Europeans. And it was Calwell and Chifley who did that – and it took a lot of doing. Australia only had seven million inhabitants. Remember the "Populate or Perish" thing in the late 1940s? I think Calwell did rather well – you can see those old newsreels of him, with the Balkan babies.' There's a part of Geoff that almost places him a generation

The right side of history

older than his cohort. His triggers for radicalism are really quite fifties.

Geoff proffers that he never thought much of Labor stalwart Eddie Ward, or even Tom Uren, whom he remembers turning up at the University Union, but does concede that 'those guys were on the right side of history'.

I put to Geoff that he seems to have been concerned with social justice and civil liberties issues such as censorship, racism, capital punishment and Aboriginal rights, but he has hardly mentioned Vietnam, the hot button issue of the Sixties. I am intrigued that the war was not the huge issue for Geoff that it was for most other students – even though he had a friend who was killed in Vietnam. Geoff agrees that it was the legal injustices that distressed him most, but then adds the kicker, 'Those issues were safer in a sense'.

'Safer?' I ask.

The answer to this question floors me. He explains, 'I mean with Vietnam you were given a police bashing, or you were listed by ASIO'.

Maybe he was more anxious about taking on authority than I had thought.

I take this in as we order more Moët. I point out that in actual fact he did end up with some interest from ASIO, mainly because at this stage ASIO was convinced that Aboriginal activists were being controlled by white Communists. However, I return to his statement about 'safer'.

Geoff's voice trails off. 'Yeah, but I think I was a bit – you've got to understand …'

As usual I finish his sentence. 'You were doing law …'

'Yeah, I was doing law. I had plans to maybe go into politics or to do something where it would not look good if you had a police "blotter". And you've got to remember that Sydney University SRC [Students' Representative Council] took a poll of students in 1967 about attitudes to Vietnam. The great majority were against sending conscripts – who could be themselves – but were in favour of sending ordinary soldiers. We were a very conservative university.'

So here he is. He saw himself as SRC president representing the conservatism of Sydney University students at that time. Or was it just a desire not to end up with a 'blotter'? I remember the poll, and also the fact that a year later we took another poll and the mood about Vietnam had changed dramatically.

Geoff explains himself, 'I defended a lot of anti-Vietnam protestors', and then he mentions Phil Kerr, the son of the (later widely hated) Governor-General, Sir John Kerr. I remember this case well, as I was one of Phil's witnesses. However, Geoff reveals some juicy details that I was not aware of. 'His dad called me and I had this amazing conversation where he bemoaned the fact that it was kiss of death to be anti-Vietnam, and then he said if we mounted Phil's case first, as some sort of precedent case, he'd turn up in court and glare at the magistrate. I thought to myself, "this is more than a sympathetic father, this is someone who really cared about the war."'

I'M UP TO QUESTION FIVE AND I'VE GOT TWELVE ALL UP. 'Not denying your genuine commitment to these causes, was your involvement in student politics in any way because you thought it would be good for your career?'

'No, I don't think so. I probably had a legal career in mind, but student politics was fun. We had a very boring life, and the SRC was where you could bump into interesting people like Bob Ellis and Laurie Oakes and Michael Kirby and Richie Walsh who were the older generation.'

Geoff's reply strikes me as totally honest. He has always chased an interesting life. What some critics might see as name-dropping by Geoff is just a consequence of chasing the next exciting thing to be involved in. This is a characteristic I see in myself, and with which I can totally sympathise.

His answer leads into my next question, 'Do you think the Sixties was the most interesting part of your life? Given all the people that you talk about in the Sixties, do you think it was more interesting than later on?'

Geoff surprises me. 'I wish I could go back, because I'd have a lot more fun and do a lot more with my knowledge of the way history would go and play out. But we were on the right side of history basically.'

I interrupt as always. 'Oh, we were totally on the right side.'

Geoff then says something strange. 'I was sometimes a bit nervous about saying so, but everything we fought about was absolutely right – capital punishment, Vietnam, apartheid ...'

Unbeknown to us both, we are photographed as we enter the theatre and find our seats. The phantom paparazzo sends it out to all and sundry. 'GEOFF ROBERTSON AND MEREDITH BURGMANN ARE AT THE OPERA ...' On stage, autumn leaves are falling listlessly on an equally listless Violetta. Geoff warms to his theme about the right side of history as we whisper in our seats. He decides that the whole book should be called *The Right Side of History*. I promise him that we will at least call his chapter that.

Geoffrey Robertson

HE ALSO CHATS ABOUT HIS PRESENT CASE. HE IS INVOLVED in the defence of Luiz Inácio Lula da Silva, former president of Brazil and a Workers' Party hero, who is facing gaol on fairly contentious corruption charges. There is no need to ask Geoff my usual question about whether he still regards himself as a radical.

After the prerequisite jovial gypsy/carousing scene we return to our spot at the bar.

Now I decide to broach the subject of the Humphreys affair. This occurred in 1967, when Sydney University's out-of-touch Administration expelled a psychology student, Max Humphreys, for leading a sit-in at the Fisher Library over increased library fines. Geoff's involvement in the ongoing legal manoeuvres was crucial. I ask him whether the Humphreys affair was his first overtly political activity.

Geoff is really proud and shows it. 'Oh, very much so. I think it was certainly a radical thing to do, to sue the university with the university's own money, and it set a precedent because I think the following year Alan Cameron [the next SRC president] did the same thing. I remember the protest meeting very well. I'd never seen so many students. There were about 2000 of them turned up with a "Justice for Humphreys" banner. I remember the moment when I decided to cut the ground from under [Labor Club leader] Hall Greenland's feet and promise that the SRC would act and would take the university to court, and then we had to do it. But it worked.'

I ask, did he intentionally take what was basically a centrist position against what would have been seen as the ratbag Left? 'No, I didn't do it intentionally, but that was what happened. I mean, we were using the law as a second-last resort to sit-ins and demos, and I was just outraged at the way the Administration were behaving. I couldn't believe it, and I knew enough about law – I'd done a year of law ...' I facetiously add, 'So you knew everything ...' 'I was absolutely flabbergasted that this could happen, so I think my passion there was about a real injustice.'

I don't want to call him a cold fish, but I can't help adding, 'Over and over again what I see is you reacting to injustice, but in a very intellectual way. The rest of us were reacting in a more emotional way, but you did it all very intellectually'.

He doesn't deny this, so we move on to his description of the incident in his memoir. When Max Humphreys appeared for punishment before the mediaeval university body, the Proctorial Board, junior law student Geoffrey appeared as his brief before a distinguished panel of academics. He has written that no witnesses were called, but I actually remember being called as a witness. Geoff is surprised. 'Do you? By me? Are you sure it wasn't for Nadia?'

We are confused. I remind him that, when he inveigled me into being a witness for Max, he said to me, 'We need you because you're respectable' – and I remember thinking that's the last time I was ever respectable.

Geoff laughs and doesn't defend my reputation. 'Yes, that was the last time you were respectable.'

Then Geoff drops a bombshell. He tells me for the first time that the whole Max Humphreys hearing before the Proctorial Board was a fix. 'It had been fixed, and we agreed to drop the case if they reinstated Max. Part of the deal was that we would get a couple of student proctors (who ended up being Joe Skrzynski and myself), and there was a retrial where they agreed to hear our witnesses, because we had a lot of witnesses that they said they wouldn't allow to appear during the first hearing.'

I get strangely agitated at the thought that my first legal appearance was nothing but a 'fix'. I ponder how Geoff had so quickly become part of the way the world works. He had realised very early on that some things in life are a 'fix'. It took me much longer.

MY NEXT QUESTION PUTS GEOFF ON THE BACK FOOT. 'I WAS not going to mention this, but Nadia has raised the fact that she remembers being in Women's College the night that you and I scampered back to college, having stolen the Rawson Cup.'

Geoff intervenes, slightly too quickly. 'It's another guy – she's got the wrong man.'

I plough on. 'Is this the only time you ever did anything illegal?'

Geoff parries well. 'What's the Rawson Cup?'

The Rawson Cup is the trophy that all the male colleges at Sydney University compete for in all sports. Its importance was beyond crucial, it was sacred.

I persevere. 'I remember, we went to a Victoriana at Paul's College and the cup was sitting there in this big glass case and I remember you saying to me, "Do you think this case is locked?" and it wasn't, and you just took the cup out and we ran back to Women's College to find Nadia thrilled at our shocking slide into common burglary. Nadia remembers us yelling below her window and her tiptoeing downstairs to let us in. I recall you saying, "I think we should throw it in the Parramatta River", and I said, "Oh no, I think it's really important, we'd better keep it", so we later returned it to safe hands. You don't remember that at all?'

The right side of history

Geoff absolutely stumbles. 'I have no memory – I've blotted that illegality out. I have a vague memory, but I'm sure I would have … It was an anti-college tease.' I tell him that the colleges are still appalling. He is surprised, but adds, 'They were dreadful in those days'.

Even though this escapade could easily be dismissed as a 'student prank' or 'hijinx', I feel that for both Geoff and me it had a more serious intent. For me it was fighting back at the stifling 'boyo' culture that entrapped us female college students, but for Geoff it was an integral part of his anti-privilege view of the world. The same forces that led to his anger about his censored version of *The Tempest* led to him wanting to poke fun at the privileged college boys. The time was definitely 'out of joint' for the cloistered elite colleges, but we still had no formal way to express our anger.

I ask him, did he ever think that we revolutionary students were ratbags? Or did he just think he and I were using different tactics?

The mention of ratbags seems to jolt Geoff's memory and he segues to the *Honi Soit* elections of 1967, when he supported the Left ticket of Hall Greenland and Keith Windschuttle (then a left-winger). He stood up for them when they campaigned in *Honi Soit* in support of those who were raising money for medical aid for the Vietcong, which Geoff describes as 'funds to repatriate the Vietnamese to help them kill more Australians'. He is diffident in his reply to my original question. 'So I suppose that was being supportive of the Left, but I didn't agree with their tactics.'

Finally, I ask: did the Sixties make him the person he is today?

'Yes, I'm sure. But that was because of doing law in the way I did it. It was because of Vietnam and hanging and

South Africa and all the raging against the stupidities of the Menzies era.'

Geoff ventures into difficult feminist territory with his next rumination. 'I remember saying to you once after you'd been arrested for sitting down in the middle of the scrum during the racist Springbok football tour, that we were a great combination – my brains and your bum.'

It is my turn not to remember. 'I don't recall that!'

He had always wanted to defend me, and got the chance in 1974. Briefly back in Sydney, he appeared for me, to ask (successfully) for an adjournment of my long-running Springbok case. He could not stay for the trial – he had to appear at the Old Bailey for a mutual friend, anti-apartheid activist Peter Hain (now Lord Hain), who had been framed on an armed robbery charge – but for a few brief moments at Central Court of Petty Sessions in Liverpool Street, 'the bum and the brains were briefly aligned'.

Geoff valiantly continues, defending his use of words. 'Which, arrogant though it was, probably gave a sense of my feeling that I should be respectable enough to be a creative force, or at least a legal force behind things that I might want to do and have fun in doing and passion in doing, while I had to keep myself …'

I say, 'Tidy?'

He refines his thought. 'I had to keep myself un-gaoled. Put it that way. I had to keep myself out of gaol, and to negotiate my role behind the scenes. So I always felt that fidelity to law, keeping hold of law, would enable what I saw as law-fare, before that term was invented.'

So here is Geoff – the self-confident, even brash, public school boy with that strange English accent – drawn to excitement and even law-breaking, but hard-headed enough to know where his value lay, keeping his nose clean and defending those who did not do so.

'The Nancy Young case was a good example of the protests we made in that way. In that we showed that injustice had to be seen to be done before justice could be done.' The case Geoff refers to was pivotal in the 1960s to the political battle for human rights and decent living conditions for Aboriginal communities. In 1969, Aboriginal mother Nancy Young had been convicted by an all-white male jury for the manslaughter of her baby, who had died probably of scurvy – at the unsanitary Aboriginal Reserve at Cunnamulla in Queensland. Geoff wrote stirring articles in university and mainstream media pointing out that it was the conditions in which Aboriginal families were having to live that had caused the death. 'You had to persevere with investigative journalism, with exposure, you had to use the media and work with the media.' This case and the earlier murder trial of Aboriginal South Australian Rupert Maxwell Stuart had so impacted Geoff that for a short while he even served on the board of the Federal Council for the Advancement of Aborigines and Torres Strait Islanders.

HE DOES THE WISE MAN THING. 'THEY WERE LEARNING experiences in the Sixties – was there something in the air? Well, there wasn't cannabis or LSD.'

So I pop the question, did he ever take drugs? His reply is judicious – and judicial. 'Not at that period, no.'

'But there was something in the air, wasn't there?'

Geoff hardly stops for breath to agree. 'There was. And I'm just trying to think what it was. Certainly it was despair over Menzies and his useless successors. There was no inspiration, and yet I think the people who left Australia in the 1950s never struck me as very political – Clive James being a good example.' Geoff refers to that generation of artistic and literary Australian talent, which included Clive James, Barry Humphries, Germaine Greer and Robert Hughes. 'They had no anger. Australia for them was just a BORING place. For us, Australia was a BAD place.' This distinction hits me. I had never thought of it that way, but he is entirely right.

For me, it was Vietnam that was the major Bad Thing, but Geoff returns to his original trope. 'Well, it was also the White Australia Policy.'

Then Geoff fires up about his greatest passion – censorship. 'You know my particular anger about censorship? It was the gaoling of Richie Walsh, Richard Neville and Francis James in 1964 over some very passionate Martin Sharp satires of right-wing hoon behaviour in the satirical magazine *Oz*. It was outrageous.'

I reinforce his early point. 'Isn't that interesting, that you're talking about anger when you weren't one of the angry young men? I think you're right. It was anger.'

Geoff elaborates on how this anger grew: 'it wasn't there to start with'. He then takes a surprising turn and ruminates about how folk music changed the world in the Sixties. He remembers that Americans Pete Seeger and Phil Ochs sang 'We Shall Overcome' without anger. 'It wasn't an angry anthem. It was a defensive anthem. It wasn't until the students went down to the south and saw the bombed churches and the hanged corpses, and got beaten up by the cops and felt up by the dogs …' He doesn't finish his sentence.

'When they got beaten up, they got angry, and Phil Ochs wrote, "Here's to the State of Mississippi", a really angry song, but I think we in Australia got angry eventually. And that was a really important factor.'

We both then riff on how important Phil Ochs was in our lives and our personal political journeys. It's interesting that, apart from the culturally active Margret RoadKnight and John Derum, few others whom Nadia and I interviewed for this book have really talked about the folk singers.

Geoff points out that when he talks to students about the importance of folk, he always plays Phil Ochs, 'Love Me, I'm a Liberal'. I remember out loud that bit in Ochs's song: '"*I cried when they shot Medgar Evers, but Malcolm X got what was coming.*" It was so true about how people thought at that time, wasn't it?'

Geoff continues my refrain. He knows it all off by heart, '"*But if you ask me to bus my children I hope the cops take down your name.*" Yeah.'

I agree. 'And the poor dear committed suicide.' Geoff even knows the year that Ochs died, 1976. We are in danger of getting maudlin, so we move on.

I tell him: 'It's one of the things that you don't really write about in your book much, but the civil rights agitation in America was very important for people like me'.

Geoff agrees. 'And for me. And then Jim Spigelman came back from the US and said he'd been on Freedom Rides in the States.'

Geoff then refers to the famous NSW Freedom Ride of 1965, organised by Aboriginal activist Charlie Perkins. The bus left Sydney University with thirty students on board and travelled around the racist towns of western New South Wales, picking up fellow Aboriginal activist Gary Williams on the way. Among the students on the ride was the future chief justice of New South Wales, Jim Spigelman.

I mention that I talked to Jim about this book, and that I had asked him whether the Sixties had turned him into a radical, and he had replied, 'Meredith, I'm still not a radical'. Geoff agrees with the statement: 'No he's not'. Jim had elaborated on his statement, adding, 'For me, it was about racism'.

Geoff finishes the thought. 'Jim identified as a Jew. I have no identification, I guess, except as a state school boy. And it may be that I was always trying to prove myself, and what I really was reacting against was the class system, the privilege, yeah.'

'And that's why *The Tempest* was such a huge issue?'

Geoff agrees, and then, boom, there's the sentence: 'I would show how superior I was to those with privilege by absorbing opera and …'

This is fun. I've never had Geoff be this open with me before. Surrounded by the genuine glamour of the most famous building in Australia, Geoff is strip-mining his life in front of me.

Then he decides he's probably overshared. 'I just think this whole idea of suddenly coming back to where I started from is really interesting. Anyway, I think that's everything.' He adds, 'Well, if you need any more just email me. I could never embarrass my mother by being arrested'. What a way to finish the interview. His beloved parents, Frank and Joy, died a few months apart in 2017. Does this mean Geoff is now free to test the limits of judicial law-breaking?

GEOFF DECIDES TO LEAVE BEFORE THE DEATH SCENE, BUT I'm determined to see the end of my first opera in twenty years. As I race up the stairs, Geoff explains, 'I have to go home and do prep to save Lula.'

The phantom paparazzo has a field day. Out it goes on the Twitter universe: 'GEOFF LEFT MEREDITH AT INTERVAL AND SHE HAD TO WATCH THE DEATH SCENE ON HER OWN'.

MARGRET ROADKNIGHT
Troubadour

Meredith Burgmann

I am anxious about starting an interview with Margret RoadKnight. I remember her incredibly well. How can you not remember a woman who appears almost seven foot tall, with the most glorious voice and extraordinary hair, who sang from the back of a truck at many of our important anti-Vietnam marches along the streets of Sydney and Melbourne? However, I don't know much about music and I certainly have no knowledge of the Melbourne folk scene of the Sixties.

Margret has replied to our tentative emails with great kindness and enthusiasm, and we arrange to meet her one very chilly Melbourne day outside her … well, she doesn't like to call it a 'retirement village'. She describes it as a 'home for impoverished thespians'. Margret takes great delight in showing us the old plaque outside her 1891 cottage, which tells us that it was built by a Mrs DR Long, a Melbourne citizen of distinction.

Nadia and I walk into her tiny, very crowded, living space; from floor to ceiling each wall has vinyl records, DVDs, CDs, instruments and books – lots and lots of books. Quick snaps taken on my phone give the impression of the whole precarious thing about to topple.

Margret – these days with shortish light chestnut hair – is tall, yes, still immensely tall, and is wearing a long, floaty, warm cardigan in blue and olive. She seems little different from how I remember her, still imposing and still with that beautiful speaking voice.

Although most folk singers of the period would have killed for a stage name like 'RoadKnight', Margret explains that, with her predominantly Irish family background, this is in fact her real name. She believes that she is indeed a road knight – a troubadour.

MARGRET WAS BORN IN 1943 AND GREW UP IN EAST Melbourne, 'before it was terribly posh', she says. At the time she was born, her mother was a 'homemaker' and her father was away at war. He served in the RAAF, and after returning from the war became deputy director of what Margret refers to as 'Air Force Intelligence'. However, when he was thirty-six, he developed heart problems and retired on an invalid pension. Her mother, the homemaker, had to go out to work as a receptionist.

When we ask Margret where her singing and her love of music came from, she says that there were the usual school and church choirs, but music was not a central part of the family's life together. Her father had been in 'St Patrick's Boys Church Choir', but Margret never heard him sing, whereas her mother sang a lot, and the family briefly had a piano. Other musical influences were standard 1950s fare, primarily the radio. Margret particularly remembers having in the house 'that Father Sydney MacEwan record'. It was probably the ubiquitous *Songs of Scotland and Ireland*, which I can remember also being in our house.

St Patrick's, which Margret has mentioned, was in fact Melbourne's Catholic cathedral, which was only ten minutes walk from the family home. And, indeed, Margret sometimes saw Archbishop Daniel Mannix walking down Albert Street towards his power base.

Growing up in 1950s Australia, Margret's world was divided into Catholics and non-Catholics. But all was not simple. On Sundays her father put on a suit and pretended he was going 'off to St Pat's'. She sees this pretence as being a kindness, a matter of 'doing the right thing', rather than any particular need to hide the fact that he wasn't going to church.

Margret attended the local Catholic school, St John's, in East Melbourne, and went to Mass every Sunday, but when I ask her, 'Do you think you really believed?' she sounds quite definite when she says, 'No'.

She describes herself as a cultural Catholic, and when I say, 'Was there an actual moment when you stopped believing?' she admits with a laugh that when the Church changed its edict about eating meat on Friday being a mortal sin to it being OK, it lost its credibility for her. They couldn't even hold fast on that small point.

Although Margret went through the motions of Catholicism, she did at one stage make a point of saying to her mother, 'If I come to you and say I want to be a nun, you'll stop me, won't you?' Margret understood well the pressure that the Church could apply to young minds.

IN 1956, WHEN MARGRET WAS THIRTEEN, HER FAMILY moved to a Housing Commission home in the suburb of East Reservoir, in Melbourne's north. Describing her parents as having 'the pride of the nouveau poor', Margret adds sardonically that 'the nouveau poor had no strategy of how to cope'. She explains that the long-term poor knew how to get their due benefits from the welfare system. In contrast, her family lacked this kind of skill.

For high school, Margret attended Santa Maria College, Northcote, which she left at the end of 1960 at the age of seventeen. The next year she started work with the Playgrounds and Recreation Association of Victoria – an organisation based in parks and recreation centres around the inner city. Already familiar with the association because she and her siblings had used its facilities while they were growing up, for the next two-and-a-half years Margret would teach art and craft and sport to toddlers and teenagers. She explains this career choice by saying, 'I'm basically a drifter', though later she did move to a better-paying job, as a 'pen pusher' in the public service.

MARGRET'S PARENTS WEREN'T PARTICULARLY POLITICAL, but were classic anti-Communist DLP (Democratic Labor Party) voters – believing, for example, in a threat from the yellow hordes to Australia's north. Despite this, Margret is at pains to say that they were 'nice people', with no racist intent.

To demonstrate this, she tells us that, when the Black American singer Paul Robeson visited Melbourne in 1960, her father and mother thought she and her sister should go to his concert – despite the fact that he was one of the best-known Communist supporters in the world. Perhaps her parents' love of good music and their opposition to the persecution of this great man was more important than their anti-Communism.

In a further account of this episode, Margret wrote in the program notes for *Deep Bells Ring*, a musical play about Robeson's life:

> When Robeson performed in Melbourne I persuaded my younger sister that we must go. Because of the demand for tickets we had to sit behind him on the stage but we nonetheless considered ourselves very lucky and were mightily impressed (this in spite of an upbringing placing us diametrically opposite him on the political spectrum).

This episode links with another significant political moment in Margret's youth. She describes reading about the way Black American singer Marian Anderson was treated in 1939, when the Daughters of the American Revolution refused her permission to sing to an integrated audience in Washington DC's Constitution Hall. A kind of resolution came about when First Lady Eleanor Roosevelt helped organise for Anderson to sing to an integrated audience of 75 000 on the steps of the Lincoln Memorial. Margret, still angry today as she recounts this incident, says, 'That situation occurred simply because she was black – I remember crying when I read about it'. With obvious delight she goes on to recall how she later managed to see Marian Anderson in concert at Melbourne Town Hall.

Asked what her first vote would have been, Margret ponders. 'I think I would have voted DLP.' Then she shakes her head. 'No, in fact I did vote DLP.' This was the 1963 election, when sectarian issues and the Communist bogey loomed large. A major campaign issue was state aid for church schools – for which the Catholic Church and the DLP were fighting tooth and nail. (Margret's ingrained Catholicism reveals itself when she says, 'We knew there was a truth – that we paid twice for education'.) In Melbourne, this fight was particularly virulent.

When we ask Margret for her light-bulb moment, that instant when she felt her social conservatism give way to more liberal ideas, she says, 'I can tell you that it was through folk music'.

However, there was no actual 'moment' of change. Her 'conversion' was a muted and drawn-out affair. She laughingly says that at one time she used to describe herself as one of the only right-wing folk singers in Australia.

She then mentions a name that crops up over and over again when we discuss the Sixties in Melbourne, and that is Emerald Hill Theatre. In addition to its innovatory drama program, on Sunday afternoons the theatre was a venue for concerts where various groups of musicians played both folk music and jazz. Margret recalls that a friend suggested she should go along to one of these Sunday music sessions. This was in 1962.

In talking about her introduction to this scene, she immediately mentions Glen Tomasetti, who, as well as being one of the musicians at Emerald Hill Theatre, also played an important part in putting together the musical program. Glen was a politically active singer-songwriter who appeared regularly on commercial television during the 1960s performing satirical political songs. Margret avows that Glen was a pivotal influence for her. Early on in her involvement with Emerald Hill she also met a singer named Paul Marks, with whom she felt an instant musical rapport. 'He was a little bit like me. He was interested in trad jazz, the blues and English folk.' (Of herself, she says, 'I was very eclectic'.)

Margret's overseas influences included Mahalia Jackson and Harry Belafonte. (Oh, how well I remember those names.)

Once again, we get back to folk music – the connection between politics and folk music. Margret is quick to draw a distinction between the range of music she encountered at Emerald Hill and some of the traditional folk songs, which she describes as 'the terrible stuff we'd been taught at school'. 'Dashing Away with the Smoothing Iron' seems to have got up her nose the most. Given the misogynistic and repetitive lyrics of this ballad, about a woman washing, drying, ironing and finally wearing her linen, it is easy to see why.

By 1962, folk music was, Margret says, 'big here, but still underground'. It was a hidden world, with a repertoire comprised of bush ballads and what were then called 'Negro' work songs. Glen Tomasetti even introduced a Chinese lullaby to the program, and the Emerald Hill musicians were also 'doing political stuff – Irish political stuff'.

Initially, Margret did not find political songs engaging. Coming from her right-wing background, and having a disdain for 'weak songs' and 'simplistic songs', she was dismissive of those numbers whose lyrics seemed like 'slogans from placards set to a chant'.

In summer, these concerts transferred to a coffee lounge in inner city Little Collins Street, called the Little Reata, which had recently been opened by Hungarian immigrant

Tom Lazar. The Little Reata was a spin-off from the original Reata in Prahran, which was the first coffee lounge in Australia to have a resident folk singer.

Although Margret was increasingly drawn into this alternative music scene, she wasn't yet singing, or at least, not in public.

Early in 1963, Margret was attending a Sunday concert at the Little Reata, where Paul Marks was the house singer; hoping for a break, Marks asked, 'Would anyone like to sing?'

Margret obliged with 'Sometimes I Feel Like a Motherless Child', an African-American spiritual that had recently been released in America by Odetta. When Glen Tomasetti applauded the unknown performer, it was a significant moment in Margret RoadKnight's lifelong musical career.

On the strength of this unplanned audition, Glen offered Margret her first paid performance at Emerald Hill's winter season. For her first gig, Glen asked the newcomer to sing three songs, accompanied by bassist Graham McLean. But when they had to do an encore, Graham didn't know Margret's chosen song. So she performed the unexpected encore *a capella*. Glen announced with prescience, 'Margret will be back'.

Although this performance had gone well, Glen stipulated that Margret accompany herself for the promised return booking. Margret went off and taught herself the guitar. Three weeks later, she played a Latvian lullaby with backwards arpeggios. Thus began Margret's self-contained act. 'Have guitar, will travel', is how she describes it.

WHILE THE MELBOURNE FOLK SCENE AND SOME OF ITS musicians provided the environment that fostered Margret's 'conversion', her repertoire turning point came when she heard a recording of Joan Baez singing a cover version of 'What Have They Done to the Rain?', written by Californian singer/songwriter Malvina Reynolds. Her reaction was, 'At last ... a poetic, melodic "protest song" with a subtle message'.

She is emphatic that 'What Have They Done to the Rain?' was as close as it comes to her 'aha' moment. She explains: 'It's not immediately obvious, but that song is about nuclear fallout'. The powerful effect that these lyrics had on Margret makes total sense because, in the early 1960s, nuclear bombs were the big radicalising political issue, before the Vietnam conflagration overtook all other worries.

Malvina Reynolds also wrote 'Little Boxes' (later made famous by Pete Seeger), 'Turn Around' and 'Morningtown Ride'. Margret taught herself various Malvina Reynolds songs, and she reiterates that Reynolds is still a favourite songwriter.

Margret delightedly adds that in 1974, when she visited the United States on a scholarship tour, she was Reynolds' houseguest in San Francisco. As Malvina was driving her from the airport she actually pointed out those 'little boxes on the hillside'.

At this, the three of us start humming, as we all remember the song – especially the bit about the little boxes that were made of 'ticky tacky'.

Margret then says something really interesting. 'Never give up on anyone. You can vote DLP all your life and then still change.' Talking again about voting DLP when she was twenty-one, she says that she's proof that even adults can change politically. She describes herself as a late bloomer.

Her second vote, in 1966, was definitely not for the DLP.

Underlining the way this change was based around the music, and the other musicians she was interacting with, she says, 'It just became obvious, hanging around the people I admired, such as Jeannie Lewis'.

Jeannie Lewis was what Americans call a 'red diaper baby'. The child of well-known Communists Sam Lewis and Ethel Teerman, by the Sixties Jeannie was regularly singing at left-wing concerts and fundraisers. Margret says she had (and still has) many political conversations with Jeannie.

In 1967, Margret was invited onto the program of the Port Phillip District Folk Music Festival (which was inspired by the Newport Folk Festival in America). This festival, commonly called the Melbourne Folk Festival, has now morphed into the National Folk Festival, held in Canberra each year. The festival's organising committee included left-wing social activist and folk historian Wendy Lowenstein, and David Lumsden, whose father had helped raise money to assist Pete Seeger in his trial for 'Un-American Activities' during the McCarthy period. Glen Tomasetti (by this stage heavily involved in anti-Vietnam activity, especially Save Our Sons) was on the committee too.

Describing these organisers as 'very serious', Margret explains that this festival 'had a very political intent'. Although 'the trad jazz and bluesy scenes were a little wilder', folk music was regarded as 'important music ... music that can change attitudes and make society better'.

If it wasn't already clear that Margret RoadKnight was accepted by the left-wing music scene, her participation at this folk festival – vetted by its highly political committee – was an endorsement; although, as Margret points out, there were many apolitical singers at the gig.

When we ask her how she came to be more deeply involved in the anti-war movement, she replies, 'I just sang at things I was asked to sing at'.

If once again there's this feeling of her drifting into things, by 1971 the drift was complete. She shows us a picture of herself, dressed in a mini skirt and with her signature afro, singing to a huge crowd at that year's Melbourne Moratorium, which was led by eminent Labor Party frontbenchers Jim Cairns and Tom Uren. Although (as she mentions) she 'still only had a nylon-string acoustic guitar and there was only one microphone', her huge voice and commanding presence were easily powerful enough for the occasion.

Two years later, Margret's first album, *People Get Ready*, was released. While the title gives a real sense of her new-found activism, the album's songs were very influenced by Black American material. Margret also took a South African song about land rights and 'made it into an Aboriginal one'. She became known for performing African songs and playing the African thumb piano.

While Margret's interest in the American civil rights movement remained intense, by this time she was also involved with 'some early environmentalism' and with Women's Liberation.

Another musical highlight was the series of 'SHE' women's concerts organised by Glen Tomasetti, which took place in Melbourne, Sydney and Canberra in 1973. Margret had been tapped on the shoulder by Glen to join this overtly political bunch of feminist singers. The first half of each concert was made up of traditional songs and the second half featured more contemporary music. The group finished with a triumphant rendition of Helen Reddy's 'I Am Woman'. It was during these concerts that Margret first sang Bob

Hudson's 'Girls in Our Town', which was released as a single in January 1976 and became her breakout hit.

Towards the end of our conversation, Margret again talks about 'that period where I was up on the back of a truck singing at the Moratorium'. At the time, she had no idea that fifty years later her Moratorium performance 'would still be an important thing'.

'Some of the most interesting people I shared the stage with were not musicians', she adds. 'They were Jim Cairns, Nelson Mandela, David Suzuki and others.'

Nadia asks about the overall effect of the Sixties on her life and her career. Did it provide opportunities? 'Absolutely! It was my university. I learnt about politics, history and poetry through folk song.'

Having said that she was a drifter and having really downplayed the political aspect of her life ('as performers, we're the front people, we don't really do the hard yards'), Margret then says something quite telling. 'You have to entertain but why would you just do that when you have the forum, the time and the focus of people?' As she wrote of Paul Robeson, in her notes for the *Deep Bells Ring* program:

> I've long cited [him] as a luminous example of the possibility, indeed the necessity, of combining social relevance with entertainment and art. How satisfying it always is to be involved in projects which can strike that balance.

THE POSTSCRIPT TO THIS INTERVIEW IS THAT, IN SEPTEMBER 2019, I attended a concert produced under the flag of the 'Sedition' festival, which took place in the old Cell Block Theatre in Darlinghurst, Sydney. Margret was the MC and occasional singer, while other performers were Sixties and seventies icons Jeannie Lewis, Janie Conway Herron, Shayna Karlin, Jan Cornall and Elizabeth Drake.

Watching Margret perform again is a treat. She loves the crowd and the crowd loves her. She looks even taller and more beautiful when she performs. Meeting someone in a Melbourne winter in a long woolly cardigan is not the way to see a performer. Up there on the stage, she comes alive in a way I can't believe.

In between sets, Margret chats happily to the audience amid only slightly controlled chaos. Many of the other singers mention Margret as one of their mentors.

Actor John Derum, sitting beside me in the happy audience, comments, 'She is so wonderfully not Show Biz'.

My own observation is that I have never seen someone look so cheerful while singing the blues.

After Margret performs a zesty duet of 'Takes Two to Tango' with Jeannie Lewis, all the women come together for 'Girls in Our Town' – almost our own feminist anthem.

> *Girls in our town get no help from their men*
> *No one can let them be sixteen again*
> *Things might get better – but it's hard to say when*
> *If they only had someone to talk to …*

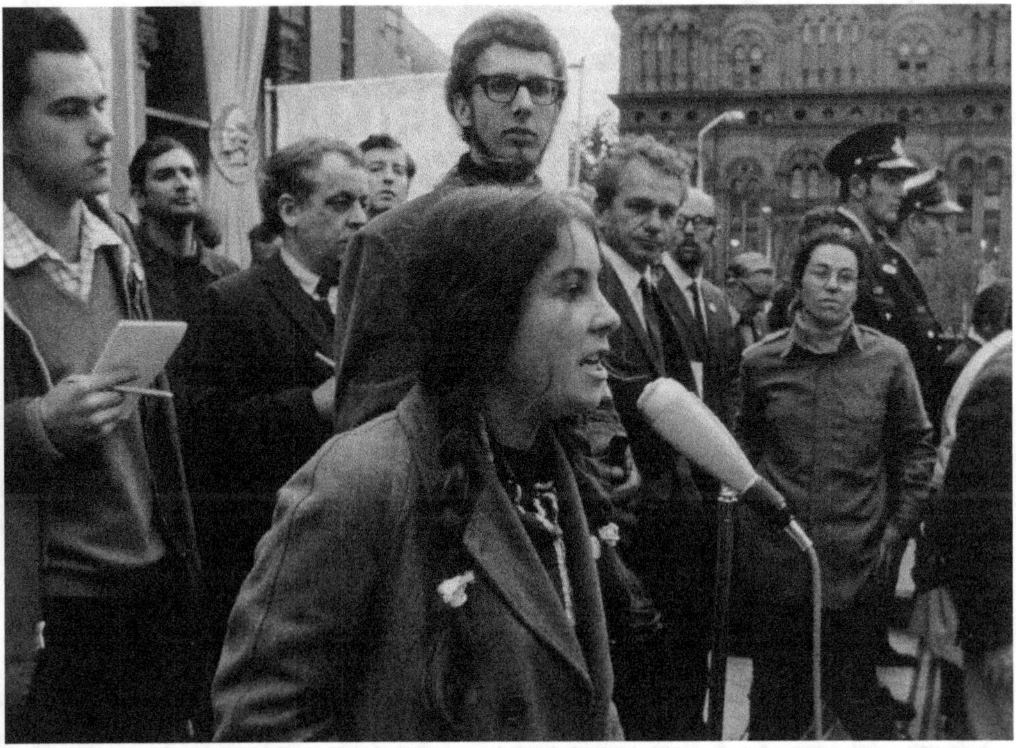

BIGGEST WEEK-DAY SALES IN NSW

ALL THE BETTING PRICES

Daily Mirror

THE INDEPENDENT PAPER

LATE FINAL EXTRA

Sydney, Friday, August 2, 1968

No. 8440 — 5c

● Lottery: Special 1641 P 56 ● Finance P 20 ● TV P 37 ● Weather: Dry, cool

ARREST

George St today: students protest

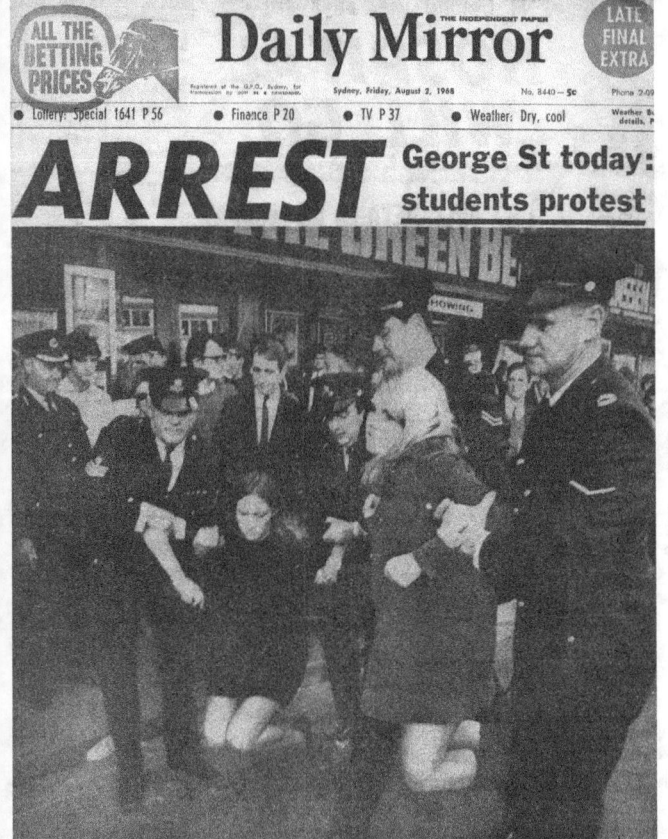

Above 18-year-old Helen Voysey addresses 20 000 people at the first Sydney Moratorium, May 1970. In the background are Moratorium convenor Ken McLeod (wearing spectacles), draft resister Mike Jones (with notepad), and lawyer Tony Blackshield (goatee beard).

Richard Brennan, Or Forever Hold Your Peace

Left Protest against John Wayne's pro-war film, *The Green Berets* at the Regent Theatre in George St, Sydney. Marie Ely (left) and Nadia Wheatley (right) are being carted off to Regent St Police Station.

Daily Mirror, *2 August 1968. Newspix*

Oz editors, Felix Dennis (giving the V sign) with Richard Neville (centre) and Jim Anderson, sprung from Wormwood Scrubs Prison, UK, by their hairy lawyer Geoffrey Robertson (far right), 1971.
Penguin Random House

Brian Laver addresses a meeting at the Forum, University of Queensland, in the lead-up to the elections for the Student Union Council, 1967.
AC20.008 UQ elections; Greg Perry, Brisbane, courtesy of State Library of Queensland

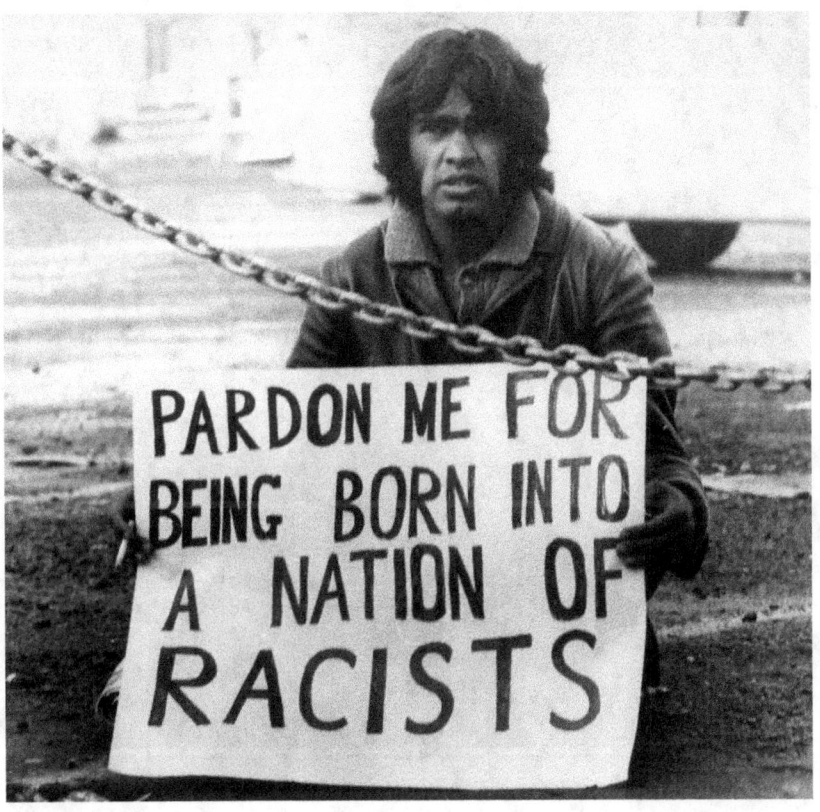

Anti-Springbok campaign, July 1971. In the image that flashed around the world, Gary Foley sits in the rain outside the Springboks' hotel in Bondi Junction. The placard reveals Gary's unique sense of humour.

Sydney Morning Herald, *10 July 1971. On request by Nine Publishing*

Springboks game, Manuka Oval, Canberra 21 July 1971. Meredith Burgmann gets busted and charged for something Gary Foley and Gary Williams actually did.

Courtesy Meredith Burgmann

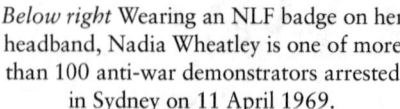

Above Bronwyn Penrith, wearing a blonde wig, personifies White Power in a street theatre performance publicising the Black Moratorium and the Gove land rights case.

This Day Tonight, *Australian Broadcasting Corporation, 1972*

Right Bronwyn Penrith, aged five, appeared on a page titled 'Some of our Ladies' in a 1957 issue of the Assimilationist government publication, *Dawn*.

Dawn, *issued by the NSW Aborigines Welfare Board, Vol 6 #10, October 1957*

Below right Wearing an NLF badge on her headband, Nadia Wheatley is one of more than 100 anti-war demonstrators arrested in Sydney on 11 April 1969.

Sydney Morning Herald, *12 April 1969. On request by Nine Publishing*

Margret RoadKnight in mini skirt and afro singing at the Melbourne Moratorium 1970, watched by Jim Cairns and a huge crowd of protesters.

Australian Performing Arts Collection, Arts Centre Melbourne

Margret RoadKnight and her great friend and political mentor Jeannie Lewis put on the razzle dazzle, 1970s.

Courtesy Margret RoadKnight

Bringing out the heavies. Meredith Burgmann arrested by Chief Inspector (later Assistant Commissioner) Stackpool outside the Regent Theatre, Sydney, which was showing the John Wayne pro-Vietnam movie *The Green Berets*, August 1968.

Photographer Wayne Davies

Freedom Riders Brian Aarons and Gary Williams test the colour bar in the Bowraville Hotel, February 1965. 'I was nineteen and I was not a drinker at this stage, I was just Aboriginal'.

Sydney Morning Herald, 25 February 1965. On request by Nine Publishing

Peter Batchelor (centre) with long hair and duffle coat arguing with police during a picket line set up by Furnishing Trade Union members at Olympic General Products, a factory in the west of Melbourne. The argument proved successful and the police withdrew.

Courtesy Peter Batchelor

Margaret Reynolds (holding 'Women's Abortion' placard) marching in an Abortion Rights protest in hostile Brisbane, 1970s.

Courtesy Margaret Reynolds

Anti-war demonstration outside US Consulate, Brisbane, 1 July 1966. Despite being accompanied by his wife Janita (pregnant at the time) and young daughter, Brian Laver is being arrested on a charge of carrying a placard (confiscated by the arresting officer).

Photographer Graham Garner. Courtesy Brian Laver

An awed Peter Manning is taken by his *Bulletin* editor, Donald Horne, to meet Gough Whitlam, some time between 1969 and 1972. Even Gough looked youngish then.

Courtesy Maria Manning

The famous Sydney University Proctorial Board Hearing, April 1967. Defendant Max Humphreys (left), Tribune of the people Geoff Robertson (centre) and Student Advisor Weir Wilson (right).

Honi Soit, *19 April 1967, University of Sydney, Students' Representative Council*

Vietnam Moratorium, Adelaide 1970. Peter Duncan (left) and David Wilson (right). Two very nattily dressed young lawyers.

Courtesy Peter Duncan

The traditional Sydney University graduation photo: David Marr, BA 1968.

Courtesy David Marr

Above Helen Voysey (second from right behind the banner) as High School Students Against the War take part in an anti-war march, Sydney, 1969.

Courtesy Helen Voysey

Left Gary Foley prepares to deliver another diatribe. His famously outspoken style of public speaking shows the influence of soapbox orator, Webster.

University of Melbourne Archives UMA/1/603, image number 1999.0081.00409

May Day March in Townsville, 1970s. Left to right: Bill Timms (Townsville TLC), Senator Jim Keefe, Stewart West (Federal MP), Col Emery (ETU), Alex Wilson (State MP for Townsville). Bit blokey ... but Margaret Reynolds (in sunglasses) soldiers on.

Courtesy Margaret Reynolds

An impossibly young Gary Williams and an older Charlie Perkins pictured in the quadrangle on their first day at Sydney University in February 1963. They were the first Aboriginal students and Charlie was an important friend and mentor for the young Gary.

Courtesy Gary Williams

Angry Redfern, 1971. Gary Williams, Dennis Walker, Billy Craigie and Gary Foley (front). The spectre of Black Power gaining ground in Australia consumed the fevered imaginations of NSW Police Special Branch and ASIO.

Photographer Barrie Ward. Sunday Australian, *5 December 1971, Newspix, 1270986*

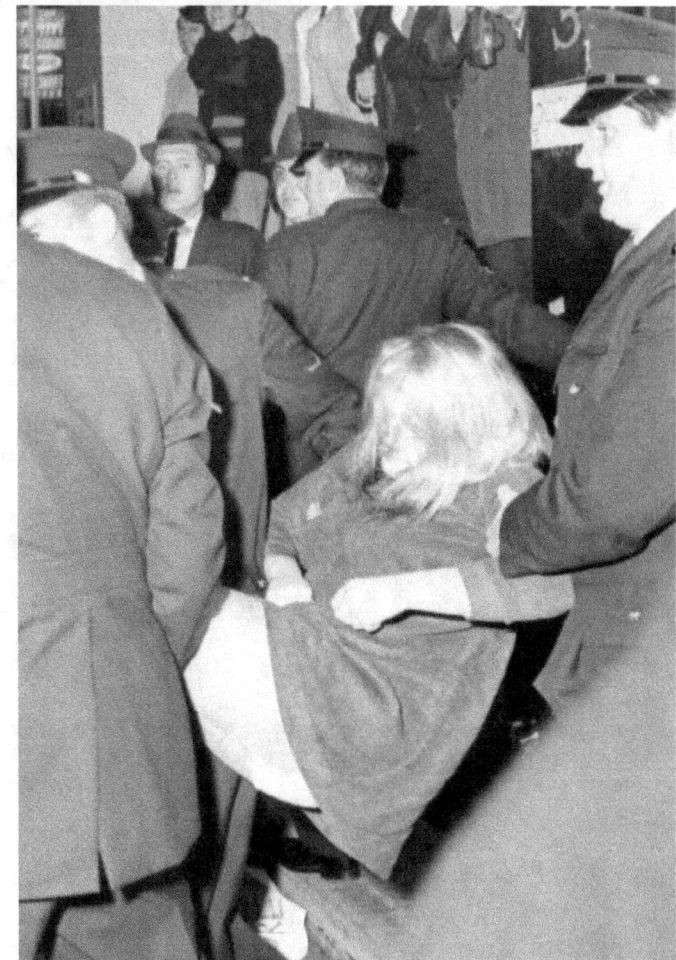

Nadia Wheatley displays her Cottontails as well as the recommended limp body-position when she is dragged out of the Liberal Party's Sydney headquarters on Independence *from* America Day, 4 July 1968.

The Sun, *5 July 1968. On request by Nine Publishing*

Ellis D Fogg (Roger Foley) demonstrates his mist machine to John Hopkins (centre) and Peter Sculthorpe (right) as part of his collaboration with the Melbourne and Sydney Symphony orchestras.

Courtesy Roger Foley-Fogg

One of Ellis D Fogg's famous Lightshow posters which proliferated on Sydney streets in the Sixties. Design by Gary Worley and Jim Anderson.

Courtesy Roger Foley-Fogg

Jozefa Sobski confronts the enemy in a 1973 demonstration demanding the right of women to drink in public bars. The drinker seems to have body space issues.

Photographer Adrienne Martyn.
Mejane March 1973

Described by her priest as 'too serious a Catholic', Jozefa Sobski makes her First Holy Communion, St Patrick's Church, Guildford, 27 October 1957.

Courtesy Jozefa Sobski

Albert Langer rallies the troops during an occupation of Monash University administration offices, August 1969.

The Mirror, *date unknown*, Monash University Archives #4333. Newspix

Albert Langer and his wife Kerry Miller enjoy a day away from the barricades.

Photographer Darce Cassidy. Labour History, Melbourne

In this publicity shot for the WOOM Environmental Happening at Watters Gallery, 1971, Vivienne Binns (right) poses with her new lover Yve Repin and her kindred spirit and former lover Mike Brown.

Courtesy Vivienne Binns

Vivienne Binns's installation 'Yipes! What a Mess' riled the critics when it went on display at Watters Gallery in 1967. The Establishment was easily scared in the Sixties.

Courtesy Vivienne Binns

Robbie Swan ... experimenting with everything in the Sixties, even dress ... with Pleasance Ingle at the Canberra Girls Grammar School function at the Federal Golf Club, 1970. Robbie had just taken a microdot.

Courtesy Robbie Swan

Two 'found bush marihuana plot'

Two Canberra students were found throwing buckets of water over more than 600 marihuana plants in bushland in the Brindabella Ranges, police alleged in Queanbeyan Court today.

The students, Werner John Baltgavis, 19, of Carnegie Crescent, Narrabundah, and Robert James Swan, 20, of La Perouse Street, Det Sgt Lambert of the ACT Police.
"They walked 300 yards to a cleared patch in dense undergrowth surrounded by netting fence. "On the area inside I Sydney Drug Squad returned to the scene in the Brindabellas.
"I saw two male persons known to me to be the defendants Swan and Baltgavis", Sgt Gudgeon

Very Sixties. Robbie Swan caught tending 600 marijuana plants, March 1972.

Canberra News, 1 March 1972.

Anti-Vietnam demonstration outside US Consulate, Sydney, 1969. Meredith Burgmann helped (or hindered) by fellow protester Dave Clark. Not quite showing the Cottontails, but almost.

Photographer Mervyn Bishop. Courtesy Josef Lebovic Gallery, Sydney

Peter Duncan addressing the crowd on call-up day outside Keswick Barracks, Adelaide, 1970. Behind him is the Chair of the Vietnam Moratorium Campaign, Lynn Arnold (later Premier of SA).

Courtesy Peter Duncan

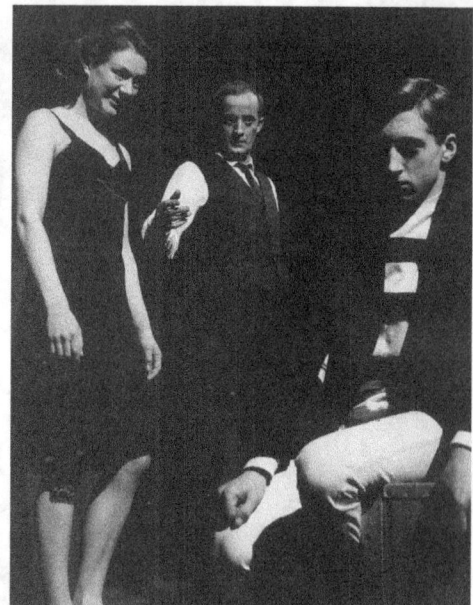

Above left Emerald Hill Theatre, Melbourne, 1964. Cast of *You'll Come to Love Your Sperm Test*. Left to right: John Paton, Michael Boddy, George Whaley, Gerda Nicolson, John Derum (seated at front). The title sure raised a few eyebrows. Some media refused to accept advertisements for the production.
Courtesy John Derum

Above right Emerald Hill Theatre, Melbourne, 1964. Cast of *Death of a Salesman*. Gerda Nicolson, George Whaley and a very young John Derum. George Whaley was particularly important in John's political awakening.
Courtesy John Derum

Right On a Newman Society excursion to Adelaide in 1962, Peter Manning (up the ladder) takes part in a mock elopement. It's a spoof, but the couple's 'marriage' (by the priest in white) is a reminder of how young Catholics often missed out on the sexual permissiveness of the Sixties.
Courtesy Barbara Cleary

ALBERT LANGER (ARTHUR DENT)
Hardened apparatchik

Nadia Wheatley

In the Sixties, every university had its own distinctive political organisations. Even within a single city, what was happening at one campus might be very different from what was going on at another. Between the cities of Sydney and Melbourne, the traditional rivalries played out.

As a Sydneysider, I remember comparing the sizes of demonstrations (usually greater in Melbourne) and the seismic level of the rage on the streets (again, usually greater in Melbourne). But if Melbourne was the Paris of Australasia, its revolutionary hotbed was the Monash University Labor Club, and its best-known activist was Albert Langer – described by political journalist Mungo MacCallum as 'the youngest and most brilliant of the Australian student revolutionary leaders'. Under Langer's influence, the Monash

Albert Langer (Arthur Dent)

militants had a political alignment that was unique among student organisations. Many were Maoists.

Since 2005, Albert Langer has been 'incommunicado' under the name Arthur Dent (borrowed from *The Hitchhiker's Guide to the Galaxy*). It's a bit hard to track him down but eventually Meredith's sister, Verity, sets up a meet, and Meredith and I fly to Melbourne on a cold, grey winter's day. As we enter the appointed cafe, I half expect Arthur to be wearing a dressing gown and carrying a bath towel, like Douglas Adams's fictional anti-hero. No such thing! With his bushy beard and black Polish hat, complete with fur-lined earflaps, Arthur Dent looks like a revolutionary. The real surprise is his beaming smile.

Somewhat later, as I consider the way Langer had been excluded from postgraduate courses at every Australian university, I mention the sacrifice that had resulted from his political activism. Arthur Dent looks at me as if I simply do not get it. 'What sacrifice?' he demands. 'It was *fun!*'

Fun? I knew we had fun in Sydney, but I had always imagined that the Monash Maoists were so committed to the capital-R Revolution that having a good time would have been seen as reactionary. Not a bit of it.

'We had a slogan', Arthur elaborates, 'that, in order to have a revolution, you needed to have a revolutionary party. So we had one every Friday night'. These shindigs were held at a former bakery in Prahran that by 1969 was the headquarters of the Maoist-aligned Worker-Student Alliance, and also the home of Langer, his wife Kerry, and a number of other cadres. (A history of The Bakery, written by former resident, Ken Mansell, has the terrific title, 'The Yeast Is Red'.)

But what came before the parties – or the Party?

Hardened apparatchik

IN KEEPING WITH THE THEME OF THIS BOOK, MEREDITH and I begin by asking Arthur about the early life of Albert Langer. I have read online that his Polish-Jewish parents reached London shortly before the Second World War, and that they had divorced when he was six. Arthur is reluctant to say more than that the year of his birth was 1949, and that he was ten or eleven when his family – whom he describes as 'bourgeois' – came from London to Melbourne, where they settled in the affluent suburb of Toorak. He tells us his mother was a Zionist and his stepfather wasn't.

Clearly, Albert Langer was one of many radicals of our generation (including myself) whose activism was forged in opposition to their background. Indeed, he makes a point of saying, 'My politics did not in any sense come from my family'. He adds that he 'had an orthodox instead of a liberal bar mitzvah because the liberals required pretending to believe in God and the orthodox did not'.

Albert's cultural background did, however, connect with one of his early political interests. Because of their historic experience of anti-Semitism, many members of Melbourne's Jewish community were strongly opposed to South Africa's policy of apartheid. To young Albert, the South African government's systemic oppression of Black people was an extreme form of bullying – and already a hatred of bullying had emerged as one of his 'fundamental personality traits'. At the age of fourteen he joined South Africa Protest and was made secretary of Youth Against Apartheid. In this capacity he organised a folk concert with singer Glen Tomasetti and other well-known musicians.

That same year, Albert joined the Young Labor Association (YLA). Organised in local branches, the association had quarterly conferences. For Albert, the YLA provided a training ground in political debate and organisation. Very soon, he was on its Victorian State Executive.

In the anti-apartheid movement, Albert was meeting members of the Communist Party of Australia, and others who had left the CPA because they were more radical. As a YLA apparatchik, he was aligned with the Victorian Central Executive of the Labor Party. In this period following the split with the Democratic Labor Party, these ALP leaders 'saw themselves as hard-left socialists' and 'ran the party with an iron fist'. On first encountering the 'spectrum of left-wing people' in these two organisations, Albert decided the Communists were 'boring', and less radical than their opponents. Already starting to read Marxist texts, he decided that 'as a Marxist, I would much rather try to see what could be done in the Labor Party' than in the Communist Party. So he remained in the ALP.

In 1964, the fifteen-year-old became involved in an episode of ALP 'gang warfare' with someone who 'ran a corrupt mafia in the Prahran City Council'. On discovering that Albert was too young to be eligible for party membership, his enemy arranged his expulsion from their local ALP branch. He could not, however, expel Albert from the YLA State Executive. Rejoining the party on turning sixteen, Albert immediately became secretary of the branch. ('By this time the gangster had himself been expelled', Arthur explains.) This personal experience of political bullying was both a learning curve and a radicalising force. All in all, these ruthless factional manoeuvres meant that Albert Langer was what he proudly calls a 'hardened apparatchik' while he was still so young that he had to climb out the window of the family home in order to go to branch meetings.

Alongside this busy political life, Albert had another

interest. In what he calls 'a very odd bit in my personal history', he was passionate about electronics. It is easy to picture him as the kind of kid who today would hole up in his room with his computer, connecting with other like-minded nerds across the World Wide Web. But in the Sixties, the international method of communication was amateur radio.

A member of electronics clubs from the age of fourteen, Albert qualified for his amateur operator's certificate the next year. Again, the precocious boy hit the age barrier. Ineligible to use a licence to transmit until he was older, Albert joined the informal community of young short-wave listeners who used to send signal reception reports to international broadcasting stations, which in turn sent back an acknowledgment by snail mail on a type of postcard called a 'QSL card'. These were highly prized by the recipients. Although this hobby might seem akin to train-spotting or collecting cigarette cards, it put Albert in touch with the world beyond Melbourne High School and the local branch of the ALP. With his postal address freely available to international radio stations, he 'got bombarded from the Voice of America, and from Radio Peking' with a barrage of pamphlets, polemics, and copies of *Peking Review*. Although he cannot recall being assailed from Moscow, he 'must have got some of their stuff' as well.

Through 'this postal propaganda', the teenager was 'acutely aware that there were these big debates going on about nuclear disarmament' – debates that reflected the widening schism between Moscow and Peking. In the left-wing circles in which Albert was moving, the ideological difference between the two Communist states 'was presented as: "The pro-Chinese are warmongers who are in favour of nuclear war, and the peace-loving Moscow-liners are in favour of disarmament.'"

This seemed to give Moscow the moral high ground, but Albert Langer found himself wondering: 'How could you be a Communist and think it's a good idea for the Americans to have nuclear weapons and for the Chinese not to?' This was so 'bizarrely illogical' to him that he 'started looking into it'.

The question quickly went beyond the nuclear debate to the essence of Communism. 'And it was utterly clear to me that, yes, the Chinese were right, and there was nothing resembling Communism in anything the Russians were saying. And though the Chinese were writing in a very strange way, using Chinese-English expressions in a hyped-up manner, they were basically on the right track.' So he went to the state library and started studying the history of the split that had occurred over 1963–64, when some members of the Soviet-aligned Communist Party of Australia had left to form the China-aligned Communist Party of Australia (Marxist-Leninist), led by local ideologue, Ted Hill. Arthur explains that: 'Only after studying the polemics did I make contact with any of its members'.

Over this same period, the bookish boy, who was 'attracted to left Communism', also 'studied Trotskyism and revisionism carefully'. Although he 'concluded that Maoism was correct', he retained an affection for anarchism. With a self-deprecating laugh, Arthur Dent says, 'I still accept being called an anarcho-Stalinist'.

By his final year at Melbourne High, Albert Langer was a Maoist, albeit a somewhat anarchistic one. He was also a first class honours student, his specialty being mathematics.

Hardened apparatchik

IN 1966, MONASH UNIVERSITY HAD ONLY BEEN RUNNING for eight years; student numbers were still so low that most people knew each other, at least by sight. Situated in Clayton, 20 kilometres from the CBD, it was one of the first of the new-style universities based in the suburbs.

When Albert Langer arrived on the campus, the Labor Club was 'very strong, but it was an ALP Club, 100 per cent', and the leadership supported the Whitlamite right wing of the party. Although Langer himself was still in the ALP, from the time of his arrival he was 'part of a cohort' within the club that was 'aiming to take it in a more radical direction' – that is, towards the ALP's left wing, led by Jim Cairns. This cohort was led by Dave Nadel, who was a couple of years older than Albert and had been one of sixteen students arrested in a highly publicised anti-Vietnam demonstration in Canberra the previous year. In the Labor Club's elections of 1966, the leadership passed into the hands of the more radical group, with Nadel winning the presidency and first-year student Albert Langer becoming vice-president. Arthur describes how, at one particularly hostile confrontation with former officers of the club, he 'saved Dave's bacon' by dampening down hostilities as 'the neutral chair'. (The mind boggles.)

In November of that same year, the win by the Liberal/Country Party Coalition in the federal election meant that there would be no weakening of Australia's commitment to the war in Vietnam. This was the catalyst for a further shift to the left in the Monash Labor Club.

Another radicalising force was police brutality during demonstrations against visits by the American President, Lyndon B Johnson (October 1966) and South Vietnam's Prime Minister, Air Vice-Marshall Ky (January 1967).

Albert Langer (Arthur Dent)

In a pamphlet detailing demonstrators' experiences, Langer described what had happened to him after the LBJ protest:

> While I was in the cell a policeman – wearing plain clothes – came into the cell. He pushed me away from the door further into the cell. He held me against the wall and asked me what I was studying. I didn't reply. He then bashed my head against the wall of the cell. He asked me again. Before I had a chance to reply he bashed my head against the wall even harder. I then said I was studying for a Science degree. Then he pushed me away, saying if I had said I was studying to be an idiot he would have knocked me unconscious.

Discussions of these off-campus events among Labor Club activists over the long summer holidays meant that 'all emerged by the beginning of term with a revolutionary socialist activist perspective'. As Arthur Dent recalls, it was in 1967 that 'things really got moving' at Monash University.

The main sign of change was a regular publication, *Print*, produced with the assistance of radical journalist Darce Cassidy, who lived in a share house with Dave Nadel. Paraphrasing Chairman Mao, Cassidy used to proclaim that 'Power comes out of the barrel of a Gestetner' (a reference to the brand-name of the duplicator used to produce radical publications). The new Labor Club bulletin began in March 1967, and came out two or three times a week over that year and the next. By 1969, it would be a daily.

The Labor Club's ability to spread its message among students would be crucial in its first big campaign. This would result in the radicalisation of Monash campus, and it would also further radicalise many of the Labor Club's own members.

Towards the end of July 1967, after seven hours of discussion over the course of five heated general meetings, the club passed a resolution to raise money for the South Vietnam National Liberation Front (NLF). An action committee led by the Labor Club's new president, Martha Campbell, and Peter Price, co-editor of the student newspaper, *Lot's Wife*, was set up to organise two funds – one for medical aid for civilians in NLF-controlled areas and the other for unspecified financial aid for the NLF.

That was a Friday. On the following Monday, the furore began. Newspaper editorials declared that the support by the 'ratbag minority' of Monash students for 'the Vietcong' was 'treason'. 'Government must stop Cong aid', the RSL thundered. Liberal and DLP politicians joined in, as did the bully-boys of BA Santamaria's National Civic Council.

Special Branch police questioned students on campus and made dawn raids on some activists' homes. Whipped up by the hysteria, some pro-war students (one wearing a jumper with swastikas and the words 'Third Reich' on it) threw flour bombs and other missiles at Labor Club members. Peter Price and Martha Campbell received death threats written on toilet paper. 'It was a very tense thing', Arthur Dent remembers. 'We had to manoeuvre a lot.'

Within the week, however, there was a complete turnaround. When the DLP Club and the Students' Representative Council (controlled by the Right) called a mass meeting to debate the issue, everyone assumed that most of the student body would oppose what the Labor Club was doing. It was a shock when a majority of the 1000 students who turned up resolved their support for 'the

Labor Club's right to any political views', and went on to declare their opposition to the Vietnam War. This early win was proof to the Labor Club militants that, by taking a hard line, they could shift students to the left.

In a deal struck with the university authorities, the Labor Club agreed to restrict on-campus collecting to the medical aid fund, but more and more politicians and organisations publicly damned the 'treachery'. After the issue had dragged on in the press for six weeks, the federal government passed the Defence Forces Protection Act, which made collecting funds for the NLF punishable by up to two years gaol and/or a fine of $2000.

Fearing that the notoriety the university was receiving would upset its funding, Monash Vice-Chancellor Louis Matheson jumped the gun by banning the collection of NLF aid on campus, even before the new bill came into effect.

Undeterred, Langer and two other students set up a table in the Union, where they collected $60 for the medical aid fund in an hour. In the fledgling university's first-ever disciplinary proceedings, they were charged with, and later convicted of, misconduct.

The vice-chancellor's handling of this issue caused the first major breach between Monash students and 'the Admin'. When the three were disciplined, students rallied to their support. This ended the isolation of the Labor Club, which emerged as the defender of civil liberties.

At the same time, the campaign also caused the Labor Club to strengthen its line. Reflecting on this fifty years later, Arthur Dent states that it 'consolidated the whole shift to the revolutionary communist position'. This position, of course, was Maoism, and Dent rightly takes the credit for initiating this shift. Among the cadres, there was Kerry Miller (soon to be married to Langer), Mike Hyde (later a teacher and the author of Young Adult novels) and Jim Bacon (later premier of Tasmania). Their opponents within the club used to call them 'the Ruling Clique' – a derogatory term, which they cheerfully adopted.

THIS SURGE OF MILITANCY ON CAMPUS IN 1967 SET THE Monash Labor Club up nicely for the revolutionary year of 1968. It was then that the media singled out Albert Langer as a major target.

July 4 was American Independence Day – or Independence *from* America Day, as we called it. Anti-war rallies were scheduled for most capital cities. In Melbourne, it was early evening by the time the march – numbering around a thousand people, and including trade unionists and older peace movement supporters as well as students from all three universities – arrived at the US Consulate, where a large squad of police was in force.

From the ranks of the marchers, a 45-year-old waterside worker named Dave Rubin made a dash for the flagpole and managed to cut down the flag. While it was being burnt, the police weighed in with batons. What was described in the next day's *Age* newspaper as 'several "hard core" groups' responded with smoke bombs, rotten eggs and firecrackers. Rocks were hurled at the consulate windows. Meanwhile, most people were peacefully milling about with their placards; some were pleading with the militants to stop.

Suddenly, and without warning, 'mounted troopers were ordered at full canter' into the crowd. While this was the most violent police action yet to occur in any anti-war demonstration, *The Age* also noted that it was the first time in twenty-five years that horses had been used in this way.

> The horses, rearing and frothing from fright, sent men and women reeling to the bitumen. Other people were trampled underfoot by protesters as they tried to escape the horses.

> The horses charged into the crowd at least a dozen times to the aid of police fighting savagely with demonstrators close to the building.

Later, when the free-for-all was over and paddy wagons filled with prisoners prepared to leave the consulate yard, some fifty demonstrators sat down in front of the vehicles. Again the troopers were called in – this time, to ride their horses over people who were already on the ground.

By the end of the night, more than fifty people had been arrested. Most of the offences were quickly dispensed with in the Magistrates' Court, but Albert Langer and Dave Rubin were committed to stand trial before a judge and jury. Rubin's fourteen charges included malicious wounding of a police officer. Langer was accused of 'inciting the whole riot'. He explains, 'They accused me of organising people to sit down and block the police vans'.

Conducting his own defence, Langer 'cross-examined [the police] at length as to whether they'd rather have people rioting on their feet or sitting down'. He laughs as he recounts this. 'It did make them look rather ridiculous.'

Unable to get a jury either to convict or acquit, the police prosecutors ran the trial three times – in December 1968, in June 1969 and again in August of that same year. As the process went on, demonstrations were regularly held outside the court, and the nearby walls were decorated with graffiti declaring RUBIN – LANGER INNOCENT and SAVE LANGER & RUBIN. Once again, the State was giving a fillip to the radical anti-war movement.

'That's when I became really well known', Arthur says. The statement is neither exaggerated nor immodest.

Arthur/Albert goes on to reflect that at the time he himself had been 'very puzzled' about the State's manner of handling the court process. 'This was part of my political development. I kept wondering: "Why do they keep doing this? All they're doing is helping me get publicity."' Later he deduced that the police wanted to lock him up for a long time. 'A major strength of the political system', he explains, 'was that in normal times a government could not just order this, but needed a public jury trial to do it'. Eventually, however, they had to abandon the proceedings. Langer was convicted on the minor charge of obstructing police, and fined $150 – paid by the Prahran People's Movement.

This was only the first of Langer's theatrical court cases. After another riot, on May Day 1971, he was charged with 'incitement to assault police'. This time they even had a recording of him saying 'Kick the shit out of them', but Langer insisted he had said this *after* it had already been done'. The jury agreed he was innocent but was asked to convict him for 'attempted incitement' instead. Sentenced to eighteen months gaol with a minimum of twelve months, Langer represented himself on appeal and was acquitted, because the jury had not convicted him of the only applicable offence.

Through the press reporting of these court cases and of ongoing campus struggles with the Administration, the image of Albert Langer became that of a kind of political

Svengali – singlehandedly masterminding the protests and manipulating other students. This was a way of discrediting the increasing size and militancy of the movement. Replacing the notion of a 'ratbag minority', there was now just a single person causing trouble.

In August 1969, when 260 students occupied the Monash Administration building, the *Herald* pronounced that 'Over the whole crisis looms the shadow of rotund bearded Albert Langer'. And Langer's intelligence was also used against him. During this same 'Siege of Monash,' *The Age* reported: 'Langer is a brilliant Maths honours student – he is also a master of manipulating people'.

But to what extent was Albert Langer – by his own account a 'hardened apparatchik' – pushing or pulling people to the left?

I describe to him the tactic used by one of the student leaders at Sydney University, who boasted of 'blooding' newcomers (especially young women) by pushing them into their first arrest, in the knowledge that an encounter with the police and the courts often resulted in further radicalisation. Did Langer do this sort of thing too?

His answer is disarmingly frank. 'We were trying to recruit people, rather than push people into being more than they wanted to be. We were pushing *the whole student body* into being more than they wanted to be, but we weren't pushing the radicals to be more.'

Similarly, when I ask Arthur if he and his fellow cadres had controlled the Labor Club by stacking the numbers, he is adamant: 'Oh, no, no, no! I was fully aware of stacking from the ALP, and a definite part of the breakthrough at Monash was the rejection of that. What we were about – it wasn't just me, but Dave and the whole cohort – was mobilising the students, not trying to take control of the organisations'.

Speaking about the mass meetings that became a regular feature of campus life, he elaborates: 'We didn't mind losing votes at student meetings – what mattered was getting more people to come. We just wanted students to get involved and start thinking about things. Every time the university stopped lectures to mobilise a larger turnout of students at general meetings we got out-voted, but we were happy to see more students getting involved in further meetings and activities'.

He also frankly describes the setting up of 'small squads' of militants who acted to 'firm up the demonstrations', either going in hard to prevent individuals being picked off by police arrests, or discouraging attempts at rescue when that would only result in more arrests. These cadres also initiated changes of direction and flare-ups of action.

But while it was this sort of thing that gave the Maoists a certain reputation, Arthur points out that 'the whole purpose of every activity we did was to draw more people into thinking about things'.

OVERALL, WHAT EFFECT DID THIS HAVE?

Asked to sum up the achievements of the Monash Labor Club, Arthur says: 'In the short term, we were a major radicalising force in Australian left politics. We deliberately shifted the whole spectrum'. He repeats, 'By taking a hard stand, we moved the whole spectrum. We were totally successful in that – both at Monash and in the anti-war movement'.

Within the Melbourne anti-war movement, the hard stand of the Maoists resulted in a fight over both tactics and ideology with the Congress for International Co-operation and Disarmament (CICD). Summing up this stoush, which was fought right up to the 1970 Moratorium, Arthur Dent says: 'The CICD-Moscow peace line was *Stop the War, Negotiate*. And the line of the Maoists and Monash Labor Club was *Win the War*. They were doves. We were hawks. We were on the side of the liberation forces, fighting for victory'. He adds: 'It was a military struggle to defeat US imperialism – it involves killing enemy troops'.

Again, the hard line seemed to attract people, rather than repel them. Arthur goes on to contrast the regular meetings of the Victorian Moratorium Committee – in which several hundred people at Richmond Town Hall used to argue for hours about tactics and slogans – with the much smaller meetings of the Sydney planning committee.

'Basically, we had the hard Left being a very strong force in [the planning]. We didn't expect the Moratorium to adopt the position of *Victory to the Vietcong*, but by pushing it, we forced them to adopt a much stronger position.'

In turn, he points out, the Melbourne Moratorium was much stronger than the Sydney one. Certainly, it had the numbers: the 100 000 who marched in the first Moratorium in Melbourne in May 1970 represented half the total number that marched throughout Australia that day.

But what about the long-term achievements of the Monash militants? If they were so effective, why did the whole phenomenon just seem to wither away (to borrow a phrase from Engels).

Dent's response is unequivocal: 'One of the reasons it faded out was because we won, basically. The Vietnamese won in Vietnam, and in Australia there was a total retreat from the whole atmosphere of the 1950s'.

Hardened apparatchik

WHEN OUR CONVERSATION HAS GONE ON FOR A COUPLE of hours, Meredith and Verity need to leave, but Arthur is happy to keep talking, and so am I. He goes to the counter to order another coffee. When he comes back, the whole conversation shifts.

'So what's *your* story?' he asks me, before I can turn on the tape recorder and resume my questions to him.

What's *my* story?

This question isn't asked as if to check my left credentials, but rather it seems to come from a genuine curiosity about other people and the Sixties experience.

When I am back in Melbourne some months later, Arthur Dent and I meet again. He has changed cafes, but is still his cheery self as he greets me over a large English breakfast.

As we talk about the current era, Arthur says he can 'see nothing in common between Sixties radicalism and the various people that claim to be engaged in radical politics these days'. He is, however, optimistic. Indeed, he is 'convinced' that radicalism 'comes in waves'.

'I am very glad to have been part of a wave', he adds. 'And what strikes me is that it took only two years from being aware I was in the Menzies era to being aware I was in the Sixties. It would literally have been a two-year shift in the whole political climate. So I do expect that to happen again.'

'Why Arthur Dent?' I dare to ask, as the time comes for me to leave for the airport.

'It was because of this electoral thing that I still haven't figured out', Arthur tells me.

The story is complex, and beyond the timeframe of this piece, but over a decade later Albert Langer again became notorious, this time for recommending something that the

Albert Langer (Arthur Dent)

media dubbed 'the Langer Vote' – essentially, a way of voting that subverted the two-party system. The High Court ruled that, even though the votes had to be counted, it was illegal to publicly advocate voting that way. At the time of the 1996 election, Langer was sentenced to ten weeks imprisonment for defying a Supreme Court injunction, but was released on appeal to the Federal Court after the election was over.

After another eight years and two more general elections, the Electoral Commission tried to arrest Albert Langer for unpaid court costs. He tells me that when his family blamed him for the regular visits by bailiffs, he 'took off for a holiday, rather than try to deal with it all'. It was at this time that he used the name of Arthur Dent, 'so if I was arrested while on holiday the reports would be of the Electoral Commission arresting Arthur Dent'. He goes on to say that he 'ended up staying away for a few years', and hasn't 'settled back since'.

Tellingly, Arthur concludes, 'I can't put up with people insisting I behave like some image they have of how an "Albert Langer" should be'.

Yes, I get all of that, but why take on the particular identity of the nondescript anti-hero of Douglas Adams's novel? After all, Albert Langer is one of the least nondescript people I have ever met.

He explains that, finding himself to be in a bizarre situation, he used the name of Adams's fictional character, who 'also found himself in a bizarre universe'.

But what seems 'bizarre' to Arthur Dent is what seems normal to most people. Again, we come back to the experience peculiar to the Sixties.

'If you grew up in that period, that seems to me the way the universe is supposed to be. And then you get forty years

Hardened apparatchik

of nothing happening, and that's *not* the way things are supposed to be.'

I couldn't agree more.

Despite the bizarrely anti-climactic nature of post-Sixties life, my companion still has full confidence in the possibility of change. 'There *will* be another generation of radicals', he assures me.

DAVID MARR
Taking on the rich and powerful

Nadia Wheatley

I love it when David Marr takes on a figure of authority. A lawyer and biographer as well as a journalist, he does his research meticulously and puts his case without resorting to ad hominem arguments. Yet, whether he is arguing live with Gerard Henderson on ABC Television's *Insiders*, or writing a *Quarterly Essay* about George Pell or Tony Abbott, his rhetoric builds inexorably as he produces fact after fact to trounce his opponent.

Before Meredith and I embarked on our conversation with David, I had expected to find that his particular kind of combativeness had its roots in adolescent battles with his father. Of course, sons have been pushing back against their fathers since time immemorial, but in the Sixties there was an added edge to the contest. Many of the 'Oldies', who had grown up through the privations of the Great Depression and had suffered further in the war, simply could not understand their children, who had been given every economic and educational advantage, but who wanted something different. At the same time, the normal urgency of youth was even more pressing for a generation that had grown up through the claustrophobic dullness of the Menzies era. And so the age-old generational contest often reached a new level.

Describing the political background of his adolescence, David speaks of having 'this sense of the possibilities of my own life and of this country's life being suffocated by Bob Menzies'. He goes on to remind Meredith and me that, 'To live through that time was – as you will recall – unbelievably tedious. And there was a sense always that the possibilities of change, of openness, were being shut down, closed down'.

If the Menzies era was the crucible in which David Marr's particular type of political anger was forged, the thing that brought it to flashpoint is one of the most dramatic moments in Australian political history. For all of our generation, what happened on 11 November 1975 is unforgettable, but David has (in the phrase of that day) maintained his rage more than anyone else I have ever met. Then a journalist at the *Bulletin*, he was at his desk when the editor's secretary came to him and said, 'David, the governor-general has just sacked the prime minister'.

'Oh, no', David replied, 'it doesn't work like that'. His discovery that in fact it *did* work like that was 'the most educative moment' of his political life.

'That was when I discovered that Australian Tories are willing to bet the house on power', he says. 'And that, at their worst, they are not constrained by law. And that they are willing to do almost anything for power, and to prevent change.'

David Marr

DAVID HIMSELF GREW UP IN A FAMILY OF WHAT HE CALLS 'Australian Tories', but when he describes the set-up it sounds like something from nineteenth-century Manchester rather than Sydney in the 1950s.

'The family trade was iron', he begins. Over three generations, the firm of Gordon Marr and Sons had been making gratings, man-hole covers, postal pillar-boxes and suchlike, mainly for state government departments. When David was growing up, his territory spanned the city, from his home in Pymble on the upper North Shore and his private school at North Sydney to 'the works' across the harbour in the industrial suburb of Waterloo. To the 200 men employed there, David's father was known as 'Mr George Jnr' and David himself, for a few years from the age of about twelve, was 'Mr David'.

Within the formal structure of the Marr dynasty, Mr David had a special privilege. He was the second son – 'the spare'.

'And there was never any suggestion that I would be going into the family business', he explains. 'It was always understood that I would be looking for a career elsewhere. I never ever resented it, never wanted to be part of the family company. That was always my brother's designated duty, and he was very happy for that duty to be his.'

BORN IN 1945, TWO YEARS BEFORE DAVID, ANDREW WAS 'the perfect older brother', and the perfect son. At Sydney Church of England Grammar School – known as Shore – he was the perfect schoolboy and the perfect officer in the cadet corps. He was also a very good football player (rugby union, of course). 'To this day Andrew is perfection, he's wonderful!' David concludes, in a tone that combines affection with admiration. He quickly adds: 'Of course, I fought like hell with him when I was a child'.

Polar opposite to this paragon, David loathed all sport (apart from skiing), loathed the school cadet corps, and played loud music on Saturday mornings – classical, not rock-and-roll, but it drove the family crazy nevertheless. But David's most anti-social act was taking on his father. At a later time, David's feelings would undergo a complete turnaround; with no self-consciousness, he says, 'My falling in love with my father came later. Then it was total'. But to the teenage boy, this father was 'a figure of cool authority. He was the source of rules, and he was inflexible in his running of the house'. And so the contest was declared.

Like any good fighter, David used to pick the moment when his opponent was weakest. There was a particular time of the year when his father's defences were down. Because Mr George Jnr was 'quite a soft employer', the firm of Gordon Marr and Sons was selected by the Ironworkers' union as a good place to start disputes. 'If you could get a deal out of Mr George, it was a good one to try to establish as an industry standard.' February was the month when the unions would lodge their new demands.

'As a smart young shit', David was aware this was 'a difficult time for Dad', and so he would use it to 'needle' his father. From about the time David turned thirteen, his mother, two sisters and brother would look on as he would 'barb' his father over the family dinner table, and his father would reply. The springboard for the argument would be something in the news – 'something the Labor Party was pushing or something Menzies had done or said'. David is quick to add: 'Dad loathed Menzies, too, but voted for him all his life. Dad loathed Menzies, but couldn't vote for anybody else'.

David goes on to explain that 'in the way of these things' the arguments 'became kind of ritualised, and I was seen as pro-Labor or a bit of a Red – which then becomes a role'.

I ask, 'In these arguments, were you pushing your father to the very limit of his patience, to test whether he would still love you, no matter what?'

In reply, David rejects this idea out of hand. 'I believed very strongly that my father did not love me.'

'Why did you think he didn't love you?' To Meredith, who had a very amicable relationship with her own father, this seems peculiar.

'Because he was clearly so very much more comfortable with my brother and my sisters than he was with me.' David goes on to explain: 'I was the troublesome child. I was cast as, and was happy to be cast as, the troublesome child. I felt I had nothing to lose in those fights with my father, because I felt I already didn't have his love'.

After saying this, David throws in something as an afterthought – something he casually calls 'an additional problem with my schooling'. But it is something much more significant than that.

In David's teenage years, there was another authority figure who, like a Colossus, straddled both family and school. This was a man known universally by the Dickensian-sounding nickname of 'Jika'. A Shore Old Boy and Rhodes scholar, Basil Holmes Travers had played rugby for England and cricket for the University of Oxford. He was the headmaster of David's school. And he was married to one of David's aunts.

Meredith, whose brother went to Shore, remembers Jika Travers's terrifying reputation. To David, 'he represented an incredibly restricted conservative notion of the possibilities of life, and how life should be led'.

Jika was a very large man, and David was 'a big fat boy' – heavier, he explains, than he is today. The scale of their battles was far beyond that of the skirmishes at the Marr family dinner table. As David describes his contests with his uncle, it is clear that Jika Travers was the authority figure who taught him how to fight.

'He and I used to fight so much at family events that we would both be sent out of the room, either by my mother or by his wife. I would fight him about politics, about school, about sport – I stood up to him, and we used to fight and fight and fight, and sometimes he would lose his block with me.'

David recalls that, 'There was a celebrated occasion when he started throwing me against the refrigerator, and he had to be stopped. But I egged him on, I provoked all this and I really *really* liked fighting him'.

In this war, there were occasional moments of armistice. For David's twelfth birthday, his uncle gave him the *Collected Poems* of TS Eliot – something that David's parents 'would never have thought of doing'. Nevertheless, the combat was of prime importance.

'These fights', David explains, 'were about how to behave, what was respectable, what was sane politics, what was the country like, and as the years went by, about the dangers or the benefits of Whitlam winning'.

BUT IF JIKA TRAVERS EMBODIED THE DOMINANT IDEOLOGY of Shore, there were more subversive ideas being mooted in the classrooms of this Greater Public School. Many of the teachers were men 'who had been broken in one way or another by the war', including a number of English expats.

Paramount among them was a 'radical British liberal', named John (Jackey) Colebrook, who spoke in 'an accent that North Shore people would have died for', but who was openly contemptuous of the royal family, Robert Menzies, 'the stuffiness of Australian public life' and 'Tory values as practised in Australia'. In addition to showing David that it was possible to challenge such shibboleths, this history teacher was the first person who taught him that 'learning could be thrilling'. 'He saved my life, really', David says. There were other teachers who brought a sense of a larger world and who – while not being in the slightest pro-Labor – were 'not Tory'. 'And that was important to me', David concludes.

By 1964, as David began his final year of school, it was time to start thinking about a career. From the age of thirteen or fourteen, he'd 'had this notion' that he was going to be 'in some way or other a writer'. The family insisted he had to have 'something to fall back on'. And so David decided on an Arts/Law degree at Sydney University. This meant two years of Arts on campus, followed by four years at the Law School in the city centre. Between lectures, in his final couple of years he worked as an articled clerk at a law firm.

IN OUR DISCUSSION TO THIS POINT, THE RECURRENT THEMES of possibilities and change have had a political context and a national focus. But through these years David Marr was also privately tossing back and forth ideas about his own possibilities, and about his own need to change (or not). As we are about to move into the university period in his life, David interrupts the flow of the conversation. 'I want to say one more thing about my school days.'

He immediately goes on: 'I was aware from the time I was about fifteen that I may be gay, and it terrified me, and I suppressed it completely, but it was always there as a question mark over my future. And it presented itself to me often enough as a question: "*How do you build a life around this?*"'

After putting this rhetorical question, David continues without pause: 'And this confusion I took with me to university in 1965. I didn't know what I wanted to do except I'd like to be a writer. I didn't really want to study law but I was going to study law. I saw the necessity of being heterosexual but I was wondering whether I was in fact homosexual'.

A little later in our conversation, Meredith checks with David: 'OK, so you get to uni and you're not sure you're gay? Or you *are* sure you're gay?'

With his unfailing frankness, David replies, 'Oh no, I'm sure that I can beat it'.

'Sure you can beat it?' Meredith sounds astonished.

'Oh yes, sure that I can beat it. Because it was a violation of respectability so total that it was inconceivable to live – to be gay.'

But for the seventeen-year-old who had only just left school, the matter of sexual identity was eclipsed by the excitement of moving into the next phase of life.

Big brother Andrew was living at St Paul's College, and one evening, when the family was dropping him back there, David 'just fell in love with the buildings'. With their sandstone Gothic style, they seemed to offer 'a kind of Oxford existence in Australia'. For a literary boy who was also a 'tremendous Anglophile', the appeal was obvious. And so in 1965 David became a Paul's fresher. With his boundless enthusiasm, his everything-or-nothing approach to life, he also instantly 'fell in love' with the people and the culture of the place. It was no big leap.

The St Paul's College ethos was that of a GPS boarding school, but one where you could drink yourself senseless and rampage around the neighbouring Women's College at night. In recent years, the formalised bullying of freshers that goes on at male colleges has received a bad press, but David 'enjoyed the hazing process very very much'. In his last year at Paul's he would lead a movement to rein in these excesses, but he remembers those wild nights in his first term fondly. 'It worked for me as a way of making friends and letting off steam.' It helped, of course, that he was big and used to being knocked about on the football field at Shore. He also very much enjoyed the 'phenomenal' level of college drinking, finding it 'the perfect way of dealing with all kinds of disturbances and fears'.

In all, the institutionalisation was an escape not just from the broader society, but even – especially – from the university. 'Although you went every day to lectures (in a sports coat and tie!), all the things that were beginning to stir on campus stirred in my absence.'

I know exactly what David means. I arrived at Women's College, on the other side of the hedge from St Paul's, the next year, and for my own first two years at college I too lived in a hermetically sealed world. We girls from Women's College were forbidden to wear slacks (let alone jeans) to campus. Our 'uniform' was the tailored Fletcher Jones skirt, the pastel twin-set, and the single string of pearls. I had none of the requisite items, but paid lip-service to the dress code by wearing dowdy dresses that I sewed myself. Meredith, who arrived in 1967, horrified the traditionalists by wearing white boots and a hot-pink mini frock that barely covered her knickers.

But if David was outwardly conforming to a world in which the only thing of importance was the Rawson Cup, awarded annually to the college that won the most sporting contests, he was aware of larger issues. In particular, it was 'just absolutely fucking obvious' to David 'that the Vietnam War was wrong'.

'It was clear also that America was losing the war. And that Australia becoming involved was the best evidence yet of the subservient second-rate hopeless nature of Australian politics. We were a vassal state. We were being dragged into a war that was clearly wrong.'

Like all young Australian men, David faced the prospect of being conscripted into the war. In 1967, he was due to turn twenty. This was his third year of university, and the year when he began the law component of his degree. As it happened, his birth date wasn't picked from the lottery barrel. His perfect brother was not so lucky. With his excellent record in the school cadets, Andrew was chosen for officer training; as an engineer he wasn't going to end up on the front line of the combat troops, but he still had to go to Vietnam.

David's response to his brother's fate reveals something of his frustration with the politics of the whole thing, but also perhaps a sense of guilt about his own good fortune. In 1968, when Andrew was due to fly out, a farewell party was held on a ferry. At one point in the festivities, David – 'furiously angry about the whole thing and terribly drunk' – pushed his brother into the water. It is something he agonises over to this day.

The next year, David was articled to the prestigious city law firm, Allen Allen & Hemsley. Now living out of college, he swapped his sports coat and moleskins for a suit. He was still not involved in campus politics, let alone a member of any of the proliferating anti-war organisations, but by now he was sometimes slipping out of the office to join a street march or demonstration. On one occasion, as he was protesting outside the US Consulate, a mate handed him a flour bomb, and said, 'Chuck it at the cops'. Nervous about getting arrested, David dropped it on the ground. The mate chucked his, and was duly lumbered. In an email, David later adds, 'Can't tell you how emblematic that moment remains. It's the Pymble that never leaves me'. Perhaps. But it was also standard for law students to avoid any risk to their career. Whatever the reason for it, David rightly sees this decision as pivotal.

Although in this anecdote David has a companion, when he describes this period he gives the impression of being alone in his political views. Naturally, his parents were horrified at him protesting against the war in which his brother was fighting. And as the approaching 1969 federal election brought the prospect of Gough Whitlam winning, David's arguments with his father and uncle became more heated.

For David, Labor's loss at this landmark election was 'a huge disappointment'. So was the career that he seemed to be ending up in, by default. In the ruthless environs of Allen Allen & Hemsley he felt demoralised, even 'useless'. There was only one case in his time there that seemed worth fighting. Penguin Books, one of the firm's clients, was prosecuted for publishing an Australian edition of Philip Roth's hilarious novel *Portnoy's Complaint*. For a few days while the case was being heard in the NSW Central Criminal Court, David was the dogsbody of the defence team. His duties included sitting outside the courtroom for half an hour with Patrick White, who was there as one of the book's defenders. In the end, two Sydney juries refused to convict the book as obscene. It went on sale across Australia.

But David's time at Allens was up. He wasn't going to hang about and wait for the country to change, or for Whitlam to have his next crack at the prime ministership. Four days after being admitted as a solicitor, David was on a plane, bound for Europe. He didn't expect he would ever come back. 'I'd had enough and I was going.' He recalls: 'I was fed up with this country. I was fed up with myself'. After arriving in Britain, he made enquiries about becoming a citizen. It was a possibility that, in the end, he didn't pursue.

Like many young Australians of our generation, David lived in London, doing odd jobs through an agency, getting enough cash to go travelling, then returning to London for another temporary position. Then, in what he describes as a 'life-changing accident', he was offered a job in a ski hotel in Austria. He grabbed the opportunity. Jennie DeLisle, another Australian expat in London, took a job there too. While the two young foreigners were working at the hotel, they were taken in by an intriguing and delightful Austrian family. Through their influence, David discovered what he found to be a very novel idea.

'You could laugh at your country. You could laugh at the kinds of people your country turned out. You could laugh about its politics. You could be exasperated by its failures to live up to its potential – and still *love* it!'

It was an epiphany that drove David's growing sense of his identity as an Australian. He no longer wanted to live overseas as a foreigner. He wanted to go home. Not right at that moment, but eventually.

NATURALLY, WHILE DAVID WAS AWAY HE HAD BEEN KEEPING an eye on what was happening in Australia, and he was increasingly confident that in the 1972 elections there would be a Whitlam victory. On a hitch-hiking holiday in East Africa, he was watching the television news in the Nairobi Youth Hostel where he was staying when he heard the words 'Edward Whitlam' in the midst of a torrent of Swahili. He knew Labor had won.

By June 1973, he and Jennie (now a couple) were back. Australia wasn't going to be the same, and nor was David. Turning away from law, he was going to be a journalist. He fired off letters to a number of newspapers, and immediately got a phone call from Trevor Kennedy, editor of the *Bulletin*.

'If you want the job, say "Yes" now', Kennedy told him.

'Yes', David said. As he modestly points out, in those days it was 'extraordinary' for someone with a Law degree to seek a job in journalism.

Initially employed as a research assistant to Peter Manning, over the next couple of years David worked alongside 'a remarkable group of people' who included Robert Drewe, Marion Macdonald and Ian Moffitt. Although the owners of the newspaper were the Packers, in the office itself 'there were almost no conservatives around'.

'That was finally, fucking finally, when my political

education began to happen', David declares. Summing up this learning process, he explains: 'I'd gone through university almost untouched except for the Vietnam War, the street marches, the prospect of me being conscripted. I'd gone away to Europe and discovered I was actually an Australian. Had come home in part because Whitlam would be running the country. And finally, at the *Bulletin* office, I started to learn about politics'.

After all the hope David had invested in Whitlam, it is unsurprising that he came to be 'profoundly disappointed' in the Labor government. He was optimistic again after the 1975 Cabinet reshuffle. 'It looked as though at last a professional government was in place.' But it was too little, too late. 'And then the campaign to get Kerr to sack him began.'

As a journalist, David was watching the events of the final period from the front line. As far as he was concerned, 'the rights and wrongs' of the constitutional case were 'beyond argument'. Just as the expat had discovered he was an Australian, the journalist discovered that he was a lawyer at heart. But despite reading many of the auguries, for this lawyer-cum-journalist the Dismissal was literally incredible. Impossible. As he told the editor's secretary when she arrived at his desk with the news: the political system didn't work like that.

At this moment, which in many ways spelled the end of the era of 'the Sixties' in Australia, David Marr's political education was well underway. As David describes it, his time at the *Bulletin* was 'secondary school'. In 1976 he went over to the *National Times*. This was 'university'.

Again, his teachers were his colleagues. He names John Edwards, Paul Kelly, Andrew Clark, Elisabeth Wynhausen ('a phenomenal powerhouse of sensible thinking') and Anne Summers, who raised women's issues in a way that until then had been limited to fringe feminist magazines. As the ancient printing press used for the newspaper was incapable of printing good-quality photographs, cartoons and line drawings had to be published instead. And so six artists, including Patrick Cook, Jenny Coopes and Michael Fitzjames, were employed there. Their eccentric brilliance permeated the paper.

Not long before David started his new job, his marriage had ended, and Jennie had gone back to Europe. Although 'determined now to get on with life as a gay man', he was 'still incredibly closeted and incredibly cautious about' what he was doing. His liberation received a kick-start from one of his colleagues.

A couple of months after David began at the *National Times*, he came in to work on a Monday and Betty Wynhausen, 'a cigarette in her mouth', shouted across the room, 'Did you find a bloke to fuck this weekend, David?'

'I thought I would completely die', David concludes as he recalls this episode, 'but a sixteenth of a second later I realised it was one of the best things that had ever happened to me. It was all out, and it was all fine'.

Discussing his delayed emergence as a gay man, David points out that it means he escaped the bullet of the HIV/AIDS epidemic. 'If my sex life had got under way in my late teens, when I was at university, I'd be dead. But I am alive because it didn't get under way until my late twenties.'

Coming out (or being outed) was only one of the great benefits of being enrolled in the university of the *National Times*. The other was what David calls the paper's 'syllabus'. The small, renegade newspaper 'had a real focus, and that was the power of money. The *National Times* was about the power of money in society and politics'. Stories commonly probed corruption and tax evasion, exposed the ruthlessness of the powerful and were critical of the judiciary. There was also 'a much more sceptical view of international relations and obligations'.

'It's been my core syllabus ever since', David says, 'but then I added to it later when I became very interested not just in the power of money in politics, but the power of faith in politics, the power of the churches'.

His inside knowledge of what he calls 'Australian Tories', together with his own outsider role, make him perfectly placed to take them on.

MARGARET REYNOLDS
Born feminist

Meredith Burgmann

It was the year 2000 and the Sydney Olympics. I was part of a women's demonstration against the seven countries that had refused to have women in their sporting teams. We had a petition to deliver to Juan Antonio Samaranch, president of the International Olympic Committee, at his hotel down near Circular Quay. We approached the front door. I was roughly seized by security guards and thrown back into the street. The only one of us who made it through to the foyer was (former) Senator Margaret Reynolds. Tall and dignified, she swept through the lobby, went up the lift, and delivered the petition to the man himself. When I asked her how she had managed to do this, she grinned and replied, 'Confidence, Meredith, it always works'.

Born feminist

I HAVE MANAGED TO GRAB MARGARET FOR AN INTERVIEW during a brief layover in Sydney from her Tasmanian home. She is on her way to a meeting with the ABC in her capacity as chair of the Friends of the ABC. Ever the activist, she is even busier in retirement than when she was Bob Hawke's Minister for the Status of Women. We start the first of many cups of tea and I begin my inquisition.

Margaret Lyne was born in 1941 in Launceston, Tasmania. She was an only child.

The family was nominally Church of England. Margaret was baptised but her parents did not go to church often. She describes herself as really having no religion. She joined the church choir at age eleven because she thought it might be interesting, but it didn't last long because she got more interested in bodgies and widgies – particularly the bodgies (the male side of the subculture), it would seem.

Her family's political views were divided. Margaret's mother, a schoolteacher, was firmly Labor and always on the side of the downtrodden. Her maternal grandmother, who was obviously very important in Margaret's upbringing, was one of many women of the period who just *loved* Mr Menzies – a love that Margaret's maternal grandfather, and her mother, would often dispute. Her grandfather used to carry on loudly about 'Pig Iron Bob', and it wasn't until many years later that Margaret discovered Pig Iron Bob and the lovely Mr Menzies were the same person. In fact, she got to university before she discovered this dual persona.

When Margaret was five, the family moved to Melbourne. Coming back home from war service in New Guinea, her father had enrolled at the University of Melbourne under a Returned Services education scheme. She says that while he was there he began to get involved with university politics and was friends with several Communist Party members.

The family lived in a two-room apartment within the converted stables of a large Queens Road mansion in South Melbourne. Margaret remembers her three years there as a fascinating opportunity to become friends with the many families who lived in cabins or caravans, established as cheap post-war housing within the grounds of the original grand home.

In 1948, the family moved to the outer Melbourne suburb of Parkdale – Margaret's father had developed a serious lung condition, and his doctor recommended a change of housing. A few months after this move, Margaret's father died. She and her mother returned to Tasmania, living in Launceston, near her maternal grandparents.

Margaret moved school several times in her early years, following her mother's work, but then settled into a fairly predictable pattern of life in Launceston, attending Trevallyn Primary School and Launceston State High School. Throughout this period, her mother was teaching, and Margaret took for granted the independence that this situation afforded her. Her mother's income enabled a comfortable lifestyle, including outings and holidays, but having a working mother also meant Margaret had to do her share of housework and cooking.

With both her mother and grandmother being teachers, Margaret was coached to guarantee her place at Launceston's selective high school, and the expectation was that she would probably also become a teacher. While she was always urged to study so she could go to university, a more important message was that she needed to be independent. This was a bit unusual for the times, because she could also have been pushed to find a nice boy and get married. She laughs her wonderful full-on laugh when I mention this, and says she did in fact meet some nice Catholic boys from university when playing at an interschools hockey carnival – and fell for one of them.

In 1957, Margaret matriculated for entry to the University of Tasmania in Hobart. Because she was only sixteen, both her teachers and her family recommended another year at school. But, with her romantic interest dominating her plans, Margaret insisted on leaving home and heading to the capital city, where she lived in a strictly run girls' hostel.

She was not interested in politics during her time at university, although she says she was 'influenced by the radicalism of the period' and describes her friends as 'bohemian'. In the coded language of the time, this means liberal-minded and interested in intellectual ideas and constant socialising.

She had 'an older boyfriend who was a poet and they smoked and drank too much'. Once she was even offered marijuana – a pretty radical act for Hobart in the very early 1960s.

In Hobart, Margaret joined the Old Nick Company, the theatre group that presented the annual university review, satirising the politics of the day. She believes she would have been perceived as 'not conservative and one of the "In Crowd"'. She is, as always, brutally honest about herself.

Margaret had a Commonwealth scholarship for a two-year teacher training program, which meant that by the age of eighteen she had already qualified as a primary school teacher. On completion of her course, Margaret went off to the country to teach at a Tasmanian area school on the north-west coast, just out of Burnie. While enjoying the job, she missed her social life in Hobart, and so she applied for a special education training course, knowing this career move was more likely to result in a transfer to the city. Ever honest, Margaret recounts that when she was accepted and sent to Devonfield, a school for 'crippled children', she immediately felt guilty about her motives in making this choice. Ultimately, though, working with children with disabilities set her on a career path that led to her becoming much more politically aware.

At age nineteen, she found herself in charge of her own school – what a way to either build or destroy confidence! But Margaret was up to the task. She worked with a community committee concerned with the needs of disabled children, and saw herself as a professional doing something useful. She describes the situation of being in charge and having to undertake her own fundraising activities as very liberating.

It was at this school that she learnt to speak in public, as she needed to address organisations like Rotary and the Lions Club to raise money for her school. As part of this fundraising process, she was asked to be an entrant in the Miss Tasmania Quest. Well before the feminist critiques of beauty pageants, Margaret refused to be involved. She doesn't think she thought it through at any level of complexity, but she did realise that it wasn't for her.

By now she was in a relationship with (later husband) Henry Reynolds, an academic historian who was influential in increasing her awareness of progressive politics. But the morality of the era was still very conservative. Margaret remembers a moment in November 1963: 'I was staying at Henry's family home the morning that JFK had been shot. His father burst into Henry's bedroom to tell him the news and I had to hide in the wardrobe as I was supposed to be sleeping in the guest bedroom'. Well, at least she remembers where she was when she heard the news!

After two years as teacher in charge at Devonfield, Margaret was transferred to a school based inside the Royal Derwent Hospital, a secure institution housing both the intellectually disabled and the mentally ill, among others. This school was located between the Alcoholics Ward for men and the Delinquent Boys Ward. The hospital was then Tasmania's 'dumping ground' for many disabled children, and for teenagers who couldn't be controlled in the community. By this stage, Margaret felt she knew a bit about running an alternative school program that suited different abilities. She had four staff, but only a few students, because it was considered that most of the children living at the institution were not worth educating.

This experience was very political. She describes the bizarre atmosphere as 'like *One Flew Over the Cuckoo's Nest* ... It was a confronting environment for a pretty sheltered girl'. But Margaret, ever optimistic and pragmatic, says it was a great experience for her.

Furthermore, as she was to discover, the Department of Education wanted to close the school and leave responsibility to the Department of Health. Despite lack of resources and some push-back, she managed to expand the school's enrolment from sixteen children to about a hundred, and ran classes on a sessional basis so that all children had some access to education.

One night, at a dinner party, she complained about these limitations to a fellow guest, Harry Holgate – who was at the time a journalist, but later became premier of Tasmania. Harry asked if he and a photographer could visit the school so that he could he write a human-interest story. Margaret agreed to an article for the *Sunday Examiner*, but it didn't occur to her that as a junior public servant she was flouting all the rules.

She was reasonably circumspect in the interview, but when she got to school on Monday, she was told 'the minister has asked for a briefing'. She was so naive she thought that it must be a minister of religion, because she was pretty used to seeing them around the institution.

Margaret survived the fallout from the interview and her indiscretion had the desired effect. Perhaps because 'the times they were a changing'. An additional trained teacher was appointed, and equipment arrived by the truckload. There was no more talk of closing the school – instead, an announcement was made about the building of a new school.

I reflect a little on how moments in one's life can so dramatically change your projection. Margaret reaffirms this. 'That year at Derwent Hospital radicalised me.'

She adds, 'I couldn't work out how those conditions could exist in a government-run school. My story was really highlighted by the media. It was fairly formative in my views about policy and government. Why decisions are made in a certain way – who gets to make the decisions'.

IN 1963, SHE AND HENRY MARRIED AND THEN WENT travelling in Italy and France, settling in London to teach for two years. Their oldest child, John, was born in London in November 1964, and Margaret returned to her teaching job when he was three months old. Labour, under Prime Minister Harold Wilson, was in power. Margaret and Henry, who were both teaching in the East End, kept up with local politics by reading the *Guardian* and the *London Review of Books*. They became very aware of discrimination, especially in the areas in which they lived – Willesden Green and, later, Islington – where local advertisements for rental accommodation read: 'No Irish, no blacks, no dogs'.

They both enjoyed living in London, but knew their working holiday visas would end after two years. Henry started applying for academic jobs in Australia. One dismal, grey weekend, while they were on a train trip to Oxford, Henry opened a telegram offering him a job in sunny Queensland. They decided, on that day, on that train, that they would go to the University of Queensland campus in Townsville. Another of life's 'sliding doors' moments.

Living in London had made Margaret aware of different cultures, and she describes how, when she knew she was headed for Townsville, she had announced the 'patronising intention [her words] of wanting to help Aborigines up there'.

In late 1965, the couple moved to Townsville. Henry arrived six weeks earlier than Margaret, who was staying with her mother in Tasmania. Margaret wishes she'd kept his letters from this time. Henry was confronted by both the environment and the social realities of the Queensland frontier: it was very hot and dusty, and Townsville itself seemed like the Wild West. Most of the main streets were still unsealed. It was a very masculine and violent society. Indigenous people constituted about 10 per cent of the population, but it was obvious that they were not welcomed by the majority of the community.

Henry and Margaret, fresh from the finer understandings of swinging London, found the place racist and sexist. One shocking event remains seared in her memory.

Without a car, Margaret walked everywhere. Her first

experience of racism occurred when, as she was out walking with baby John in the pram, a young Aboriginal man was thrown out of a bar and landed in front of them. John, who was about fourteen months old, kept saying 'Look, look', pointing at the young man lying bloodied in the street.

Margaret ran into the hotel for help, but at the sight of a young woman entering the bar everyone simply stared at her in horror. When she explained the situation and asked 'Can you ring the ambulance?', the barman shouted, 'This bloody sheila reckons we should help the nigger we just threw out'.

Finally, she found a phone booth at the post office and rang the ambulance service herself. But they were no help at all. They wanted to know the patient's membership number and other bureaucratic information, before asking 'Is he drunk?', and finally, 'Is he *only* an Aborigine?' Margaret, in exasperation, then rang the police. They said they'd send a patrol car – and they actually did. The police picked up the young man and took him away.

Margaret hoped he would get medical help, but was worried he would be blamed for the situation. She rang the police again to make it clear what had happened, explaining that the young man had been thrown violently to the ground. 'They thought I was mad, and they said, "Listen lady, we can't spend all our time running after the blacks up here."'

'I was disturbed by this incident', Margaret recalls. 'The memory of those drinkers' derisive laughter lingered as I tried to explain to myself why I had been so powerless ... It was that incident that made Henry and me aware how racist and violent the town was.'

AT THIS POINT IN MARGARET'S DISMAL NARRATIVE, I ASK IF there were others like her and Henry in Townsville, and she says, 'Yes. That's how I got involved with the Communist Party and the trade union movement'.

On one of her walks into town, Margaret had discovered a small political bookshop close to her home. It was run by the CPA. They would offer her a drink of iced water when she came in – and because it was at the bottom of the hill leading up to her house, and had air-conditioning, she would drop in there often. They got to know her – 'They knew me as the woman with the baby' – and would occasionally tease her and say she only came into the shop because she wanted the cold water.

The Trades and Labor Council was actually around the back of the little shop, and it was through this connection that she eventually got to know Senator Jim Keefe and his wife Sheila Keefe, who were based in Townsville.

(I remember that name. I still have the now-faded telegram that he sent me when I was given my gaol sentence. What a nice man.)

It was through Jim Keefe that Margaret and Henry were invited to meet Labor Party leader, Arthur Calwell.

Henry had come home from university and said, 'We're going out to dinner'. Margaret was very excited, but disappointingly it turned out to be a Labor Party event. She says that they had dressed very inappropriately, 'me in my only decent outfit – short mini and sandals – and Henry and I were the youngest people there by thirty years'.

The MC for the event was a funny old guy in a grey cardigan. There was an Australian flag draped across the lectern. Henry kept entreating Margaret to look more interested. She believed her Saturday night was definitely doomed; but, suddenly, the old man – Arthur Calwell – started talking about the Vietnam War and arguing against the conscription of young Australians, and she was very impressed. She remembers writing in a letter to her mother that Arthur was really concerned about the Vietnamese and that 'It seems unfair, that he is rarely reported in a good light'.

At the time, Margaret had little interest in party politics. She remembers that on the night of the 1966 election she was ironing in the kitchen, occasionally interrupting Henry's avid monitoring of results on the TV to ask, 'How's it going now, dear?'

She has often claimed it was the Vietnam War that really radicalised her.

Margaret then talks about conscription. When she came back to Australia in 1965, she discovered that the country was at war and conscription had been instituted. It might seem odd that a schoolteacher living in Britain was unaware of the Vietnam War, but as the UK never committed troops, Vietnam was never the issue there that it was in Australia. She was genuinely surprised that a government could so easily introduce a policy that chose young men at random to go off to war. 'I had girlfriends whose baby brothers were being conscripted and I was more confronted by conscription at that time than about Vietnam. I didn't know much about Vietnam, but conscription made me sit up and take notice. Also, we had a son and I could relate to the fact that this could be my John.'

In 1966, Margaret joined the Townsville Peace Committee and was encouraged by Fred Thompson, a Metal Workers' Union organiser and an active CPA member, to set up a branch of Save Our Sons (SOS) in Townsville.

Margaret had read in *The Australian* about the founding of SOS in Melbourne by anti-war activist Jeannie McLean. She asked a few friends to come to the first meeting, but no one turned up.

Margaret persevered. Eventually, the wives of the local Trades and Labor Council men came to her house on Melton Hill and helped set up SOS in Townsville. Two of these women, Lorna Thompson and Esme Hardy, became quite important mentors for Margaret.

Townsville was a military town, because of the army base nearby, so promoting SOS was hard work. However, she did manage to get an interview about her work with SOS into the *Townsville Bulletin*. The article described her as a part-time housewife and schoolteacher, 'too young to have a son eligible for conscription'. Margaret also did a radio interview with a journalist friend, Shirley Gilliver, where she spoke about SOS. Shirley had warned her, 'everyone in Townsville wants us to be in Vietnam'. Tellingly, Shirley eventually lost her job.

After the *Townsville Bulletin* article came out, Henry was in strife at the university because of his wife's activities; basically, she and Henry were sent to Coventry. One comment, reported back to them, was that 'Reynolds should control his wife'. It was considered that Margaret had brought the university college into disrepute – she was seen as endangering their hard-fought respectability as a tertiary institution. For good measure, Henry was also accused of being a Communist.

Margaret displays no bitterness about the small-mindedness of an isolated Queensland town, but it seems like a good time for a break. We renew our cups of tea and I ask Margaret whether she was much aware of protest activity outside of Townsville. She says that at this stage she had started to read more and more about what was happening down south in Melbourne and Sydney. Much of what she read about was not easily transferable to a place like Townsville.

Margaret stresses, though, that SOS managed to do some good things. 'We made a real point that we were against government policy, but not against the poor soldiers. We got snack packs such as boxes of sultanas and cheese. We prepared messages of support and our views on Vietnam and conscription and put little messages into these snack pack boxes. The troops were coming through Townsville frequently. The Save Our Sons women handed these boxes over to the guards on sentry duty and asked them to deliver the goodies to the troops.' She now believes that the actual troops probably never received these gifts from SOS.

SOS also used to conduct opinion polls, which involved standing in the local shopping centre with clipboards and directing prepared questions at the passing shoppers. On one occasion they were stopped by the police. The 'kind old sergeant' told them that they had to get a permit, and when they asked him how to do that, he said, 'I think something like that would have to go to Brisbane'. The sergeant confided that his son had just turned nineteen, and the family were very concerned about the next ballot. He suggested that the women just talk to people as they walked past, so they discarded their clipboards and were then able to lawfully engage the shoppers in conversation about Vietnam and conscription.

When Prime Minister Harold Holt visited Townsville, the Peace Committee asked Margaret and a young clergyman called John Beer to present him with a report they had prepared, which criticised Australia's involvement in the war. Surprisingly, they tracked Holt down to his motel room, and a rumpled prime minister, in a tweed dressing gown, appeared at the bedroom door to shake their hands and accept their protest.

Margaret describes herself at this time as 'still quite tentative about confronting authority, yet Townsville provided the kind of environment where I thought "someone should do something" and it seemed I was the only person available'.

She sees her early SOS activity as a significant contributing factor in her coming of age as a political activist.

Later on in 1966, Margaret read an advertisement in the local paper about a meeting of the Aboriginal rights organisation OPAL (One People of Australia League), and decided to join. There she met young black activist Roberta (Bobbi) Sykes, also at her first meeting. Margaret remembers Bobbi explaining to the group that she had grown up in Townsville and had lived daily with the racism her colour attracted. Margaret and Bobbi left that first meeting as secretary and treasurer of the Townsville branch of OPAL.

As Margaret and Bobbi continued their work together they became increasingly aware of the Black Power campaigners in the United States, particularly the Black Panthers. They had also read about the activities of Charlie Perkins, the Aboriginal activist who had led the Freedom Ride through country New South Wales in 1965: 'We wanted to bring these debates to North Queensland but we later learnt that OPAL Queensland had a much more cautious approach to Aboriginal rights issues'.

When Margaret and Bobbi went to Brisbane for the OPAL conference in 1966, they discovered that the organisation was mainly run by church people. Margaret became aware of a radical group operating in Brisbane within the OPAL context, and she remembers meeting activists Pat O'Shane (then in the CPA), Mick Miller and John Newfong at the Brisbane conference.

Another significant figure at this conference was Pat Killoran, then head of the Department of Aboriginal and Islander Affairs. (He ended up being so hated that his 2010 obituary in *The Australian* earned the headline 'Notorious Bureaucrat Who Oppressed Aborigines Dies Unlamented'.) Margaret simply describes him as someone 'who believed that Communists were trying to control our black brothers and sisters'.

During the conference discussions, Bobbi asked Killoran a question about housing. Killoran airily dismissed her, and gave her a lecture about the dangers of meddling in matters she did not understand. Margaret, who recalls being 'really, really angry', rose to her feet and demanded that Killoran answer Bobbi's question. She thought 'this is dreadful – just control of everything and no respect'.

Margaret remembers her tilt with Killoran as 'probably the first time I had challenged a male in society'. She adds, 'I was surprised by the intensity of my challenge to this figure of authority. It was another turning point – asserting myself in a world that still expected young women to meekly accept the word of men in power'.

In January 1967, Margaret and some friends opened the OPAL Kindergarten for children aged about three to four. Eddie and Bonita Mabo (later to become famous as leaders of the Native Title victory) were among the first parents to show trust in the kindergarten, and this gave other families the confidence to allow their kids to attend. She continued to work with, and learn from, the Mabos during those early years.

Townsville OPAL also raised money for the Gurindji stockmen who in 1966 had walked off the job at Wave Hill Station in the Northern Territory, as part of Australia's first land rights claim. OPAL was also active in supporting the YES case in the 1967 Referendum that proposed amending the Constitution to allow the Commonwealth to make laws for Aboriginal people and include them in the Census.

After the YES decision, Margaret became secretary of a group called the Inter-racial Citizens Committee, which organised a two-day seminar about what was to follow the Referendum. The event was a huge success, with 300 participants, and keynote speakers Faith Bandler, Joe McGuinness, and Professors Charles Rowley and Colin Tatz. Margaret found the seminar very challenging 'as it was the first time that I had participated in a discussion which seriously addressed the racism I knew was endemic in North Queensland. It was, in a sense, almost reassuring to have the two-day debate confirm the doubts and fears I had of my own society'.

OPAL head office had made it clear that its members were not to be associated with such a radical event. Shortly afterwards, OPAL in Townsville ceased to function, as the activists in the group, including Margaret, wanted to stay involved with the more radical Inter-racial Citizen's Committee.

NOW I THINK IT'S TIME TO ASK THE QUESTION THAT SO often provides surprising answers. Where did Margaret's feminism spring from?

Margaret explains, 'I was a bit different from other girls of my generation. My mother had always worked, and I had a well-educated, very radical grandmother, despite her love of Menzies'. At secondary school, Margaret was an avid reader of the *Women's Weekly,* and she can clearly remember her grandmother saying to her, as she devoured the usual content about weddings and the royal family, 'one day women won't marry'.

There were other elements of Margaret's upbringing that fed into her later feminism. She and her mother did not sit up at the table but ate their meals chatting on the sofa – more like sisters than a mother and child. She had also accompanied her mother to concerts and plays from a young age.

So when had she become aware of second wave feminism? In London in 1965 she had attended an abortion rally, and had started reading Betty Friedan, Kate Millett, Eva Figes and Simone de Beauvoir. She was particularly attracted to Eva Figes's *Patriarchal Attitudes*, with its subtitle, *My case for women to revolt*. The words inspired her, and she quotes them to me, sitting at my dining room table. 'It's a man's world and to the extent that it is and remains a man's world it's going to remain a shabby deal for one half of humanity … and for the other half too.'

She had even attended consciousness-raising sessions in London – although she adds with great comic timing that there was a problem with this, because she had confessed to the gathered sisters that she got on well with her husband.

But another circumstance had also created fertile ground for feminism. After her first year of teaching in London, her appointment was terminated because, as a married woman, she was only a 'temporary' teacher. She was assured she would be employed again after the (non-paid) holidays. 'I was indignant that my marital status had an impact on my professional role, and I started to question the different way men and women were treated.'

A patronising male local government official in Townsville, who told her, during some administrative snafu, 'there's no need to get hysterical', also helped jolt her along the road.

Margaret's 'see a problem – fix it up' personality had led her further and further into the workings of the Townsville City Council. The women activists lobbied to have a Women's Advisory Committee established but, as the local paper reported, the mayor replied, 'Women have no particular needs. Most of what you ladies have talked about are social welfare needs'.

Margaret remained calm in the face of these provocations, but her nascent feminism was bubbling away.

Early in 1972, when women activists established Women's Electoral Lobby (WEL) branches around Australia, Margaret and her friend Patti Kendall started a group in Townsville. For Margaret, an important aspect of Gough Whitlam's election later in 1972 was the opening words of his victory speech: 'Men and women of Australia'. It indicated to her that equality was at last on the political agenda.

By 1974, WEL Townsville was confident enough to hold a cocktail party and forum for the candidates in the coming federal election. One hundred and fifty women turned up to check out the (mostly conservative) male candidates. The candidates' general level of apathy and arrogance towards the women disillusioned many of Margaret's Townsville friends, but it also led to a general resolve to become more actively involved in the political process through membership of parties and nomination for preselection.

Shortly afterwards, the conservative state member of parliament made a speech attacking both WEL and the preparations for International Women's Year. Margaret was asked to debate him on television, and she emerged from the debate feeling 'somewhat triumphant', with her confidence boosted considerably.

She remembers being particularly involved in abortion issues because 'a couple of friends at uni had botched abortions and one nearly died'. Many of her contemporaries were in the National Council of Women (NCW), which she joined in the 1960s. NCW was campaigning for 'family planning' clinics, but Margaret's view was that they should be called 'birth control' clinics.

As she ponders her own feminism, she remembers the time when she stood up to Killoran. Another moment that she thinks was important was her last day of primary school. She took her precious autograph book into school, and the headmaster wrote in it – a piece about cricket. Margaret remembers an incredible sense of anger that 'he hadn't written about me or directed it to me. He'd written in my book in big spidery writing and he'd written about cricket!' Her grandmother saw, and understood why she was so upset.

As I have said, I often get unexpected answers when I ask women where their feminism springs from.

I realise that throughout our conversation we have discussed women and confidence continually without even thinking about it. I have never met a more unconscious feminist. The issue of how women relate to the world around them and to the men in their lives is forever at the forefront of Margaret's discourse. Her final anecdote describes a familiar trope.

Born feminist

Margaret remembers attending an important academic conference in 1974. She was going to present a paper on a program that she had been running in the school she was teaching at in Townsville, 'but I was very worried because I wasn't an actual academic and I felt that I wouldn't know anything and everyone else would be excellent'. She was succumbing to this 'impostor syndrome' experience when she started listening to 'the Canadian bloke who got up and gave a paper before me'. She suddenly thought to herself: '*What was I worried about?*'

We both giggle about this common experience – the sudden revelation that the men around you are pretty mediocre. We don't have time to properly sum up Margaret's life experience as, ever on the move, she dashes out to catch a taxi down to Ultimo – her life, one long quest for a better world.

BRIAN LAVER
Fighting fascism

Nadia Wheatley

When I was growing up, tennis was one of my bugbears. Regularly forced to make up the fourth in a doubles set with my three foster siblings, I used to stand weeping on the court as tennis balls flew at me at high speed. Naturally, I didn't follow the game, but even I could not fail to know that there was an Australian tennis player called Rod Laver, who in the latter part of the 1960s was the world's number 1 professional.

Over those same years, I knew of Brian Laver as one of the leaders of the student movement at the University of Queensland.

It was only recently, however, that I discovered that he and Rodney (as Brian calls him) are cousins. And indeed, Brian Laver, as well as being a student radical, was a university Blue in tennis. But if elite-level sport is an unusual backstory for an Anarchist with a capital 'A', Brian Laver's family history makes his left-wing credentials even more remarkable.

Fighting fascism

The Lavers were cattlemen, reputedly the third family to take up land in the Fitzroy River region of North Queensland. As Brian tells me this, he is quick to add that historian Paul Memmott has assured him that the Lavers arrived *after* the massacres of the traditional landowners.

By 1944, when Brian was born, the Laver clan owned a number of cattle stations. Although Brian's parents moved from their rural property, 'Lumeah', to the nearby town of Rockhampton when he was four years old, the country connections remained strong. Throughout Brian's formative years, his extended family used to gather on Sundays for social tennis on the property of one of Brian's uncles, where the court was made of pounded ant-beds and surrounded with chicken mesh. On these occasions, Brian's dad played, his uncles played, his older brother Ian played, and many of the locals joined in as well. By his early teens, Brian was regularly age champion for the central Queensland region. He also played in the Queensland State Age Championships in Brisbane from the under 11s through to the under 18s.

But sport was more than just a passion for Brian's immediate family. It was also a business. After the move to Rockhampton, his father opened a sports store, later expanded to include marine supplies and seafood. Len Laver also became a member of the town council, where he supported Liberal Party and Country Party policies. At home, however, politics wasn't discussed, and the only explicit political input that Brian remembers was his paternal grandmother getting him to sit with her as she watched BA Santamaria holding forth against Communism in his regular television broadcasts.

In all, it was a happy and loving family. A honky-tonk pianist before her marriage, Brian's mother 'let her two sons grow with kindness and love'. His father, whom Brian remembers with great affection, brought up his boys as he himself had been raised, with bush skills and a sense of independence. A keen fisherman, he often took Brian along with his mates on fishing trips, and 'from a young age' Brian was taken to an impromptu firing range in the Upper Fitzroy and 'educated in the use of weapons'.

Brian's interest in weaponry was whetted by the particular time and place in which he grew up. While everyone in our generation was shaped to some degree by the aftermath of the Second World War, for Brian Laver the recent conflict was a pervasive part of his mental and physical landscape, moulding his early understanding of the world and the course of his future life.

From 1942 to 1944, 'Camp Rockhampton' had been home to an American Infantry division, and there had been half-a-dozen other American military camps scattered through the nearby area. According to local legend, when the troops decamped, they left caches of military materiel hidden in the nearby ranges. On weekends, Brian used to ride his bike out to search for them. The Holy Grail that he sought (and never found) was an M1 Carbine.

But the jungle-training procedures undertaken by the Americans were only a part of the war history that coloured the boy's imagination. As a result of listening to stories told by his dad's fishing mates, Brian grew up with the sense that life had been 'pretty dangerous' in North Queensland, because 'the Japanese had almost invaded'. Living beyond the 'Brisbane Line', in the area that the Menzies government and American General Douglas MacArthur had allegedly decided to abandon if the enemy invaded, it was easy to think that one day the threat might return. This gave Brian

Fighting fascism

a keen interest in history, particularly the history of the Second World War and the defeat of fascism and Japanese imperialism.

Alongside this crucial extracurricular learning, Brian's formal education was underway at the two-classroom Crescent Lagoon Primary School. 'When heavy rains filled the floodplains', Brian remembers, 'all the lagoons filled with saltwater crocodiles, and snakes came into the school and sports ground'.

In 1956, Brian moved on to Rockhampton Grammar School, a non-denominational private school for boys. In many of the stories in this book, there is an influential teacher who provides the impetus or at least the information that brings about a radical shift to the left. In Brian Laver's case this is also true. Curiously, however, the teacher, Des Carroll, was himself 'quite conservative'. Brian's 'aha' moment came when Mr Carroll showed the students documentary films about concentration camps. As well as images of Nazi camps in the Third Reich, these films included footage shot in Communist countries. At first, Brian 'couldn't believe it'. Already imbued with a sense of loathing for fascism, he was astonished that the other side was imprisoning Russian dissidents. He became 'fiercely anti-totalitarian' on the spot. As radical awakenings go, this is a pretty extraordinary one, and it would underpin the way Brian Laver would go on to live his life. From this time, his beliefs would begin to set him apart from many of his peers.

In this first year of secondary school, he chose the topic of 'Anti-totalitarianism' for his speech at the school's Public Oratory competition. This was in marked contrast to the other students, who prepared talks about their pets, sports and hobbies. In fact, Brian almost didn't make the contest.

Earlier in the day, he'd been playing a game of impromptu soccer with a tennis ball when he suffered a knock so hard that he lost three front teeth and had to make an emergency trip to the dentist. Despite struggling to speak through the unaccustomed gap in his mouth, he won the competition. This talent for oratory would become one of the things for which Brian Laver was famous in his university days.

'What do you think it was', I ask Brian, when we reach this stage of our conversation, 'that prompted this amazing political response to totalitarianism, which you seem to have worked out all by yourself, and in the backwater of redneck North Queensland?'

After a long silence, Brian astonishes me by saying he's never thought to wonder about this. So I try to come at the question in a different way. 'Do you think there was something in *you* that responded to the idea of freedom, and made you oppose authority?'

After considering this for a while, Brian agrees. 'Well, I had a fairly free life', he says. 'I was independent in my tennis, and I went off and fished by myself, and there was no attempt to rein me in. There was no feeling that I couldn't self-regulate my life, so I suppose I was self-managed.'

Some time later, after our conversation is interrupted by the arrival of a parcel delivery, Brian himself returns to this question and thanks me for prompting him to think about it. He concludes, 'I think I am truthful in saying that probably my self-regulated time [growing up] led me to be who I am'.

I find it fascinating that – unlike some of the people in this book, including myself – Brian was not kicking back against a repressive familial authority. Rather, it was the personal freedom his parents gave him that caused him to espouse political freedom for everyone.

Fighting fascism

BY THE TIME BRIAN WAS AT THE END OF JUNIOR SECONDary school, it was obvious that he was bright. One of his dad's fishing mates, Des Derrington, who was a barrister in his professional life, thought the lad would make a good barrister, and recommended that he apply for a scholarship to 'Churchie' – the prestigious Church of England Grammar School in Brisbane.

No member of the Laver clan had ever gone beyond junior school, so when fifteen-year-old Brian left home for boarding school he really was a trailblazer.

The family expected him to have a career in law, but at the time he didn't foresee himself as going on to university. Indeed, he wanted to join the army in order 'to defend democracy' against the threat of totalitarianism. 'I thought, "We don't have to fight these forces now, but we might have to fight them again one day."' The stories he'd grown up with, about the threat of invasion in his home area, were always lurking in Brian's subconscious.

At his new school, he made friends with another boarder, John Purcell, whose father was a brigadier-general. Together, the two boys put in an application for Duntroon, the officer-training academy in Canberra. At a school like Churchie, it went without saying that everyone was in the cadets; everyone, that is, except Brian Laver, who wrote a position paper criticising the school corps, which he saw as a useless outfit with outdated weapons and training. 'I was interested in fighting very efficiently against fascism', he explains. As punishment for his non-compliance, Brian was sometimes forced to run around the sports field on training afternoons, carrying a pack full of bricks. Fortunately, 'the teachers soon lost interest in the supervision and went to the pub'. In this early act of resistance, Brian revealed his characteristic doggedness, as well as showing that he had the courage of his convictions.

The school may have deplored his attitude to the cadet corps, but tennis was another matter. With Brian Laver in its 1st IV team, Churchie won the Greater Public Schools championship in 1961 and 1962. As far as his studies went, history continued to be Brian's main subject, and the school's curriculum focus on imperialism, Nazism and Stalinism was right up his alley. In his final year exam, however, Brian suddenly decided to write about the war in Vietnam, as well as European history. It was a decision that, with hindsight, assumes significance.

Although he was still preparing for a career in the army, in 1963 Brian enrolled in a Bachelor of Laws as well as an Arts degree.

AT THAT TIME, THE UNIVERSITY OF QUEENSLAND WAS A sleepy sort of a place, with about 8000 students.

In his first year, Brian studied history, played competitive tennis, and fell in love with Janita, a student in her final year at St Aidan's Anglican school for girls. By the next year, Brian and Janita were married, with a baby on the way. The young couple had to grow up very quickly, and, as Brian goes on to talk about his extremely busy student days, I keep having to remind myself that simultaneously he had the responsibilities of a husband and father. Over this initial period, however, nothing political was happening on campus, and Brian's own politics were, by his own rueful account, still fairly naïve.

'I remember Kennedy being shot, and crying', Brian suddenly says as we get to this period of his life. As he describes the impact of hearing this news on the car radio, he is overcome with emotion once again. 'At the time, I believed Kennedy was the saviour of democracy', he explains. His tone is wry, and he adds that he would soon start reading about what the Americans were doing in 'placing fascist dictatorships' in Third World countries. 'So that crumbled my whole view about American democracy.'

These new ideas led Brian to get together with fellow student, Mitch Thompson, to found the Vietnam Action Committee (VAC). Under the influence of a young American academic named Ralph Summy, who had recently arrived from the legendary Berkeley campus of the University of California, the VAC students were strongly attracted to the ideology and activism of New Left groups in America, especially Students for a Democratic Society (SDS). By August 1966, the University of Queensland radicals were calling themselves Students for Democratic Action (SDA).

The group's platform went beyond conscription and Vietnam to embrace the ideals of participatory democracy and non-violent civil disobedience espoused in the American organisation's Port Huron Statement. In Queensland, however, the state government's use of Brisbane's repressive Traffic Acts to prevent street marches meant that the first campaign was to claim the right to protest. 'People who were radicalised at Queensland University were more radicalised about the right to march than about Vietnam', Brian explains.

On 5 October 1966, as part of an Australia-wide anti-conscription protest initiated by the National Union of Australian University Students, about forty University of Queensland students resolved to march the 8 kilometres from the campus to the city centre. A five-minute film montage, shot over the course of this day, shows the students setting off with handwritten placards, but no banners or flags. The young men have short hair and wear white shirts (some even have ties), and the girls are in frocks. They are barely out of the campus gates when they are stopped in their tracks by about the same number of police (plain clothes as well as uniformed), who start shoving selected marchers into a paddy wagon and a number of cars. The notes accompanying the footage record that 'Eye witnesses report the use of excessive police force (not photographed in this film record)'.

Later in the same day, after a small public meeting held in a room at the university, the students drove to the city to continue their demonstration. Again, police were quick to break it up. The twenty-seven people arrested throughout the day represented a majority of the demonstrators – and included Brian Laver.

When the court case over these arrests took place in the new year of 1967, Brian – along with fellow activists Mitch Thompson, Barbara Jane Gaines and Gail Salmon – elected to go to gaol rather than pay a fine, in order to underline their right to march on the street.

'What was your parents' reaction to your political involvement?' I ask.

'They never put any pressure on me, but they were deeply concerned', Brian replies. His paternal grandparents were 'very disappointed', especially his Santamaria-fan grandmother, who 'thought I was pro-Communist'. Brian's mother, too, was 'deeply worried'. However, he reiterates, 'none of them asked me to stop'. This surprisingly tolerant response was in keeping with the way Brian had been raised.

Fighting fascism

WHILE THIS INITIAL SKIRMISH WITH THE FORCES OF THE state energised the radicals at the University of Queensland, the vast majority of students were oblivious of any political issues. For the movement to grow, there needed to be an education campaign.

'We started our own university', Brian says, 'at this place called the Forum'. Setting themselves up in the open space between the Refectory and the Relaxation Block, speakers from SDA began to address students making their way to lunch. But first, the territory had to be won.

'Let me tell you how dangerous it was', Brian says. He proceeds to describe how, in the early days of the Forum, the bully-boys from the engineering faculty would 'come up and form an Indian circle and throw us in it and push and shoulder us around, to teach us a lesson. On one occasion it got so rough that girls intervened to stop it'. Other people have described how Brian Laver would talk on under a barrage of apples and oranges. But no matter how much opposition he faced, he would come back again to talk the next day.

'It was the influence of tennis', he tells me, when I ask how he managed to keep going. He cites quick thinking, quick reflexes, an ability to strategise, good concentration, and endurance. I had never thought of tennis as training for revolution, but certainly, those skills would come in handy.

As the weeks and months went by, more and more listeners gathered on the grass in front of the speakers, or on the surrounding pathway and paved area. 'It was an experience as much as a place', writes one of the contributors to a recent Brisbane Discussion Circle blog, in which former attendees describe how the Forum educated them.

Of course, on every university campus in the Sixties there was a place where public debate happened, but it does seem that the style of discussion was different at the University of Queensland – perhaps because Queenslanders lived in a place where speech was patently not free, and perhaps too because Brian Laver, with his libertarian views, insisted that all could speak, even opponents from the Right.

'I remember, some of the Marxist-Leninists tried to ban the fascists', Brian reflects. 'And I said, "No, they're speaking. The ban on the fascists occurs when they start to shoot people. And then we'll kill them."'

'That's how I spoke in those days', he adds, 'and I still believe it today'.

Brian's anarchist philosophy also meant that his radical rhetoric was different from that of many other student leaders of the era. He refers, for instance, to how anti-Vietnam protestors in other states used to yell, '*Ho Ho Ho Chi Minh*'.

'But I knew that Ho Chi Minh was a murderer', Brian says. 'He'd killed every nationalist who wasn't a Communist, he'd killed every anarchist, he'd killed every libertarian Marxist. I didn't ever support him. I supported the National Liberation Front, but that's because I saw them as the heroic resistance to Chinese imperialism, French imperialism, and now to the imperialism that was manipulated by America and led by the South Vietnamese.'

This is a viewpoint consistent with Laver's even-handed opposition to totalitarianism. Jumping ahead slightly to the time when Joh Bjelke-Petersen became premier, Brian says, 'Bjelke-Petersen used to call me a Communist, but every day the students heard me denouncing Communism'. Brian adds, 'He was the joke on campus. The students thought his stupidity was hilarious, along with the disgusting gutter journalism of the *Courier Mail*'.

IN THE EARLY MONTHS OF 1967, A NEW CAMPAIGN GOT underway at the university – a push to take over the Student Union Council. The New Student Movement had a five-page platform calling for change in the relationship between students and the university authorities. This was similar to 'student power' demands across many campuses, in America as well as Australia. But Brian Laver had a different aim – to abolish the Council and replace it with communitarian democracy. His popularity is shown by the fact that, when he ran for president of the Student Union as an Independent, he won 40 per cent of the popular vote.

Over these same months, the civil liberties campaign was building up a head of steam under an action committee made up of Brian Laver, Mitch Thompson and Ralph Summy (who brought skills learnt in the Free Speech campaign at Berkeley). The broader Co-ordinating Committee included representatives from various religious and political clubs (including the left wing of the Liberal Club), and members of staff. As the daily gatherings at the Forum went on, the hundreds in attendance swelled to thousands, and discussions often continued throughout the afternoon.

The issue was simply the right to march on the street. When the conservative president of the Student Union brokered a deal with police for a permit to march on the footpath, the majority of students resolved to burn the permit – which was duly done in front of television cameras.

On 8 September 1967, a huge crowd gathered to listen to speakers advocating a march to Parliament House *without* a permit. In the vote that day, 5000 students supported the proposal, and 4000 (half the campus population) went on to march illegally on the road. This evidence of the broad base of support that the radicals had built up is confirmed by the fact that Laver's 'minders' in the march that day included members of the university regiment and the martial arts club, as well as fledgling actor Jack Thompson in his trademark amber sunglasses.

Despite being prepared for battle, Brian and the other leaders had trained the students in the classic technique of the non-violent sit-down. Upon coming around a bend in the street and seeing the size of the police force massed against them, one of the leaders at the front of the march screamed, '*Shit!*'

Hearing this as the order to '*Sit!*', students in their thousands immediately plonked themselves down on the roadway. Silent film footage of the event shows them being removed, line by line. Most consented to being pushed onto the footpath, but every so often someone was hauled into a car or police wagon. By the end of the afternoon, there were 114 arrests.

Although the streets of Brisbane had been claimed, to Brian Laver the victory seemed limited. Writing a few months later about this campaign, he noted that the 'depressing thing' about the outlook of the students, and even of many trade unionists, was that 'they see no connection between the suppression of civil liberties in Queensland and the suppression of the civil liberties of resistance fighters in Vietnam, fighting for their liberation from French imperialism and now American imperialism'. For most students, the government's attack on their civil rights was 'only one aberration of an otherwise fulfilling system'.

Obviously, their radical education needed to be taken further.

BY 1967, BRIAN AND JANITA HAD HAD A SECOND CHILD, and Janita too was studying at university. Despite his family commitments and the long hours he put into political organisation, Brian completed his final honours year in history. Taking up a job as a research officer for the Trades and Labour Council, he proceeded to bring together young workers and student radicals in a peculiarly Sixties style of fun known as 'Foco'. (The name came from Che Guevara's theory of revolutionary warfare, which was to be led by small guerrilla groups called *focos*.)

Although many people – from the trade unions, from the Communist Party, from SDA, and from the broader music and arts industry – played their part in this phenomenon, Mitch Thompson insists that 'There is absolutely no question that Foco was the brainchild of Brian Laver. He provided the concept, the name, and he negotiated the premises'. Brian himself describes Foco as 'a cultural guerrilla event for rest and recreation'.

On Sunday 3 March 1968, the Foco Club opened on the third floor of the Trades Hall. This multifaceted extravaganza, incorporating music, poetry, political discussion, film, literature and theatrical performance, was unique in Australia, and was probably ahead of anything happening at that time in New York or London. And when the local member of parliament, Don Cameron, labelled the venue 'Australia's most evil and repugnant nightspot', Foco's success was guaranteed.

Brian Laver

IN 1968, EUROPE TOOK OVER FROM THE UNITED STATES as the centre of the radical movement, with charismatic leaders such as Daniel Cohn-Bendit (France), Rudi Dutschke (Germany) and Tariq Ali (Britain).

In Australia, we all thrilled to the documentary footage of the May protests in Paris: this seemed to be the revolution we were all waiting for. Brian Laver, too, closely followed the events, and when he was invited to attend a youth festival in Bulgaria's capital of Sofia in July of that year, he 'saw it as a chance to look behind the Iron Curtain'. He took with him Janita (who was pregnant again) and their two children, aged five and three. 'Wanting to see totalitarianism' for himself, he intended to travel on to Moscow, but developments in Czechoslovakia brought a change of plans.

Prague! Throughout our conversation, Brian has alluded a number of times to this experience, which was obviously a radical turning point for him.

Arriving in the city in mid-August, he paid a visit to the Metalworkers' Union, which had an office near Wenceslas Square. Because of his connection with sport, the unionists appointed as his guide a member of the women's Olympic rowing team, who quickly became friend and minder to the visiting Australian family. By this time it was clear that the Soviet leadership had lost patience with Czechoslovakia's reformist regime, and Brian – mindful of what had happened in Hungary in 1956 – thought it likely that the country would be invaded. Sure enough, one evening he and Janita came out from a performance at the Black Theatre of Prague to see tanks in the streets.

Naturally, Brian wanted to join the action. As soon as he'd seen Janita safely back to their accommodation, he made his way through the huge crowd in Wenceslas Square

Fighting fascism

to the union office, where 'the metalworkers thanked me for offering my support'.

Brian recalls: 'I said, "Do you think it's going to be an armed struggle?" and they said, "Well, we're trying *not* to make it an armed struggle, because if it is, we'll lose."'

He continues, 'You know, there were tanks and troops everywhere! It was obvious it couldn't last for long. We held the buildings, and their tanks and troops dominated the streets and squares'.

Worried about his family's safety, Brian went back to the hotel and moved Janita and the children to their guide's family home on the outskirts of the city. Then he returned once more to the Metalworkers' Union office. He spent the next few days mingling with the demonstrators in Wenceslas Square and 'forming lines of communication with other workers and student activists'. Meanwhile, Janita joined the women who were changing the positions of street signs in order to confuse any invading Russians.

When it became clear that the Czech regime was going to give in, the militants decided to get foreign supporters out of the country. A car was organised to take Brian, Janita and the two children to the border with Germany. Inside the nappy of the younger child, Janita hid documentary film footage of the events in Prague, which was passed on to Tariq Ali after the family finally arrived in London. This was the first footage of the invasion to be shown in Britain, and Tariq Ali also published in his newspaper the pamphlets that Brian and Janita had smuggled out.

Around the world, the Soviet government's brutal crushing of the Prague Spring widened the chasm between the New Left and the Old. I remember that on the day the tanks rolled into Czechoslovakia, Meredith and I were in court to face charges arising from an anti-Vietnam demonstration. We raced down afterwards to Martin Place for an impromptu protest against the invasion of Czechoslovakia. Significant though that event was for us all, for Brian Laver it was proof positive of the belief he had held since adolescence, of 'the brutality of Marxist-Leninist and Stalinist totalitarianism'. And now, he had seen it for himself.

SINCE THEN, BRIAN'S LIFE HAS BEEN AN ENDURING commitment to the cause he variously describes as libertarian socialism and anarchism. These days, he explains, he usually calls himself 'a social ecologist'.

'Any regrets?' I ask.

Only the fact that, after about eight years, his marriage to Janita ended, he tells me. Although he later went on to form another long-term relationship, and to have two more children, he is still clearly remorseful about the hardship that his activism caused for Janita and his first three children. This included terrifying threats by police and other right-wing forces. As well, Brian's reputation caused him to be black-banned from a number of jobs, both in Queensland and in Victoria.

Eventually securing an interview for a position at a Zionist school in Melbourne, Brian was daunted to see his name on a file on the principal's desk. Expecting the usual political interference, he said, 'I see you've got my ASIO file'.

'Oh, no', the principal replied. 'This is your Mossad file.' Opening the folder, the man continued, 'It says here that you would fight fascists. Is that true?'

'Yes, that's true', Brian assured him.

'Well, that's good enough for us', said the principal. And Brian got the position.

Later, after returning north, there were appointments at Queensland and Griffith universities. It has been tennis, however, that has given Brian Laver the freedom to live as an anarchist and activist. It was during his employment as 'Head Pro' at Laver's International Tennis Resort in Florida that he travelled to Scotland for a three-day coaching gig at Gordonstoun School, where his select group of students included the young Prince Andrew. Of his £3000 payment from the royals' alma mater, Brian gave £1000 to the Scottish National Party, and donated a further £1000 to the British Voluntary Euthanasia Society, in memory of Arthur Koestler. He put the rest on the bar at the local pub at Oban, where they are probably still talking about the crazy Australian.

AFTER WE HAVE LUNCH, AT A VIETNAMESE RESTAURANT near his Brisbane home, Brian is going on to give his regular Friday afternoon tennis lesson at a local primary school – something he has been doing for over twenty years. 'It's the longest job I've ever had', he tells me, before insisting on escorting me to the bus stop. This isn't paternalism masquerading as courtesy, but 'anarchist military practice'. As we march shoulder-to-shoulder down the footpath, I feel that, if the fascists were suddenly to mount an attack on Brisbane's West End, it would be great to have this comrade at my side.

BRONWYN PENRITH
Miracle child

Nadia Wheatley

'I was a miracle child', Bronwyn says.

In another context, this might mean she was a baby conceived against the odds, or perhaps a baby who survived a difficult birth. But in Bronwyn Penrith's life, the miracle was simply that she wasn't a Stolen Child. She repeats, 'It really was a miracle, considering …'

In the crowded Redfern cafe where we are meeting, it can sometimes be difficult to hear Bronwyn's soft voice, but at this point she lets her thoughts trail off, perhaps because she herself is considering how the odds were stacked against her having the loving family and stable home life that she goes on to describe to us. As in many Aboriginal families, the roles in the Penrith family did not follow the nuclear model that was the Anglo-Australian norm in the 1950s when Bronwyn grew up.

'It's a bit complicated', she explains. 'I lived with my grandparents, but I called them Mum and Dad.'

Bronwyn's grandfather-cum-father, Charlie Penrith, was a Yuin man from the Country around Lake Tyers and Wallaga Lake, on the South Coast of New South Wales. 'We're traditional owners of Wallaga Lake', Bronwyn says proudly. Although this was their homeland, Bronwyn succinctly describes the Penriths as 'comers and goers'. Their travelling was often connected with the itinerant work the family would get, following the picking seasons of various fruits and vegetables.

In the 1930s, Charlie had married a woman named Lily MacRae, who came from Coranderrk Reserve in south-central Victoria. The couple had two sons and a daughter, Irene, but Lily died of tuberculosis when the little girl was about two years old. As part of the so-called 'Welfare' policy of that era, Irene and her brothers were subsequently taken away and put in Bomaderry Aboriginal Children's Home, on the South Coast. Charlie did his best to keep in touch with his children – even taking fruit and vegetables to the institution as a way to see them – but a few years later Irene was sent to the notorious Cootamundra Aboriginal Girls' Home. Cut off from her family and her community, 'she never had anybody'. Bronwyn repeats the stark phrase: 'She never had anybody'. After leaving Cootamundra, Irene ended up in Newcastle where, at the age of about seventeen, she became pregnant.

Meanwhile, Charlie Penrith's comings and goings had taken him to the Snowy Mountains, where he married Emma Hickey-Williams, a Wiradjuri woman from the Country around the tiny township of Brungle. After getting a job on nearby Red Hill Station, Charlie built a house out of kerosene tins, close to the river. Over the coming years, he and Emma had four children – three boys and a girl. There was family living on the local Aboriginal Mission, but the Penriths kept their independence by living on the property where Charlie worked.

Before her marriage, Emma Hickey-Williams had worked for over ten years as an indentured servant in Sydney; while she was there she'd met an Anglo-Australian woman, appropriately named Mrs English, who was an inspector for the Aborigines Welfare Board. In this role, she visited every mission and reserve in the state, including the Cootamundra Girls' Home. It must have been there that she first encountered Irene, who by 1952 was in Newcastle, and ready to give birth.

As seventeen-year-old Irene was still a ward of the state, it would be up to the Welfare authorities to decide the future of her child. In this way, the government policy enforced a vicious circle of inter-generational trauma, whereby a girl who had been a Stolen Child faced the likelihood that her own child would be Stolen in turn.

This is the point at which the miracle kicks in.

Aware of the relationship between the young Irene Penrith and the Harry Penrith whom Emma had married, Mrs English got in touch with Emma and asked if she wanted to look after the baby.

That baby was Bronwyn.

She tells us: 'I said to Nanny, "How come I came to live with you?" and she said, "Well, love, I said you was coming, and that was it."'

Emma's forthright character as well as her fiercely protective spirit shines through in this simplification of a complex and bureaucratic process.

Miracle child

EIGHT YEARS YOUNGER THAN THE YOUNGEST OF EMMA and Charlie's other children, the new addition to the Penrith family would always be the baby.

'Did they dote on you a bit?' Meredith asks.

Bronwyn roars with laughter: 'Of course not!'

As well as being loving parents, Emma and Charlie were very protective of their youngest child. 'In a way, I was really sheltered.' Although Bronwyn had escaped the system once, this did not mean she was safe. Throughout her childhood 'there was always the threat of the Welfare' hanging over her. Casually, Bronwyn speaks of accessing her file in the departmental archives. 'From what I've seen in the records, there were regular reports on me.'

Even though the Penriths lived independently, they were not free of surveillance. Bronwyn describes how the proprietor of Brungle's only shop used to make reports about his Aboriginal customers to the Welfare. To pre-empt accounts by busybodies and bureaucrats, sometimes Emma herself used to write in to the Welfare Board about Bronwyn's progress, to 'safeguard' her.

At this point in our conversation, we talk about the attitude to the police that we had when we were growing up. Like all white Australian children of our generation, Meredith and I were always told that if ever you got lost, you should find a policeman to help you.

For Bronwyn, police were to be avoided at all costs. 'You spent your life trying to make yourself invisible around them.' But that wasn't always possible. The Penriths still followed seasonal work – Bronwyn lists Batlow for the apples, Young for the cherries and other stone fruit, Oberon for peas – and there were occasions when the family was on the road and would have to go to a police station to get rations. From reading her Welfare Board records, Bronwyn knows she was sometimes shown to the police, to prove that she was clean and healthy and well cared for. 'You was always fearful.'

Also pervasive was the sense of segregation. At Brungle's small primary school, Aboriginal children were in the majority. Nevertheless, 'all the white kids would congregate on one side of the classroom, and closer to the front, and all the black kids would be across the other side'. On weekends, Bronwyn would go to the Mission to play with the other Aboriginal children, but the white kids and the Aboriginal kids never got together outside of school. In a wry tone, Bronwyn says, 'I think we all knew our place'. She adds, 'That was the way it was'.

In 1965, Bronwyn moved on to Tumut High School, half an hour away on the bus. In this larger school environment, her life 'intersected' a bit more with that of her non-Indigenous classmates, because she was involved in choir and sport. She was also a keen student. At home, she used to stay up so late reading her brothers' cowboy books by firelight that her mum said she'd probably go blind; some sort of grant enabled Bronwyn to buy a Tilley lamp. But more important than any book-learning was Emma's own storytelling, which went together with the strong sense of love and security that enfolded Bronwyn.

'For as far back as I can remember, I always slept with someone. And those were the occasions when the stories were told. You'd get in close to Mum to hear the stories. Even though you heard them every night of the week, you still wanted to hear those stories.'

Charlie too was a great storyteller, and Bronwyn credits the knowledge passed on by both her parents with the development of her sense of Aboriginality. 'We're all strong on

Miracle child

identity in our family. We know who we are – we know our family's generations.' In these accounts, the ancestors 'were like real people, because of how Dad and Mum talked about them'.

But although Bronwyn's parents asserted their identity and their independence in so many ways, they were not overtly political. For example, she does not remember any discussion at home about the 1967 Referendum campaign.

IT WAS THE YEAR AFTER THE YES VOTE THAT BRONWYN started her own 'coming and going'. Now sixteen, she left school and followed her sister and one of her brothers to Griffith, where she did a secretarial course at TAFE. Then, with her sister-in-law, she came to Sydney, where she worked in a bank in Parramatta and lived in Seven Hills (a suburb on the north-west fringe) with a woman from the Foundation for Aboriginal Affairs. Although 'the girl from the bush had come to the city', she wasn't yet in the heart of things. Homesick after a while, Bronwyn went back to Brungle. 'Till I came back to Sydney. Next time I came, I stayed.'

After this second arrival, Bronwyn found her way to the inner-city suburb of Redfern, where she soon met up with other young women – Isabel Coe, Lyn Thompson (formerly Craigie), Susanna and Alana Doolan, and also the group of young men that included Paul Coe, Billy Craigie, Gary Williams and Gary Foley. Soon in a relationship with Gary Foley, Bronwyn would have a child with him in 1971.

Becoming part of this radical group was an exhilarating introduction to politics. Bronwyn remembers that the first political speech she ever heard was given by Paul Coe, and she describes accompanying Gary Foley to meetings at the time when the new generation of Aboriginal activists was 'pushing back' against the older mob at the Federal Council for the Advancement of Aborigines and Torres Strait Islanders (FCAATSI) and the Foundation for Aboriginal Affairs. 'The young movement, of which I was a part, we wanted to do it ourselves.'

As we talk about how these crowded couple of years saw the establishment of the Aboriginal Legal Service and the Aboriginal Medical Service, as well as the Tent Embassy, Bronwyn says, 'You lived and breathed politics! You didn't have time to work!'

Through taking part in marches and demonstrations about the Vietnam War and apartheid as well as Aboriginal issues, Bronwyn 'started getting the idea that people could make change just by sheer force of numbers'. She also developed a new attitude to the police, whom she 'no longer regarded as all-powerful'. Bronwyn explains, 'I think it gave you a certain feeling of power, to be able to come to Sydney and confront them in a group'. Gone were the days of making herself invisible around the forces of the law.

But street marches were not the only way for a minority group to get their ideas across. Theatre could be another tool for the Redfern radicals. In mid-1972, a grant of $500 was secured to bring Aboriginal actor, Bob Maza, from Melbourne to Sydney to mentor aspiring actors. By the grand age of thirty-three, Bob had had a number of television roles and he also had experience writing his own material.

Bronwyn describes how, from the moment Bob Maza arrived in Redfern with his wife and young children, his Regent Street terrace house became 'a kind of hub for all of us young ones to go to and just sit around and sing, and talk about politics'. The group who congregated in the Maza family's crowded living room included singer Alana Doolan, actor Bindi Williams, blues pianist Teddy Maza (Bob's nephew) and dancer Wayne Nicol, along with activists such as Lyall Munro, Gary Foley and Paul Coe. As Bronwyn describes those get-togethers, she concludes, 'It makes me smile to think about it'.

While non-Indigenous radicals of the 1960s were soaking up American influences through books and music, these Aboriginal activists were getting their inspiration from much closer to the source. In 1970, Bob Maza had attended the Congress of African People, in the United States.

While he was there, he had met Black American leaders such as Angela Davis, Jesse Jackson and Elijah Muhammad, and he'd also spent some time with the National Black Theatre of Harlem. As well teaching the younger generation of Aboriginal activists in Redfern about the theatre, Bob introduced them to the new ideas coming out of Black America. He himself would describe the book *Malcolm X Speaks* as one of his major influences, and Bronwyn cites Eldridge Cleaver's *Soul on Ice* as one of the books that she and the others were reading at that time. 'We were certainly very well aware of the Black Panthers.' Bronwyn also mentions the influential role of Carole Johnson, an African-American dancer who toured Australia in early 1972, then stayed on to set up a dance workshop in Redfern.

A Black Theatre wasn't going to put on plays by Shakespeare, or even by the new left-wing Anglo-Australian playwrights who were running alternative theatre companies in Melbourne and Sydney. The actor-activists in Redfern needed their own material, and they needed it fast. The political discussions at Bob's house provided instant subject matter for performance. Of course, there was not yet a bricks-and-mortar theatre for the company to perform in, but who needs a building when there is the street?

In the United States, street theatre (or guerrilla theatre, as it was often called) had kicked off in the mid-1960s in San Francisco as a non-violent way to get a message across to members of the public who would not attend political meetings or rallies. In these spectacles, absurdity and humour were often used to challenge passers-by and make them think about their views. Street theatre in Redfern was in this tradition, but it had its own distinct Aboriginal identity. Bronwyn was part of it from the start.

Meredith asks: 'When you did street theatre, was your main purpose to shock people or to educate people?'

After a long pause, Bronwyn replies, 'I think it was – to give us a voice, *and* to educate'. She points out that in that era, when there was no social media, or even community radio, 'You had to make it up for yourselves!'

The performances the group put on might take place on a Redfern street corner, then move to another corner. Or they might be part of a rally or a march downtown.

On one occasion, the trigger for the protest was the Gove land rights case. In this first Native Title case, the court ruled against Yolngu plaintiffs trying to prevent the mining company, Nabalco, from mining their traditional Country in Arnhem Land.

For this performance, Bronwyn Penrith, wearing a long peroxide-blonde wig, had the starring role as a symbolic representation of White Power. 'I was dressed up as a white woman, in a gaudy dress and with white flour on my face', she remembers, 'and I had an umbrella with words on it like "mining companies" and "multinational interests". Other people were demonstrating against me. And then there were

Miracle child

the police. They were blackfellas too, but they had masks on'.

This particular dramatisation was picked up by the producers of the ABC news review program, *This Day Tonight*, who asked the group to do a repeat performance for broadcast to a national audience. Out of the streets and into the living rooms! For the performers themselves and their Redfern audience, it was empowering to see Aboriginal people impersonating police in an absurd or mocking way. And no doubt for many members of the white television audience it was confronting to see a young Aboriginal woman provocatively representing themselves and their authority.

While street theatre, as performed by the young radicals of Redfern, shows a unique mix of international ideas and Indigenous attitude, Bronwyn connects it with a much longer tradition.

'The corroboree tells a story through gestures, and it signifies certain things that affect the everyday lives of the people that are watching. And I don't think it's a far step from that to telling a story with actors.' She adds: 'That's why I became interested in street theatre. I think I kind of fell into it, as well as marching and demonstrating, as a way of getting messages across'.

Redfern's street theatre soon developed into the more formal performances of the National Black Theatre, but Bronwyn – preoccupied with family – was no longer involved.

BY 1972, BRONWYN WAS IN A NEW RELATIONSHIP, WITH A man whom she describes as being 'extremely violent'. Now her coming and going took a different form as she frequently moved house around Redfern, or sometimes went back to the Snowy Mountains for a while. 'My first four kids I had at home', she says (meaning Brungle). However, she retained the powerful knowledge that people could change things, by force of numbers. Her ongoing friendship with other women, such as Alana Doolan, was the source of another sort of power.

'We pooled money, shared houses, supported each other's children, and drank endless bottles of cheap white wine.' Bronwyn laughs as she rattles off the popular brand-names: 'Porphyry Pearl! Rhine Wine!'

Obviously, the support these women gave each other was a crucial survival strategy, but when the new wave of feminism first began to roll into Sydney in the early 1970s, how did Bronwyn and her friends perceive it? The question is important, because the women's movement is often portrayed as a middle-class Anglo organisation that had little or no relevance outside its own privileged circle.

Bronwyn replies, 'I've always thought that the women's movement was about practical things, like refuges – which I was in a lot, at that time'. As well as spending the occasional week or two at 'Elsie', the women's refuge in Glebe, Bronwyn sometimes went to a refuge at St Peters or Marrickville. Although these places were run by radical activists from Women's Liberation, Bronwyn doesn't remember these women having any political influence on her. Preoccupied with her domestic situation, she and her children would stay for a few days or a couple of weeks, while she was organising somewhere more permanent for her family to move.

Yet while she didn't form friendships with the women running the refuges, Bronwyn speaks warmly of informal support from non-Indigenous women whom she generically describes as 'the students who supported the movement'. She adds, 'They weren't like they are like today – wanting to be up in the lead of it. They did practical things, like babysitting so we could go and get arrested'. As she goes on to talk about her 'real appreciation of that kind of practical support', Bronwyn names Heather Goodall (later the author of a ground-breaking history of land rights) who, on one occasion in 1972 when the Tent Embassy was under threat, looked after Bronwyn's infant son and Lyn Thompson's baby daughter so the two women could go to Canberra and take part in the struggle.

Among the Aboriginal women of inner Sydney, the main conduit for feminism was the activism and influence of Bobbi Sykes, who produced a little magazine called *Koori Bina* and organised meetings in her own flat in Surry Hills or in one of the other women's houses in Redfern. Bronwyn remembers Germaine Greer being present at a couple of these informal get-togethers, but the Aboriginal women developed their own style of feminism.

With Aboriginal men being bashed and locked up by police at an alarming rate, and with land rights as the overriding cause, Indigenous feminists were unwilling to adopt the anti-male attitudes expressed in some of the rhetoric of the international women's movement. 'We didn't want to be in a movement against the men', Bronwyn explains. 'That was our sentiment at the time.'

She goes on to talk about a controversial article by Suzanne Ingram – 'Silent Drivers / Driving Silence' – which had been published shortly before our interview. In it, Ingram set out to appraise 'the cost that has since been borne' in the area of domestic violence because Aboriginal women, from the 1970s onwards, have taken the line: '*We're not against our men*'.

Bronwyn tells us, 'I said to Suzanne, "Forty or fifty years ago, nothing came before the strength of the Aboriginal movement, the people's movement."' She adds the proviso: 'I think *today*, we'd have more expectations of our men'.

After talking about this change from the Sixties to the current era, Bronwyn moves on to compare her own generation of Aboriginal women with the generation that came just a little before, and who felt obliged to follow what she calls the 'Assimilationist model'. By this she means the idea that an Aboriginal person should strive to advance upwards through the white hierarchy, whether in education or in employment.

'You know, I came here to Sydney at the time of Assimilation, so I was probably a very good candidate for it. Because, you know, I was all right at school, went to Year 10, and then I did Secretarial.' The expectation was that 'Then you get a job, and climb your way up the ladder. Maybe go on to higher education, a bureaucratic job'.

In discussing why this did not happen in her life, Bronwyn credits the effect of being in Redfern in the Sixties: 'It changed my life totally. Made me more of a thinker, an examiner. And I've never wanted to work in the establishment. I understood early, that's what I was like'.

A significant part of Bronwyn Penrith's work *outside* the system has been her role as chair of Mudgin-Gal (literally 'Women's Place'), the Redfern-based women's centre that describes itself as 'a service run by Aboriginal women, for Aboriginal women, addressing family violence and providing a safe haven'. On the centre's website, a mission statement by Bronwyn declares:

> Healing has to start from within, right back at the point where we say, this is our country, these are our lives. Where we can live in hope and pride and have the same chance of achieving our dreams as any other Australian.

Having been to various events at Mudgin-Gal over the years (I've even got the T-shirt!), I know something of the high level of sustained support that Bronwyn has provided to her community through her role there. But when I describe this as 'giving back', Bronwyn is quick to point out, 'I think that it's quite different to the kind of "giving back" people say they do today – going back to the community to work for paid money. I don't think that's really giving back, it's not the same'. Her own work, like that of all the women at Mudgin-Gal, has been as a volunteer.

She goes on to say, 'I think my healing work today came about through *doing*. It's true of a lot of blackfellas. You get involved because of what you see that is wrong, and because of what has had a lot of impact on you personally. So I've been able to work in that space, and help other people'.

While Bronwyn's whole philosophy of working outside the establishment is pure Sixties, it also reflects the powerful grassroots community practice of the core Redfern radicals of that era. Further, Mudgin-Gal is a formalisation of the support that Bronwyn and the Redfern sisterhood gave each other, over the kitchen tables and the Porphyry Pearl.

Overall, if Bronwyn Penrith made the choice to avoid the Assimilationist way that she derides, her life might have had a very different outcome again, if she had not been a 'miracle child'.

Bronwyn Penrith

ALTHOUGH BRONWYN DIDN'T PURSUE A PROFESSIONAL acting career when her time in street theatre ended, some years ago she had the lead adult role in the opening episode of a television adaptation of my children's book, *My Place*. As the character 'Auntie Bev', she was cast as a community leader and a matriarch of her extended family. This of course is Bronwyn Penrith's real-life role. There was also no need for any transformation of her appearance: she was elegant as always in a long skirt and flowing top, with her dark curly hair (no peroxide wig this time) and the walking stick that always looks like a fashion accessory.

A particularly powerful scene in this drama (filmed in a local hall) showed members of the Redfern community gathered to see the Apology to the Stolen Generations on a big television screen. Allowed to be part of the live audience watching this re-enactment, I was moved even more profoundly than I had been at the time of the actual speech. But although my friendship with Bronwyn began during the making of that series, I did not then know how the history of the Stolen Children connected to her own family history.

Early in our conversation for this book, when Bronwyn was talking about the 'horrific life' of her birth-mother, Irene, she said, 'I've lived the life she could have had'.

Yes, she has.

Just to sit in a street-front Redfern cafe with Bronwyn Penrith, and to see how she is constantly being greeted by passers-by, is to realise the huge size of the life she has created in her inner-city Country.

ELLIS D FOGG (ROGER FOLEY)
I hate being bored

Meredith Burgmann

Nadia and I are about to interview Ellis D Fogg, and I don't know what to expect. I can remember seeing the name on every lovingly silk-screened poster advertising a fundraising dance or Happening in the Sixties; however, it's only recently that I have discovered he is not just a mist machine but a real person.

He arrives for the interview wearing bright-purple glasses, a purple shirt, red braces and a sheer black jacket with sparkles on it, which I later discover was specially made from a curtain he found in New Delhi. He still obviously sees himself as an exhibition piece. Sitting happily in my highly coloured living room he looks like a cleverly camouflaged parrot. However, he ruins the tableau by hesitating before we start. He screws in his hearing aid, and I notice he is wearing very ordinary sandals – though later he assures me they are Birkenstocks.

Ellis D Fogg (Roger Foley)

ROGER FOLEY WAS BORN IN JANUARY 1942. HIS FATHER AND pregnant mother were on the last flight out of New Guinea before the Japanese invaded – Roger's father had been working for an airline in Port Moresby. The flight hopped down the Australian coast and Roger was actually born in Cairns. This event may well have been the forerunner to a chaotic life.

By the time of Roger's first memories, the family had settled in Raglan Street in what he calls 'leafy Mosman', on Sydney's lower North Shore. It was a devoutly Liberal-voting area, and Roger remembers that at Mosman Public School, when the bullies wanted to pick on a kid, they would jeer: 'You voted Labor! You voted Labor!'

In Roger's home, politics wasn't discussed. His father came from a strong Irish Catholic family and his mother was from a Protestant Irish family, but both had given up religion before Roger was born. They were humanists 'because that's what they realised they were', but were not members of the Humanist Society.

Roger's father worked at various accountancy jobs. Describing him as 'very sensitive' and 'not a strong man', Roger says quite randomly, 'I think he should have been gay'. He adds that his father was 'downtrodden by strong women'. (Roger often brings up the issue of strong women, and mentions apropos of nothing how terrified he himself was of Germaine Greer.)

One particular strong woman was his father's sister, Eileen M Foley, a well-known concert pianist, whom Roger describes as 'domineering'. During the 1930s, she had travelled through Europe, where she had met Adolf Hitler – and been so impressed by him that she had a photo of herself with the Führer displayed in her house in Sydney. Roger remembers his aunt reading Leon Uris's novel *Exodus* and exclaiming: 'My God! My God!' The book was an epiphany for her. After learning more about Hitler, she cut his head out of the photograph. Eileen was also the first woman in Sydney to run a radio station that broadcast from a ship, the *Kanimbla*. Amid these very mixed memories, Roger recalls one peculiarly prescient moment when Aunt Eileen said to her ten-year-old nephew: 'Roger, you should take up guitars or lighting'.

In contrast to this weak father and all-too-powerful aunt, Roger's stay-at-home mother, Hazel, was his major influence. From a family so upper class that 'they even had servants', she was very bright. As a young woman, she had wanted to be a lawyer, but had to give up her career ambitions to look after her brothers and father after her mother's premature death and the loss of the family business in the Great Depression.

It was Hazel, Roger sums up, who encouraged his creativity. His father went along with whatever she said.

Roger describes himself as a shy, introspective and silent kid with particular sensitivities. Like many an only child, he amused himself by giving full flight to his imagination. 'I think I could actually see auras', he tells us. 'I could see when people had something wrong with them.' He remembers an experience he had as a child, while bathing: 'getting that little bit stoned that you get in a warm bath' and seeing 'stuff going on' in the bathroom windows. It later becomes evident in our conversation that this 'stuff' was a moving pattern of light and shadows being cast by the leaves of a tree outside. After this experience, young Roger moved on to experimenting with his bicycle torch, coloured glass and mirrors. He doesn't elaborate, but you can easily see where

Roger's fascination with the interplay of light comes from. He also describes being at Balmoral Beach, looking at the waves crashing into the rock pools and watching them form perfect circles. He was mesmerised. The 1960s psychedelic experience was there just waiting for him.

To encourage her child's artistic side, Roger's mother would show him prints of Leonardo da Vinci's drawings of water and clouds. He'd stare for ages at the clouds. Roger and his mother would go to art exhibitions – he recalls seeing a Malevich painting that was all white and pondering, 'It could be about nothing or it could be about everything' – which is pretty deep thinking for a child. His mother also took him to puppeteer classes run by Joan and Betty Raynor, two well-known, independent-minded entertainers who lived in a caravan in Centennial Park. They taught him puppet-making and working with clay.

Other outings included visits to La Perouse, where on Sundays Aboriginal residents used to put on displays of boomerang throwing. Roger says his mother had loved playing with children from Aboriginal communities as a child living in the Harden-Murrumburrah district. He started experimenting with making boomerangs as the result of these trips.

Among the Foleys's neighbours in Mosman was the Neville family. While the two mothers were friends, Roger was school friend and playmate of one of the Neville children. Later famous, or infamous, as a founding editor of the counter-culture *Oz* magazine, Richard Neville was already a rebel. Roger vividly remembers his friend's twelfth birthday, for which Richard had bought himself a gun, sent through the post from America. Of this 'scandalous' act, Roger's mother said, with a smile, 'That Ricky Neville, he's a very naughty boy'. Young Roger thought, 'I want that smile for me'. Overall, he concludes, 'I was influenced by Ricky's phenomenal energy and bravery, so in a sense Richard liberated me'.

Around this time, however, the two friends were separated, when Roger began his secondary schooling at North Sydney Tech and Richard went as a boarder to Knox Grammar School. Roger was happy at North Sydney, which he says had a great music department and a very good library, but in 1957, after his parents' marriage ended, he was sent to Newington College, a posh private school in Sydney's inner west. Here there was no good library and 'just football and bullies'. Describing himself as being 'traumatised' there, Roger adds that to keep himself sane he used to draw and make sculptures. He offers, 'Shy people often start in theatre. I wanted to be in the wings'. Already he was working on Saturdays in a children's theatre in Tempe.

At the end of 1959, Roger did his Leaving Certificate and left school. His mother said that he must learn something practical because he loved making things, and so he obtained an apprenticeship as a fitter and turner at Email, a whitegoods manufacturer in Zetland, where he worked in the washing machine department. Roger enjoyed his time at Email. He recalls that there were lots of migrants working there, and 'they had wonderful parties'.

He found this liberating new life in the inner city very different from Mosman, which he describes as being 'like a cloud of poison gas had descended on it'. Roger would soon move out of Mosman, into share houses across eastern Sydney, from Coogee to Kings Cross. 'Kings Cross was so much better than Mosman', he reminisces. 'It was wonderful. There was a woman there who would walk around with a pink rabbit on a lead.'

Ellis D Fogg (Roger Foley)

At the same time as starting the apprenticeship, Roger enrolled part-time in engineering at the University of New South Wales. He quickly became part of the vibrant arts scene at UNSW, with which he would be associated for most of the coming decade. One of the main movers and shakers in this scene was Roger's old neighbourhood friend, Richard Neville, who was already involved with the UNSW student newspaper, *Tharunka*.

Still very much drawn to the theatre, Roger joined the UNSW Dramatic Society, later becoming its president. He also began a combative friendship with experimental film-maker Albie Thoms, who was president of the Sydney University Dramatic Society (SUDS). Although Roger acknowledges that it was Thoms who educated him about theatrical concepts such as the Revue of the Absurd and the Theatre of Cruelty, Roger felt that SUDS was essentially negative when he wanted to be positive. He says that SUDS was a bunch of guys all dressed in duffle coats sitting around being gloomy. He then adds that he did not like the French existentialists, like Samuel Beckett, 'who never got out of bed'.

Early in Roger's association with the UNSW Dramatic Society, when he was still an apprentice at Email, he started making light sculptures out of stainless steel, using tools and materials from his workplace. Initially built as part of Roger's idea of becoming a set designer, these sculptures soon became a theatrical art form in their own right.

As he describes how he made his sculptures by moving light through leaves, Roger explains that animals and humans love getting stoned from the visions created by sunlight flickering on their closed eyelids. Obviously, this was a development or extension of his childhood experience of lying in the bath and watching light and reflected shadow from the trees coming through the patterned-glass window. He adds, 'You can make an artwork yourself from the shadows of your spread fingers rapidly moving back and forth on your closed eyelids which make patterns in your brain'. He keeps repeating, 'Everything is made of vibration'.

Talking about his first light sculptures leads Roger to recall reading an avant-garde magazine from the French publisher Maurice Girodias, called *Olympia*, which Martin Sharp had given him. In it there was an article about how American beat generation writer William S Burroughs and his lover and technician, Ian Sommerville, had built a 'Dreamachine' – a form of stroboscope intended to affect the brain via alpha-wave activity. For Roger, the idea of a machine that 'created amazingly beautiful patterns' was an inspiration. He believes the effect of the movement of light on the brain is tied to evolution and governs what people need to do to become properly evolved.

Some important reading material recommended to Roger by Albie Thoms was *The Synthetic Futurist Theatre: A manifesto*, by early twentieth-century Italian poet, Filippo Tommaso Marinetti. Futurist theatre is characterised by short scenes, nonsensical humour, heavy use of machinery props and attempts to subvert normal theatre traditions. One such subversion was the collaboration between the public and the actors. Paraphrasing the Futurist student actors, Roger explains that, 'The idea is to shock the audience like a Brecht play does, with random acts such as getting madmen off the street and giving them free tickets to the show'.

For Roger, this whole concept was an invitation to follow his own iconoclastic ideas about the theatre. He explains: 'I would find material not written for stage and put it on'.

Ellis D Fogg (Roger Foley)

One of the things he put on – at the 1966 UNSW Uni Review – was a performance of the poem known as 'The Word Flashed Round the Arms', a cutting satire about the mating habits of North Shore schoolboys, which Martin Sharp had published in 1964 in the satirical magazine, *Oz*.

At this point in our conversation, Roger laughs and starts to recite the piece that he still knows by heart. '*The word flashed round the Arms that there was a gas turn up at Whale Beach Rd ... so we piled into the Mini Coopers and thrashed over ...*'

What a poem to know by heart! 'The Word Flashed Round the Arms' is one of the pieces that in 1964 resulted in Sharp, together with Richard Neville and Richard Walsh, being charged with obscenity and sentenced to six months gaol by famously vicious Sydney magistrate, Gerald Locke. For Roger, reporting on these events fifty-five years later, it's as if this outrage happened yesterday.

By now, Roger's brain is banging away as fruitfully as his backdrops and he is already onto his next love – Destruction art.

In September 1966, a 'Destruction in Art Symposium' was held in London, attended by the international counter-culture underground. Roger gleefully claims that (performance artist) 'Jenni Nixon and I staged a "Happening" straight after that – in Orientation Week 1967. People would bring things that they loved to us and we would destroy them. It was a way of destroying the old way of looking at things'.

Meanwhile, as Albie Thoms and his film-making collective, Ubu Films, moved into increasingly experimental modes, Roger's various artistic arguments with Albie were ongoing. Roger wanted even 'experimental' films to be watchable. Declaring himself to be a fan of counter-culture guru Marshall McCluhan (presumably for his 'the medium is the message' edict), Roger says, 'I thought our shows had to be entertaining, to be popular, to be POP, to get a message through'.

In 1967, Roger answered Albie's *Handmade Film Manifesto* with what he called his *'No Film' Film Manifesto*. In it, Roger argues that 'In a *No Film*, anything goes ... *No Films* are constantly and infinitely changing, never to be repeated ... They are ephemeral and leave no easily measured evidence'. His ongoing refrains continue, with: 'Even the sunlight filtered through the leaves on a tree branch moving in the wind is a *No Film*' ... and, finally, '*No Films* can exist even when there are no witnesses as they also exist in the subatomic world of vibrations'. There's that word again.

ROGER WAS CONVINCED THAT EXPERIMENTAL FILMS WERE more interesting when smoke was added for atmosphere. He says that Albie didn't realise lightshows were an art form in themselves until he saw Roger's shows. This would eventually bring about a collaboration that was important to both artists.

In 1969, Albie made a film about Filippo Marinetti's work. It was a totally new form of film-making, and many in the audience walked out. Eventually Roger convinced Albie that the film should not be shown on a rectangular screen. He argued that if a rectangular screen is used, people want a beginning, a middle and an end – in fact, a narrative film. Instead, the film should be presented a bit more as a lightshow. So they produced *Marinetti* as a lightshow, and it worked. Albie would later tour Europe with this film/lightshow.

Ellis D Fogg (Roger Foley)

Of these collaborative productions, art critic Elwyn Lynn would later write, 'In admittedly rather hazy retrospect, it seems to me that truly experimental art (in the Yellow House) was done in light by Roger Foley and film with Albie Thoms'.

As the light sculptures became lightshows, more people and more equipment were needed to stage the performance. Although the chronology seems appropriately to have blurred into a pink and golden haze, at some stage the individual artist Roger Foley became known as Roger Foley and Friends. (He tells us that he always got the best people to work with him.) Then, because he wanted to include everybody under one name, this collective morphed into the famous psychedelic lightshow man, Ellis D Fogg, with the delicious coincidence of the name being pronounced as 'LSD' Fogg.

So how did the name come about?

Characteristically, Roger explains this in a fairly roundabout way. 'Acid's a funny thing. It's something you've got to learn to drive. A lot of the hippies in San Francisco didn't know how to do it and they ended up in San Francisco Hospital where the attending physician was often a doctor called Ellis D Sox.' Roger thought this was funny and the name stuck in his brain. The 'Fogg' part of the collective name stemmed from the fact that Roger's nickname at school had been 'Fog'.

So Ellis D Fogg was born. The team often called themselves the Fogettes, and their uniform was white cloud-decorated overalls.

I hate being bored

BUT WHAT ABOUT POLITICS?

When I ask Roger whether Vietnam and civil rights had pierced this admittedly exciting cultural cone, his response is telling. 'Politics was criminal. We were being led by criminals. [NSW Premier] Askin was a criminal.'

He says he always opposed the Vietnam War. When I ask him about his family's attitude to the war, he says he doesn't know because he gave up on his family when the psychedelic era began. 'We were fighting with each other too much.' He reiterates: 'We were all against war'. He says again that he found the political stuff very boring. He must have a very narrow view of 'political stuff', because later on he displays intense interest in political and cultural struggle around the world.

Roger Foley's political ideology is expressed in this passage from his notes for the photography and film exhibition, *Spirit of the Gija*:

> Not knowing of Aristotle nor Aquinas at the time …
> my young friends … my generation … understood
> that we have a duty to change unjust laws. In the trial
> of Adolf Eichmann in 1962 we were excited by the
> judge's decision that obeying the law of the state was
> not a defence for murder which convinced us that to
> experience JOY through doing GOOD … we have a
> duty to change bad laws. By 1968, the Vietnam War
> had led our generation of students to invest themselves
> in the same process of change … by breaking bad laws.

Roger's mainstream political activity at the time seems to have been sporadic and reactive. When anti-Vietnam student activist Rod Webb asked him to help with the 'Stop Work to Stop the War' Moratorium concert at UNSW in 1970, Roger helped by organising lightshows for the bands that donated their services.

Describing rock-and-roll as 'my generation's agitprop', he makes the link between political protest and the counter-culture, which he sees as being driven by the sexual revolution.

> The symbolism of long hair, and the exploding sexual revolution, and drug taking were allied to antiwar protests and civil rights movements under the banner – Counter Culture ... an art form that defied national, political and cultural barriers. It was a global enterprise played out under blazing lights, lightshows ... and in Australia most of this phenomena was generated by Albie Thoms' Ubu group and my group, Ellis D. Fogg.

Though Roger may understate his political involvement, in fact his lightshows were a crucial part of almost every fundraising concert for every left-wing cause. He did see these as having a political intent, although their main purpose was to be 'an expression of joy and positivity'.

AS WE MOVE FROM POLITICS TO THE QUESTION OF DRUGS, Roger says that his first joint was given to him in 1968 by Robert Taylor, the drummer from the band Tully.

His first experience with psychedelic drugs occurred soon after this, when he met and began to hang out with Gretel Pinniger (later famous as performance artist and dominatrix Madame Lash). Gretel was at East Sydney Tech,

I hate being bored

where Roger too was enrolled for a while. She was a strong-willed person, and Roger reports rather matter-of-factly that 'people were terrified of her'. I remember her at the time as being a commanding presence. She was tall, and mostly kitted out in character – certainly a remarkable sight, but not terrifying.

When Gretel asked him to do the lighting effects for her entrance as Titania, Queen of the Fairies, in a theatrical production, he suggested she appear in a cloud of fog, which proved to be a great hit. They soon became lovers. Gretel was stripping for a living while undertaking her degree, and Roger would carry her bag to the various strip clubs.

Roger believes that psychedelic drugs expand consciousness, whereas alcohol contracts it. He sounds so much like fellow interviewee Robbie Swan – no wonder the political activists drank beer and the artier types took drugs.

What is the meaning of psychedelia?

In reply, Roger quotes Aldous Huxley, saying that 'It means an epiphany ... expanding one's knowledge and awareness ... and it gives you insights into something such as the apes'. He is obviously paraphrasing Huxley's *Ape and Essence*, his novel about intelligent baboons who destroy the universe and through mutually assured destruction, kill themselves in the process.

However, there is even more complexity to Roger's layered view of the world. In his notes for *Spirit of the Gija*, he explains that 'all my Lightshows and indeed most of the 60s Counter Culture movement in Australia was inspired by the multiverse of Indian culture'. He cites Gandhi's non-violence, and India's colourful gods, mandalas and spiritualism.

Ellis D Fogg (Roger Foley)

> We tried to become Carlos Castaneda's 'honourable warriors' and used bright coloured lights in surreal ways with live performances by rock bands, jazz and symphony orchestras – words, music and dance – with our indeterminate and ephemeral Fog to stimulate the minds of the participants to concentrate on being 'Together', to become 'One' with the universal brotherhood of man – The World as One.

This is pure Sixties, as is Roger's conclusion that: 'It seemed both fortuitous and serendipitous for us to be born in the twentieth century when all aspects of the world began to change from the Industrial/Material toward a world of many realities'.

MEANWHILE, THE SHOW WAS STILL GOING ON.

Akin to the revolutions in the theatre was the arrival in the art world of performance art. Incorporating painting into the mix, on one occasion Roger asked the artist Jeffrey Rose to paint a giant banana and used it as the backdrop to a theatre piece. This was considered a curiosity.

The art form known as a Happening was also a perfect vehicle for Roger. He mentions reading Allan Kaprow's seminal 1966 work, *Assemblage, Environments & Happenings*. Kaprow was an American painter and pioneer in performance art who created Happenings in California in the early 1960s.

In February 1971, Roger collaborated with artist Vivienne Binns in the 'Lightshow Environmental Happening', *WOOM*, at Watters Gallery in Sydney (described later in this book in the chapter about Vivienne). A few months later, Roger staged another Happening at the Elizabethan Theatre in Newtown. Unhappy with what he was planning to do, the management decreed that he could not rent the theatre unless he called the production something else. So he called it 'The Un-Elizabethan Theatre'. In this performance, Binns and a team of assistants 'action painted' a bare dancer and a backdrop of a thousand square feet of bed sheets to the sounds of singer Wendy Saddington and the rock-and-roll band Chain – all illuminated by Roger's light sculptures.

An important part of Roger's life began on 1 April this same year, with the opening of the 'Yellow House' in Macleay Street, Potts Point. An homage to Van Gogh's Yellow House in Arles, it was a haunt for artists, writers, film-makers and generally way-out characters of the era. Roger describes himself as being 'The only adult in the Yellow House – the one who knew that bills needed to be paid and electricity needed to be on'.

He spent his time at the Yellow House doing lightshows in collaboration with his old sparring partner Albie Thoms. He thinks Albie's book about this period, *My Generation*, is 'excellent'. In it, Albie described his work with Foley as 'shamelessly derivative but we believed it was the art of the future … now it is all around us in movies and television and is called appropriation'.

Roger concludes that 'Everyone and every subculture needed some kind of lighting or lightshow for their events and Happenings and by a kind of osmosis my lightshows became a part of this counter-culture'.

Ellis D Fogg (Roger Foley)

SO, HOW DID ALL THIS CHANGE HIS LIFE?

In a practical sense, when his lightshows took off, Roger dropped out of university and, later, East Sydney Tech. (He was amused one day when his former university philosophy tutor wanted to come and work on Fogg lightshow projects.)

He says, 'You do stuff that just feels right at the time and it does have meaning for your audience, which you find out later'.

Then, strangely, he talks about starlings – about 'murmuration'. No one bird is in charge, but they all co-ordinate and things happen. All our cells make us do stuff in concert, as a great symphony. Once again he talks about vibrations, vibrations of the universe, of music ... then he starts to speak about the author Michio Kaku. I google Kaku and discover he is an American theoretical physicist and futurist, famous for his work on 'string field theory'. My head hurts at the thought of delving down this rabbit hole, so I let it be.

I have been taken on a journey I did not expect and I have learnt much about Roger's particular version of the counter-culture. It has been entertaining, but I'm still not sure I fully understand it. What is clear is that Ellis D Fogg was a crucial part of Australia's counter-culture scene. For many, particularly today's young, this counter-culture *was* the Sixties. And for us oldies, a Sixties Happening wasn't really happening without an Ellis D Fogg lighting and mist machine.

PETER DUNCAN
Activism works ...
and it works in parliament

Meredith Burgmann

Peter arrives looking as distinguished and politician-ready as ever. He is always self-assured, almost cocky, but these days there is a shadow of hard times and a hint of wisdom about him. Always thoughtful, life has made him even more so, and genuine concern for the underdog now seems to be his all-consuming passion.

I presumed that our interview with him would be different from our other forays. I had always thought of Peter as being more sure about his life and career trajectory than the rest of us, but I was wrong. His early life seems as haphazard and unplanned as it was for most of us. His stratospheric rise at a shockingly young age to become the youngest state attorney-general in our history led to quick and sometimes callous judgments by his detractors.

We have somehow chosen to do this interview on the

hottest day of the year, and we are sweating like pigs, but hey, Peter now lives in Lombok, so he'll cope.

Nadia puts our first question. She asks the activist/politician/attorney-general, 'Did your experiences in the Sixties determine how you became the politician you were in later life?' His answer is a very definite 'yes'.

Peter Duncan was born in Melbourne in 1945, into what he describes as a lower middle-class family. He has written a scrappy memoir of his early years – but being intellectually lazy, he says, he has never tried to put it into a readable form. What scraps I have read, however, are compelling. His description of his mother as desperately wanting to be accepted by 'the right sort of people' gives a devastating taste of class in the 1950s.

As with our previous interviews, it's amazing how often the issue of religion and Catholic–Protestant bigotry arises. Peter was shocked by the prevailing discrimination against Catholics, especially in the period during his childhood when he lived in Melbourne. His parents were strong Presbyterians, although he does suspect – as so many kids do – that his father didn't have much religion. His father's attitude to life seemed to be 'keep your head down'.

Despite a brief flowering of trade unionism among his forebears (various relatives ended up as presidents of the Labor Council of New South Wales), it does not seem to have affected his views as he was growing up. No proletarian ideas in the Duncan family home. His father worked his way through the ranks of the Commonwealth Bank to end up holding a quite senior position and, as Peter says, 'at last we had made it into the middle class'.

Peter's vague recollection of his first political action is marching in the bank nationalisation rallies of 1949 with his father, although, as he says, this might be family history rather than his own personal memory. I only realise later I'm not sure which side his father was supporting – but further correspondence with Peter puts me straight. His father was a member of the Commonwealth Bank Officers' Association, which fervently supported Prime Minister Ben Chifley's nationalisation plans.

Peter attended the fiercely selective public school Melbourne High in his early years of secondary schooling, and his main activity there seems to have been trying to dodge being in the cadets. His first protest was leading a campaign against the requirement for fourth formers to wear caps. He describes in great detail and with delight the fact that the students etched in weedkiller 'No Caps for Fourth Formers' on the school lawns. This handiwork was visible from passing trains and was a considerable embarrassment for the school authorities.

Although I interpret this protest as about authority and irrational rules, rather than Peter's desire to be particularly stylish, I feel the need to query, why the issue about caps? He points out that the fifth and sixth formers were allowed to wear hats, and the fourth formers had to wear the despised caps. Such are the first clouds that darken the souls of the young. It is so reminiscent of Geoff Robertson being offended at having to read an expurgated edition of *The Tempest* or Robbie Swan wanting to grow sideburns.

His history teacher, Ben Mundey, was important in that he taught the subject in 'a very political way'. It is remarkable how these socialist and crypto-socialist teachers of the Sixties had such an effect on students. Peter remembers in particular learning the 'proper' political history of Eureka.

Peter Duncan

IN 1962, THE FAMILY MOVED TO SYDNEY, AND PETER WAS relocated to Homebush Boys' High School – where, in 1963, he ran a book on the Melbourne Cup because he felt he 'owned it', coming as he did from Melbourne. Inevitably he was caught: in the school toilets with his transistor radio glued to his ear, listening to the race to find out how he had fared. The school hauled his father in and explained that they thought Peter 'would be better spending his time in the work force'. Although Peter was not formally expelled, he revelled in the fact that he was asked to leave school. By the following Monday, his father had organised a litho-printing apprenticeship for Peter, at John Sands, the printing company best known for its greeting cards.

Peter sees this as an important event in his unfolding political consciousness, because as part of taking up the apprenticeship he joined the printing union – this was compulsory. The printing chapter was very active, and they often held meetings. When the secretary of the union, Col Colborne, visited the factory, Peter described it as 'like a royal tour – the way in which this important individual was treated'.

Within a year he'd been promoted to a role as a junior printing executive, and he remembers the manager talking about those 'fucking unions'. When I asked him, 'Did you have sympathy with the manager when he expressed these views?', Peter answered prosaically that 'sometimes I did and sometimes I didn't, depending on the issue'.

BY THIS TIME, PETER HAD ALREADY GIVEN RELIGION AWAY. He had done that quite publicly. Unlike me (I never admitted to my parents that I had become a non-believer), at the age of fourteen years Peter simply told the Reverend Mullens at Strathfield Presbyterian Church that he wasn't attending services any more. This incident is a bit of an indicator of Peter's later life, in that he makes a decision, and just carries it out.

He told the minister of his decision in a short conversation as they were leaving what came to be Peter's last religious service. The Reverend Mullens was out the front of the church shaking hands, and Peter simply blurted it out. He reports that his mother 'was mortified', but as Peter says, 'I just didn't believe it any more'. He reiterates his suspicion that his father was probably an atheist but just went along with it all because of his belief in the importance of not rocking the boat.

AT THE END OF 1963, WHILE HOLIDAYING IN MELBOURNE, Peter made a decision that was to be a turning point in his life. His mates from Melbourne High were by now mostly at university, and superficially at least seemed to be having a great time. This made Peter determined to follow them into tertiary education, even though, of course, he had not finished his schooling.

Back in Sydney, he undertook the Leaving Certificate at night at Burwood Evening College. His job at John Sands involved delivering and collecting printed material from around Sydney, and because he always did this delivery work very quickly (as his speeding tickets would indicate), he would return to the factory in time to do an hour's study in the back of the car. He always boasts that this is why he knows his way around Sydney so well.

I wonder what would have happened to Peter if he had

not had this holiday and decided to follow his mates to uni. I suspect he would have become a pretty cut-throat printing-business owner, making oodles of money out of funny birthday cards and novelty decorations. I'm sure if I told him this he wouldn't be offended.

In 1965, he enrolled at the University of Adelaide. His parents were moving to South Australia for his father's work, and his father – still obviously trying to guide his wayward son – said that he would help Peter financially if he went to university there. When Peter was deciding between Arts and Law, his father said, 'Well, you're no good at art, you'd better do law'. So it is clear that Peter wasn't particularly sophisticated at this stage, and was still very much part of his family.

At the beginning of his university life, Peter was still living at home. We ask him about the generation gap with his parents, and he just says it was more his father's caution and his mother's social climbing that was the issue, rather than their politics. His parents were overt about voting Labor, but their social life was 'very staid'.

PETER'S MOTHER KEEPS CROPPING UP IN HIS NARRATIVE. HIS father died early, aged only fifty-seven, and his mother was 'a very dominating woman … very 1950s'. Peter disapproved strongly of his mother's 'shallowness' about social class, and shortly after enrolling at university he moved out of home. I wonder whether he was able to verbalise at the time why he was so dismayed by his mother's attitudes or whether it was something he began to understand in later life. How much do we really understand of our younger selves?

Activism works ... and it works in parliament

HE DESCRIBES HIMSELF, AS HE ENTERS THE UNIVERSITY of Adelaide, as 'with Labor sympathies, but with a pretty straight view of the world', and he certainly had not taken drugs. In my interviews, I find myself continually asking this question, 'When did you start taking drugs?' – not because I think that it's a particularly important part of the Sixties, but because I see it as a bit of a marker as to whether someone has become part of student culture. However, it does seem that Adelaide was less into the druggie lifestyle than Sydney was.

Apart from having Labor sympathies, he describes his political position as 'rejectionist'. He didn't like Menzies or Calwell, but because they kept Labor out of government he also despised the DLP. However, a hint of Peter's developing political views is that in Orientation Week he joined the ALP Club, and clearly remembers charismatic Attorney-General Don Dunstan and David Combe (later ALP national secretary) coming to campus. Later in 1965, he joined Young Labor and also the Labor Party. He joined the Sturt local branch of the ALP, based in Linden Park, and remembers being heavily involved in the 1966 federal election campaign.

Peter had been conscripted in 1965, but he says, quite nonchalantly, 'I was at uni, so it just wasn't a problem'. I suspect that he was like many of his generation, those who pictured themselves at university for the next three or four years, simply believing that the war would be over by the time they graduated and that their own conscription would never be an issue. Unlike me, he always saw conscription and Vietnam as interlinked, regarding them as essentially the same issue.

In 1966 he was living in a student share house and, as is often the way of share houses, the housemates tended to act collectively, all joining the 'soft' campaign for peace in Vietnam. (This seems to be a South Australian 'tendency' or faction that we did not have in other states.) But Peter had already started to get caught up in other student political activity from 1965 onwards. First, he became involved in what seems like a totally non-Sixties issue. It was not civil rights or Vietnam but, rather, the unfair gerrymander of the South Australian electoral boundaries, which massively favoured the conservative side of politics. Not only was this a cause without soul-stirring narratives or handsome heroes, it was specifically state-based and pretty mundane. State Labor had struggled into office in 1965 under a massively unfair electoral system, but lost again at the 1968 election. The rising star of the trendy Left, Don Dunstan, had replaced the prosaic Frank Walsh as leader in 1967, but the gerrymander was seen as the main obstacle in the way of Dunstan's re-election and the progressive reforms promised by him.

In 1967, Peter's attention was captured by the issue of 'student control of student affairs' – central to many of the student actions around the country at the time, the so-called 'student power' revolt, so vivid in the frenzied minds of Australia's more conservative commentators. A vigorous campaign was orchestrated by Peter's fellow students Peter O'Brien and Rob Durbridge to have students elected onto the university governing body. The university rejected this proposition outright.

The left-liberal Vice-Chancellor, Geoffrey Badger, tried to reason it out with the students. He invited a bunch of activists to his house in the posh suburb of Springfield. There was 'a huge amount of argy-bargy', nothing was resolved, and a month later forty students broke in and occupied the vice-chancellor's office. Peter was among them.

Activism works ... and it works in parliament

I ask whether they were aware of American students' demands around student democracy. He says that they were, and that they were also aware of French student leader 'Danny the Red' (Daniel Cohn-Bendit) and the sit-ins at the London School of Economics. Obviously they saw themselves as plugged into the global student movement, just as we in the eastern states did.

In terms of his intellectual growth, he was very lucky. In first year politics he was lectured by Bob Hetherington (who later ended up in the SA Upper House), Gordon Reid and Neal Blewett (later federal minister for Health). This was an extraordinary group of young progressive academics, and Peter says he was greatly influenced by their 'small-l liberal' views.

His academic stimulation increased sharply the following year. Graeme Duncan was appointed as professor of politics and he then brought in Brian Abbey and Bob Catley. Both Abbey and Catley were great contributors to the Australia-wide debate about Vietnam and American foreign policy. Peter says that by the time he did second year politics in 1967 it was 'a full-on Marxist analysis', and what they were learning was international politics, rather than domestic Australian politics.

Peter had become the vice-president of Young Labor in 1966. He says that until the Vietnam Moratorium movement began in the late 1960s, there was 'not much schism' in Young Labor, and ironically describes fellow Young Laborite Julian Myles, who worked for the Commonwealth Bank, as being 'the left-wing agitator' in the organisation.

In his very early time in Young Labor, he still did not regard himself as left or right. However, he soon became a supporter of charismatic Victorian left-winger Jim Cairns, and by 1967 he considered himself in the Left of the Labor Party. The fount of all knowledge for the ALP Left in the Adelaide political scene was Jim Cavanagh, a former plasterer and traditional leftist trade unionist, who would become a minister in the Whitlam government. Cavanagh appears to have mentored Peter to some degree.

Young Labor held seminars on various political topics at a place called Graham's Castle, a conference centre in Goolwa, about 80 kilometres from Adelaide. Peter remembers David Combe, Mick Young (later to become a federal minister), John Bannon (later SA premier) and Chris Schacht (also later a federal minister) being involved with these seminars, either as students or teachers. Perhaps because of its small size, students in Adelaide felt more plugged into the political power structures of the state than we did in the east.

At these seminars, members of federal caucus came to speak. He remembers Clyde Cameron (later federal minister), another dominant Left figure in South Australia, not allowing Kim Beazley senior to come and speak because he was a right-winger, and presumably because he was a member of the right-wing religious organisation Moral Re-armament. Cameron was considered pragmatic, but very close to Don Dunstan. As Peter says, 'those two were singing from the same songbook'.

I am curious about whether the political and historical material they looked at in these seminars was similar to what we were looking at in Sydney. Once again, he confirms that it was from America – so we shared ideological forebears.

At this point, I press him again about drugs, and he says he was still not into them, 'but certainly booze and birds'. He explains that he'd smoked pot occasionally, and had tried LSD once in 1968, up in the Flinders Ranges, but hadn't found it very nice. He remembers crawling around in a delirium thinking he was trekking in a desert, whereas really he'd only crawled 3 or 4 metres in either direction.

When we ask him about more radical politics and whether he was at all involved, he remembers taking part in a Vietnam demonstration outside parliament in 1967, where the police closed off the street, even though Don Dunstan was the premier by then. And he admits that, yes, he wore a National Liberation Front (North Vietnamese) badge in 1968, and understood that this was basically supporting the enemy. But he denied ever having worn a Mao badge. He also adds that there were very few Trots (Trotskyists) in Adelaide. Both Nadia and I burst into giggles at this. There are some advantages to living in a small city.

PETER SAYS HIS POLITICS HAD DEFINITELY BECOME MORE radical by the time he became co-editor (with Arwed Turon) of the university student newspaper, *On Dit*. It was a position elected by the Students' Representative Council (SRC), and the Labor group had already taken control of the Council at the previous election. His predecessors on the paper were Peter O'Brien and Julian Disney (later a Rhodes scholar). Peter O'Brien and Rob Durbridge by this stage were in Students for Democratic Action (SDA), which was an American-inspired student democracy group similar to Students for a Democratic Society (SDS) in Sydney.

Peter says – still with some bitterness fifty years later – that Peter O'Brien and Rob Durbridge, and two of their supporters, voted against him as editor of *On Dit*. It is strange how these petty treasons lie so heavily on our souls. He buried the hatchet on this issue many years ago, and while he was attorney-general employed O'Brien, remaining good friends with both men until their deaths.

As with other student newspapers of the time, *On Dit*, under Peter and Arwed, used to run traditionally sexist photos – 'Bird of the Week' – and a column called 'Abreast of the Times', but what is interesting is that they also ran campaigns about problems that later became very important feminist issues. They even ran an abortion edition. He still remembers the front page, which was a box with a woman wrapped up inside, with the headline, 'The Case for Abortion'.

Peter says that they did not have much of a problem with censorship, because O'Brien and Disney had already won that argument the year before. *On Dit* was set up so that the editors were responsible to the SRC and to no other body. The university itself had no responsibility for the paper, and so did not have the oversight role that happened with other student newspapers. He laughs about how they were 'a bit cheeky'. When it came to the special edition for the SRC elections – where each candidate gets a picture and a little space for a blurb – they put all the progressive candidates on the front page and the conservative candidates at the back. Peter never could help himself.

Peter and Arwed ran material on Aboriginal issues. In 1968, they supported the Gurindji, who in 1966 had walked off Wave Hill Station in the Northern Territory in protest against their working conditions and the dispossession of their land. This 'walk off' later morphed into an iconic ten-year fight for their land rights. They also campaigned in support of Dunstan's attempt to devise a form of land rights in the north of South Australia – the Anangu Pitjantjatjara Yankunytjatjara (APY) lands. There was also substantial activity in support of the Aboriginal scholarship organisation, Abschol, and the government program, ABSTUDY.

Peter enticed Brian Abbey to write anti-Vietnam articles for *On Dit*, and Chris White (later secretary of what is now SA Unions) was his review editor. 'We stole stuff from everywhere', as long as they thought students would be interested: from a US magazine called *Resist*, from the Communist Party of Australia's *Tribune*, from Sydney University's *Honi Soit* and other student newspapers.

Peter's mother was, strangely, very impressed by his editorship of *On Dit*. As he says, no matter how disgusting or sexist the content – and we must remember we are talking about 1968, before the rise of second wave feminism – no matter how racy the newspaper was, his mother was always very proud that this was a paper being produced by her son.

While attending a conference of student editors in Melbourne, he met Freedom Rider Darce Cassidy, who was very influential in left journalism at this time. Peter then tells a very funny story, probably apocryphal, of Darce stopping off for a meal at Gundagai on his trip down to Melbourne and discovering that there was an issue between south Gundagai and north Gundagai. The south Gundagai folk felt very put upon by the citizens of north Gundagai. Within minutes, Darce had produced his portable Roneo machine from the back of his car and was producing leaflets for the South Gundagai Liberation Front.

PETER SAYS THAT SUPPORT FOR DUNSTAN AMONG THE students was very high, especially on his social policy agenda. I think about this and can't help an internal giggle over the prospect of students in New South Wales being inspired to support our then state Labor leader Pat Hills over *anything* – all horn-rimmed glasses, brushed-back hairstyle and grey cardie.

In the 1968 state election, Don Dunstan was defeated by the shocking gerrymander, and Peter organised a special edition of *On Dit* to memorialise the occasion. More significantly, he was detained by police during an anti-gerrymander rally. The police arrested about 200 of the protesters, took them down the road and let them all out. I ask him whether he was concerned about being detained, because I remember students at Sydney who were doing law being very concerned about arrests, given the general view that if you'd been arrested as a student, you could never be a lawyer. This was not strictly true, but certainly the students believed it. Peter confessed that he had been really concerned at the possibility of arrest.

By 1970, he was dealing with the looming prospect of having to enter the army as a result of his conscription in 1965. As his student deferment had at last run its course, he received a letter that ordered him to present himself at Keswick Barracks. Peter's reaction was swift and predictable. He organised a large demonstration. When I asked whether the protest was just about him, or if it was general, he said that because he'd received a letter, he'd assumed others had also been called up to the barracks at that time. So he organised the demonstration for everyone – but in actual fact he was the only named person called up that day.

I wonder if Peter had been picked on purpose. I fantasise about some middle-order bureaucrat being so irritated by this know-all young lawyer that they decide to pull the pin on him.

Two thousand people attended the rally, which was huge for Adelaide. Peter addressed the crowd outside the barracks, no doubt using all the skills he'd learnt in his years in Young Labor. Another speaker was Lynn Arnold, later premier of South Australia, who was the chair of the Vietnam Moratorium campaign. The military personnel inside the barracks simply shut the door; no one was allowed in. The demonstrators hung around for a while, but nothing happened – so they went home. Peter heard nothing more about his conscription. This was very typical of the time. Often conscripts who were considered troublemakers discovered that their papers simply never turned up, or cases against them were mysteriously dropped.

I ask him, did he see himself as a left-wing martyr or, in fact, did he want to be a martyr and go to gaol? He answers with a definite 'No'. This is very characteristic of Peter's politics, in that his ideology is not to rail against the system, but to change it. There is nothing martyrish in his personality or his politics.

Although he was activated by the unjustness of the Vietnam War, he does concede that being conscripted himself probably did 'focus the mind'.

THE ELECTION OF DON DUNSTAN IN 1970 HAD A HUGE impact on Peter and the radicals of the young Left. They realised that they could change the world (or at least the government) by working within the system. The student body was very inspired by the young and trendy Dunstan, with his sweeping vision of a new society. During the election the gerrymander had once again loomed large – it had been leaked that the Liberals had drawn up a plan to make the gerrymander worse. And so there was huge relief when the first long-term Labor government for many years finally got elected.

Dunstan brought profound change to South Australian society. He recognised Aboriginal land rights, decriminalised homosexuality, appointed the first female judge and the first Indigenous governor, enacted consumer protection laws, abolished the death penalty, relaxed censorship and drinking laws, created a ministry for the environment, lowered the voting age and enacted anti-discrimination laws. Peter tells me, 'the Dunstan era transformed South Australia – and Australia too'.

Such was the pull of the Dunstan charisma that there was a sizeable migration south of young idealists from the other states, all wanting to work for his government. Like a herd of socialist wildebeest they gathered at the waterhole of Laborite endeavour. Many stayed there for life.

ON GRADUATION, PETER DECIDED HE WANTED TO BE AN industrial lawyer. He had become familiar with trade union people by this stage, as he used to drink with them at the Trades Hall bar. He took his articles in a law firm that he describes as barely a law firm – two brothers called Roberts, who turned out to be more like moneylenders than lawyers. But he fulfilled the requirement to become a fully-fledged tribune of the people.

Very typically, when Peter finished his articles he and another young graduate set up a law firm – at Cowra Chambers, in the city. I am amazed at their chutzpah. Peter says that the Law Society hated the fact that these young students were now a 'very troublesome' law firm. To appease the establishment, they eventually took on board an old lawyer called Charles Wheatley Reeves as a partner. He turned out to be a terrible apologist for apartheid and they quickly sidelined him, but at least the Law Society felt they had a wiser head within their firm.

Peter was still very active in the ALP, from 1970 right through to 1972. Then he went for a long trip overseas. When he returned, the state seat of Elizabeth was without an incumbent Labor candidate. He was given advice by South Australia-based federal front bencher, Clyde Cameron, that as long as he had the AWU (Australian Workers' Union) primary votes he should 'just go out and wangle for second preferences'. Which he did. He eventually was preselected against ten or eleven candidates, which caused much unhappiness within the Right of the party. In the 1973 election, he went on to win the seat at the age of twenty-eight.

Then Nadia asks: 'How did these experiences change the sort of politician you became?' He talks about his political commitment to the dispossessed and the working class, the environment and women's issues. He thinks that his period of activity in the 1960s gave him a preparedness to have a go when others were less inclined. I ask him if this was a result of the radical atmosphere of the times, and he says, very emphatically, 'Yes'. He saw that students to the left of him – such as the SDA – did force change, by occupying the vice-chancellor's office and through similar direct-action strategies, eventually getting student representatives onto the governing body.

He ruminates on these achievements. 'If you have a go, you might just win.' He then expands on this thought. He talks about the Residential Tenancies Act, which he introduced in state parliament. When everyone said that it couldn't happen, he just went ahead with it and it did happen. In the 1960s, Peter says, with a bit of both activism and chutzpah you could achieve anything. He does add more soberly, however, that 'sometimes you're beaten by circumstances'.

We then approach the issue for which he is justly best known, putting forward the first successful legislation to decriminalise homosexuality, as a back bencher in 1973. Peter has rightly been described by Justice Michael Kirby as 'the father of homosexual law reform in Australia'.

I ask when he became interested in the issue of homosexual decriminalisation. Peter says it all became clear to him when a lecturer in his law class started talking about victimless crimes. And when asked to explain a victimless crime, the lecturer had said, well, an act between two consenting adults in private – that was a victimless crime. Peter, with his very logical mind, saw immediately that homosexual decriminalisation was in fact an issue that needed to be dealt with, and it's no surprise that, in 1973, he did just that.

As the Sixties had taught him, 'activism works ... and it works in parliament'.

VIVIENNE BINNS
Searching for Truth

Nadia Wheatley

Commercial art galleries close over January. For Sydney's acclaimed Watters Gallery, the January of 1967 was no exception. Before going on holiday, director Frank Watters gave the gallery key to a 27-year-old artist named Vivienne Binns, so that she could spend the month installing her first exhibition. A couple of weeks later, Watters received a frantic phone call from a friend who had happened to walk past the gallery and look through the window.

'Someone has broken in and is trashing the place!' the passer-by reported.

'That's just Vivienne', Frank reassured his friend.

In preparation for the exhibition, Binns had painted a number of works on canvas and had made some constructions out of wood, all of which were modestly priced between $60 and $160. It so happened, however, that over this same summer the artist was moving from her rented flat-cum-studio in Paddington to a flat across the harbour in

Neutral Bay. What to do with pieces of broken Masonite, old newspapers, smashed records, discarded clothing, and all the other flotsam and jetsam of her life? Easy: stick it on the wall at Watters, title it 'Yipes! What a Mess', and put a ridiculous price of $6554 on it. (I particularly like that last $4; it seems so considered.)

In a photograph of this artwork, the self-proclaimed 'mess' is flanked by half-a-dozen press clippings about the show that have been attached to the nearby wall. Even in a small reproduction, the headline of the review by critic Rodney Milgate can still be read. 'SHE'S A SHOCKER' the huge print blares. Milgate's text elaborates:

> This show will tear you apart and make you question every social value we live by and every physical human characteristic we possess.
>
> It makes Colin Lanceley seem almost effete by comparison and Michael Brown a Middle Ages moralist.

The critic's reference to Michael Brown underpins, even more than the headline, the horror that greeted Binns's work. In December 1966, artist Mike Brown had been sentenced to three months hard labour in Australia's first – and indeed only – successful court case brought on a charge of obscenity in art. After describing Brown's paintings, exhibited in a Sydney gallery a few months earlier, as an 'orgy of obscenity', the magistrate had rhetorically asked: 'Does society permit the flaunting of sex, the debasing of the female form, or are [the images] being foisted on an unwilling community by a noisy and arrogant few?' He had concluded:

> I believe that the great majority of decent people –
> mothers and fathers responsible for rearing children
> – feel very deeply about these tendencies. These people
> look to the law and to the courts to do something
> about it.

Art patrons John Reed and Kym Bonython and critic Elwyn Lynn had spoken in court in defence of Brown. The art establishment was either silent or hostile, however, in response to Vivienne Binns's show. The works on exhibition included an image of a metre-high technicolour vagina surrounded by teeth (titled 'Vag Dens'), a huge penis and testicles ('Phallic Monument') and – most controversial of all – the piece titled 'Suggon', which had at its centre a purple hairnet (driven by an unseen motor) that pulsed in and out in an orgasmic way. Clearly, for a woman to be 'flaunting sex' was completely beyond the pale.

This 1967 exhibition of paintings and sculptures is the first entry in Wikipedia's timeline of Australian feminist art. There isn't another exhibition in this chronology until 1974.

So how did Vivienne Binns come to be painting these images at a time when the women's movement hadn't yet got to Australia? How did she have the bravery to put those images on public display in an era when this act could have landed her in gaol? Fifty years later, how does Binns assess this exhibition, and the responses to it?

HAVING CONCLUDED HER TEACHING CAREER AT THE Australian National University, Vivienne Binns lives in a bungalow in suburban Canberra, and on a number of occasions during our conversation she refers to herself as 'just a little girl from the suburbs'. Born in 1940, from the age of about five she grew up in a lower middle-class suburb on Sydney's lower North Shore. The Binns family, however, was more creative than the area's lower middle-class demographic might suggest. Vivienne credits her parents and siblings (three brothers, one sister; all older) with having taught her 'the basis of the practical skills' she has used throughout her career.

'It was a really rich life', she says. 'It wasn't intellectual. But it was active, and I was always doing things and making things – I couldn't wait for school holidays so I could get on with what I wanted to make.' She adds, 'My family were proud of my skills, too. Very supportive'.

The teenager was allowed to paint murals on her bedroom wall, and her parents didn't even object when she did a Pollock-style 'splash-and-splatter' on the ceiling. Vivienne's relationship with her oldest brother was especially important. He played records to her – classical as well as popular music – and lent her books that went far beyond what was on the school syllabus. One of these introduced the young girl to the concept of Free Love, which instantly appealed to her.

Despite the loving atmosphere, Vivienne found family life oppressive: being the youngest wasn't easy. At the same time, school disappointed. North Sydney Girls' High, proud of its reputation as a selective school, expected its students to go to university. Vivienne wanted to study art.

And so she did. There was first a year at the local tech, which Viv very much enjoyed, and then two years at the National Art School in East Sydney. Still living at home, she used to ride there on her motor scooter, but she was not acting out *The Wild One*. 'More serious' than many of her fellow students, Vivienne was 'considered a bluestocking'. Already she knew there was something she desperately wanted to discover.

'*Truth and Beauty* ...' she declares, early on in the interview. She goes on to explain that, at that time, she saw them as being in opposition. While the young artist had no doubt about which of the two she was seeking, it didn't take her long to realise she wasn't going to find Truth at the National Art School.

'As I moved on from first year, I was pretty disgusted with the level and quality of education we were getting. It was limited to this academic type of drawing and stuck in the notions that had come out of the Impressionists.'

But what of extracurricular activities? To the outside world, the National Art School seemed a place of licence and promiscuity, and indeed, a number of staff members and students had connections with Sydney's libertarian Push. In one respect, however, the art school was as narrow-minded as the rest of society.

'Lesbianism was a tainted word', Vivienne says. 'It was so ridiculed and reviled.' Feeling herself at times to be attracted to women, but seeing some of her fellow women students being 'targeted' with 'snide jokes', she feared that she too could easily become an object of vilification. 'In that sort of atmosphere it was hard to be honest, and hard to honestly evaluate who and what you were.' She 'had some very close female friendships' while she was a student, but these relationships 'didn't quite bring up the question' of lesbianism. There were boyfriends, too, but again there was disappointment.

'I was really interested in the idea of Free Love – I was a romantic, of course – but I wasn't really extremely brave.

Vivienne Binns

I was not precocious. There were other young women who were much more precocious than me – and they were sexually active. But I wasn't, and the boyfriends I had didn't really interest me all that much. I didn't have any really exciting boyfriends.'

This type of caution would have been the norm for most young women at the end of the 1950s, but it is astonishing to think that, within a few years, this particular young woman would be shocking the art world, and the broader society, with her frank images of sexual organs.

IN 1962, BINNS GRADUATED WITH A DIPLOMA IN PAINTING and Drawing. Rather than become an art teacher – the standard career path for a female graduate – she began a series of part-time jobs, at the switchboard of the telephone exchange, in an art supply shop, and in the family's wedding reception business. Still living at home, she clashed with her parents when she fell in love with a 'much older man', of whom she still speaks with great fondness. A European refugee who had fled Austria ahead of the Nazis, Robert King was a psychologist and a member of the Push. A mentor as well as a lover, he introduced Vivienne to a wider world of intellectual and philosophical ideas.

'Robert taught me what my family couldn't – that whole business of relationship, and negotiating relationship, and sexuality and eroticism. He was very generous and intelligent and taught me a great deal.'

In keeping with the ideals of the Push, Robert King regarded honesty in sexual relationships as more important than fidelity. This was the kind of Free Love that bookish Vivienne had read about; for women of this era, however, love was never free of danger. Vivienne 'was terrified of getting pregnant'.

The relationship ended when Robert returned to Europe. Needing space from her family, Vivienne set off on her scooter for Melbourne, where she spent a few months working as a scooter delivery girl. 'I had to break away from the family, I had to find what the hell I was in the world, rather than being just the youngest child.'

It was after she came back to Sydney that she met Mike Brown, who soon became her great friend and mentor as well as lover.

Although he was only two years older than Vivienne, by the mid-1960s Brown was already acknowledged as the leader of Australia's avant-garde art scene through the small group calling themselves 'Imitation Realists'. Their work – characterised by one critic as 'chaotic, exuberant and profuse' – had certain similarities with the Pop art going on in America, but Binns insists that they didn't know what was happening overseas. Certainly, Brown's work had an Australian sense of larrikinism.

Like her earlier romance with Robert, her relationship with Mike was marked by a mutual respect that was at odds with those misogynistic times. 'Mike and I were really important to each other', she says. 'We were different, but we were kindred spirits, we came from a kind of similar background.' Most importantly, Mike was also in search of Truth with a capital 'T'.

'Mike could think with a scalpel, he could cut into nooks and crannies where other people would be fearful of going. He just did things in a direct but humorous way that no one else could think of or was game to do. He hit such a nerve of raw brutal honesty.'

Still trying to 'find out what it bloody well truly and really meant to be an artist', Binns found that Mike was 'one of the few people I could really talk to'.

Like Vivienne herself, Mike Brown was a 'great talker'; the two artists would 'talk all through the night'.

In particular, she explains, Mike had 'got onto and understood the stuff about "automatic" drawing'. This was a process developed by the Surrealists, whereby the artist allowed the unconscious mind to take over. Exploring this idea, Binns began to draw without thinking about the images she was producing.

'It was a bit like doodling', she explains, 'but there was an intensity about it – I was so focused on the form of the drawing and staying in touch with the tension between the marks on paper. At the same time, I was letting what happened happen, and at some point it did just flood out'. At this point, as the artist 'started to find that the drawings appeared on the page', she realised that she 'just had to follow them'.

Going on to explain how she 'got into finding out what it was to be an artist', Binns says she 'went backwards' through her training about the 'rules and regulations' of composition and design, and discovered 'there was something fucking wrong'.

'So I started disobeying the rules, going back, back, back – cutting back, cutting back – and that brought me to the breakthrough. You know, I cracked through and came to this other place – the basic, intuitive sort of place, where you didn't have the strictures of overlaying rules – there was something else that was going on. And that was really revelatory.'

This rule-breaking that Vivienne Binns was doing in her art mirrored the rebelliousness of her times. She may have been alone in her studio rather than out with a bunch of activists on the street, but nevertheless she was embodying the *zeitgeist*. While the sexual revolution was already underway, this was also the time when (in the words of the Beatles' song), all you needed was Love.

'I woke up one morning and I thought: "Why spend so much time with people's faces as erotic symbols? Lovers, who love one another, love each other's genitals. Why don't we have portraits of genitals?"'

And so, still working out of 'this intuitive space' of automatic drawing, Binns painted an image of a vagina onto a piece of composition board in luminescent shades of green and purple and yellow. Filling the whole area of the board, this vagina is over a metre high and nearly a metre wide. Although the colours and style are reminiscent of psychedelic images from the era, Binns had 'never been on drugs'. She didn't need them: her unconscious was enough. Soon, however, she ran into trouble with her composition.

'I had the vagina, and I couldn't make the painting work – it didn't work. And I had this image of teeth, and I thought: "What on earth am I doing? That's too brutal, I can't do that." And of course it didn't work, it didn't work.

'And I had already discovered that when something really bugged me, the only way to get rid of it was to just *do* it. And I did it.

'And all of a sudden the painting worked. It was right. I could let it go, and that was it.'

WHEN SHE SHOWED THE PSYCHEDELIC VAGINA (STILL untitled) and the other paintings in the series to gallery director Frank Watters, he offered her a show. But when Watters sent Melbourne connoisseur John Reed to Binns's studio, the wealthy patron was dismissive. 'Do you think you'll keep on doing art?' he asked.

Vivienne interpreted this as a derogatory comment referring to women artists, who often, for reasons beyond their control, gave up their art in order to be wives and mothers. Incensed at this stereotyping, Vivienne thought, 'Fuck it – I'll be who I am'.

Someone else who saw the work in progress was radical psychologist Dr Peter Kenny, who had achieved notoriety at Sydney University for his Orientation Week 'sex symposia', at which he advocated 'the right to fornicate'. When Kenny saw the teeth that Binns had placed around the inside edge of the vagina, he told her this was 'an archetypal image', which psychologists had dubbed 'vagina dentata' – a term the artist instantly appropriated and abbreviated. This seemed to confirm Binns's sense that she was in touch with something beyond her conscious thought. 'I didn't set out to paint "Vag Dens"', she insists. 'How would a little girl from the suburbs really know anything about that?'

The concept of a vagina with teeth is regarded by psychologists as an expression of male fears of castration by women, so I check with Binns: 'You didn't produce this image out of a sense of feminist rage?'

In reply she points out that Women's Liberation had not yet taken off, and there had been no awareness of that sort of political view at art school. But again it is clear how much she was in touch with the spirit of the times.

'What amazed me about [the imagery of 'Vag Dens'] was

that things that were personal to me were universal. It was not just Viv turning out some pictures. I struck a chord.'

At this point of our conversation, the 78-year-old woman who is sitting with her schnauzer, Harriet, on her lap, having a 'morning cuddle', admits, 'I must have been a bit disturbing to some people'.

A BIT DISTURBING!

Helen Sweeney, the only female art critic to review the exhibition, accused Binns of showing 'an ungirlish impulse to shock'. Echoing the magistrate who had sentenced Mike Brown for obscenity, she added: 'These capers … are not for the family man or young mothers. [They] are intended to outrage and scandalise'.

But was that the artist's intention? When I ask Vivienne if she was challenging the censorship laws, she draws a distinction between herself and Mike Brown.

'In that work he was doing, Mike was definitely challenging the authorities. He was sticking his tongue out and thumbing his nose at the authorities and saying, "C'mon! Catch me if you can!"

'Whereas for me, it was about trying to find myself as an artist. Certainly, I thought it was ridiculous that you couldn't talk about these things, and you couldn't explore them but I was just putting this work out there. I didn't feel I was up against the authorities. People automatically thought I just wanted to shock, but I didn't so much want to shock as to say, "Look! I'm not necessarily what you think I am. You just don't see me."'

But surely Binns's declaration against her invisibility was in itself a form of feminist protest. It was akin to her response to art patron John Reed, but it was also part of the defiance women were starting to express towards the end of the 1960s.

Beyond the erotic images in the paintings, what shocked people in the Binns exhibition was the cumulative effect of the whole thing, and especially the work titled 'Yipes! What a Mess'. After describing the artist as using 'broken Masonite, crumpled newspaper and electric motors to mirror a decadent pagan terrifying world', Rodney Milgate announced: 'If this is to do with the world in which we live, an immediate reassessment of our entire way of life is necessary'.

Overall, Frank Watters described Binns's show to me as 'the best first exhibition by an artist' he had ever seen. Coming from the man who ran Sydney's leading commercial gallery for more than five decades, that is an amazing testimony. Watters added, 'I don't know any other first exhibition that caused such angst'.

To Binns herself, the furore in the press was irrelevant.

'I knew I'd broken through these extraordinary membranes of limitations, and I had had these revelations – this was the time of greatest revelations in my life.

'I knew that I was way ahead of everybody else. I didn't know what would be coming, but I felt I wasn't afraid of it. I felt I was utterly prepared for anything anybody could say or do. Because I'd got to a point of the truth. I knew what it was to be an artist. I'd hit it. I didn't have any doubts about it.'

SO WHAT DID THE ARTIST DO NEXT?

For me, the most shocking thing about Vivienne Binns's first exhibition is that, after it was over, she stopped painting for eighteen years.

It is easy to explain this as a case of an artist (especially, perhaps, a woman artist) being stifled or silenced by stupid critics and a narrow-minded society. But the public hostility seems to have had remarkably little effect. Rather, Vivienne explains that she knew that 'the process' of that particular way of working intuitively or automatically had 'completed itself'. She could not repeat it, she says, because '"It" no longer would come in the same way with the same truth'. The work would be, at best, 'an imitation'. So she set painting aside.

As well, now that Binns had searched for her truth as an artist, it was time to acknowledge the truth of her sexual identity. In Neutral Bay she was living close to Peter Kenny and his partner Noel, who shared a house with Yve Repin and her partner. Yve was an intelligent and cultured young woman who came from the Russian émigré family who ran the famous Sydney coffee shop of the same name, where the city's bohemians gathered. Vivienne explains that 'Peter and Yve sort of adopted me'.

Leaving her flat to join their hedonistic Mosman household, she started to get the blood back in her veins. Vivienne adds that Yve, in particular, 'really humanised' her after the long and lonesome work on her exhibition. Soon the two women were in a relationship. This was the first time Vivienne had actually lived with someone. 'I felt as if Yve was the relationship of my life'. As well, 'for the first time in my life I felt really sexually liberated'. No longer did she live in fear of pregnancy. Laughing exuberantly, Vivienne adds, 'Lesbianism was the best contraceptive in the world'.

Yve didn't want Vivienne to work, but she was determined to be independent. To earn some money, she began teaching at a private girls' school, where in one of her classes she taught enamelling – a process of using heat to fuse a thin layer of powdered glass to a metal base. This took the artist back to the kind of practical things she'd enjoyed when she was growing up, and it 'didn't test me emotionally and psychologically'. Developing her own unique take on the process, Binns would use it over the following decade to express radical subject matter that was at odds with the usual status of enamelling as a craft for jewellers and hobbyists.

Alongside this, Vivienne was also involved in another type of art that was typical of the era: the Happening. Originating in a New York gallery in 1959, the phenomenon combined visual art with elements of dance, theatre, music and poetry. Typically a collaboration between a number of artists, a Happening was also a collaboration between the artists and their audience.

In February 1971, Binns joined her talents with those of light sculptor, Roger Foley, whose professional name of 'Ellis D Fogg' captured his style. Their 'Lightshow Environmental Happening', held at Watters Gallery, was called *WOOM*. American art historian, Kirk Varnedoe, once said that attempting to preserve a Happening would be 'like trying to catch wind in a butterfly net', but a sense of this production is indeed preserved in the black-and-white artwork of the program, which maps the route spectator-participants took through a kind of fun-fair maze that had been set up in the two-storey gallery. After paying a dollar and leaving their shoes at the entrance, people progressed through coloured lights and mist towards the 'Exit through Hole in the Wall', where they could buy shoes (their own or somebody else's) for $10 a pair before witnessing 'Mystery Effect Number Eight' (whatever that may have been).

Publicity photographs for the event show Vivienne Binns

standing with her former lover, Mike Brown, and her current lover, Yve Repin – all three stark naked.

MEANWHILE, SOMETHING WAS HAPPENING OUTSIDE THE Happenings.

By 1970, Women's Liberation was getting underway in Sydney. As well as marching on the streets, the new wave of radical feminists were publishing leaflets and broadsheets and holding endless meetings in the movement's shopfront headquarters in Glebe Point Road. To Vivienne Binns, however, this upsurge of activity seemed to be something associated with the university and with women who were younger than she was. To some extent she was involved in the social activities of CAMP Inc (a gay liberation organisation founded in 1971), but she was too busy to join a group and sit around doing consciousness-raising. 'I was much more centred on my art practice', Vivienne explains.

Her attitude started to change in 1974, when she and a small group of other women artists in Sydney began to meet in order to talk about art. One member of these discussion groups, art historian Barbara Hall, had recently been to America, and so was able to tell her colleagues what was going on in the feminist art scene there. As groups of women artists in other cities began to meet, the Women's Art Movement was born.

Nineteen seventy-five was International Women's Year. It was symptomatic of the new consciousness that, in March, the feminist journal *Refractory Girl* published a nine-page interview with Vivienne Binns, which gave her the acknowledgment that had been lacking at the time of her 1967 exhibition. Only eight years had passed, but the social and political change had been so rapid that the art scene of 1975 was very different from that of 1967. *Refractory Girl* even re-published eight of the hostile critical attacks made on Binns's first show, as evidence of the maltreatment of women in general, and women artists in particular.

That same year, the Women's Art Movement got a boost when the American feminist art critic, Lucy Lippard, came to Australia to deliver the Power Lecture at Sydney University, and went on to tour the country. At Lippard's presentations she showed a collection of photographic slides, called the 'Women's Art Register', which showcased artwork produced by American women. The criterion for something getting into this register was simply that it had been produced by a woman. This idea instantly appealed to Binns, for whom it fitted the notion of prioritising Truth above Beauty. 'Selectivity was not on whether it was good or bad art', she explains. The important thing was the spark of creation.

This idea was the polar opposite of the notion of 'the artist as an individual male hero', which had aggravated Binns since her time at art school. Soon, the Women's Art Movement was establishing its own register of Australian women's art, including ceramics, textiles, photographs, posters, and what Binns describes as 'work done on the kitchen table'.

When Binns saw the women's work that Lippard was showcasing, she felt that she 'walked through a door and into this vast country'. Much of the rest of her career has involved exploring that territory, often in partnership and collaboration with other women, whether so-called amateurs or other professional artists.

In 1976, Binns co-ordinated an exhibition at Watters

Gallery titled *Portraits of Women – Experiments in Vitreous Enamel*. This was described by critic Janine Burke as the first truly feminist collaborative exhibition in Australia. Another ground-breaking community arts project, *Mothers' Memories, Others' Memories*, ran at a number of venues in Sydney from 1979 to 1981. The title encapsulates the honour that Binns gives to the lives and histories of 'ordinary' women.

A COUPLE OF MONTHS AFTER OUR INITIAL MEETING, I VISIT Vivienne again, and on this occasion there is time to see the purpose-built studio in her backyard, where a couple of large canvases are in progress.

Here, instead of enormous genitals and eye-scorching colours, there is the graceful silhouette of a nearby fig tree traced onto a pure white background. In another work, the same tree is transposed over a mosaic representing the light in a Moorish window in Spain's Alhambra palace (which Binns recently visited). No longer does Binns see Truth and Beauty as being in opposition: 'My concentration on Truth actually eventually brought me to Beauty, and by the time I reached middle age I understood much more about how they worked together'.

If this seems a mellowing, the small collages and experimental works on the 'detritus wall' reveal the sense of humour that once produced the installation titled 'Yikes! What a Mess'. Here one small work is comprised of the word 'Entropy', written in a script reminiscent of that of Sydney's pavement artist, Mr Eternity.

Coming back into the house, Viv shows me something perhaps even more astonishing than any of the individual works. This is a computer catalogue recording every work Binns has done, with its date of production, and its place of exhibition, together with a thumbnail image. In addition to her own entire oeuvre, the artist has recorded some of the collaborative work she has done over some forty years with communities of other art practitioners. Here is the ultimate register of the Women's Art Movement.

Very conscious of the continuity that runs through her whole art practice, Binns stresses that this is 'not just related to materials and images, it's related to *process*'. She also freely acknowledges the effect both of her gender and her generation. With her emphatic way of speaking, she declares, 'I see my work and the whole process as absolutely coming out of the experience of being a female, from the era of the 1960s right up to now – absolutely!'

GARY WILLIAMS
A lot of stuff just happens ...

Meredith Burgmann

Nadia and I travel up to the beautiful NSW North Coast beach town of Nambucca Heads to interview Gary Williams – Freedom Rider, Black Power activist, almost lawyer and THAT face on the poster. This poster became very famous in the seventies and even appeared recently in an episode of ABC TV's *Cleverman*. It depicts Gary's face in profile, with a smaller face, belonging to a more traditional Aboriginal man, superimposed on Gary's image. It was ubiquitous in inner-city student bedrooms of the seventies.

Now he is playing out his most important role of all – bringing the Gumbaynggirr language and stories back home.

We start the interview at the Bookshop Cafe – a typical, slightly hippie, North Coast joint – wedged between Pretty Woman Total Beauty Therapy and the main road.

Gary, who is now seventy-three, is wearing jeans and a plain blue T-shirt. He has aged gracefully. Still tall and well-structured, shoulders back and eyes looking unwaveringly ahead. He probably doesn't remember what a stunningly magnificent sight he was back in the late 1960s.

He is delighted to see us and introduce us to his home town, which he loves with a passion.

I have never been here before. But Nadia has, and has even spent time on neighbouring Bellwood Reserve.

Gary has with him his beloved dog Duuwaa, a name that means 'boomerang' in the Gumbaynggirr language. Duuwaa is half kelpie, half Rhodesian ridgeback, and has a delightfully pathetic face, reminiscent of Red Dog in the movie. On his collar, in big writing, are the words *Duuwaa Bear*. He is obviously a matrilineal-minded dog, as he has taken the surname of Gary's long-time partner, Deirdre Bear.

Gary was born in December 1945 in Mullumbimby, in a house on the banana plantation where his father lived and worked. His brother and sister were born there a few years later. Gary doesn't recall much of this period, but he remembers the railway running through the plantation where they were living. His father and his mother's brother had worked long-term on the banana plantation.

Gary's mother, Jessie, is from Nambucca, and his dad was born further north in Casino, which is Bandjalung territory. He talks about his mother's mother, who married a man from the South Coast who was living in Nambucca. Indigenous Australians from the North Coast and South Coast of New South Wales regularly intermarried, and exchanged language, stories and fun.

Gary and his family lived for a short period with his dad's people in Casino. When Gary was five, his father took the family to Burnt Bridge, out of Kempsey. He attended the kindergarten at the Aboriginal Reserve at Burnt Bridge, which still had a mission manager.

Like many Aboriginal families who move frequently to follow work or because of family obligations, they picked up sticks again, and shifted to Nambucca.

The Williams family lived initially on Stuart Island (which Gary always refers to as 'the Island'), which sits in the estuary of the Nambucca River. Gary began his primary schooling there but, within a few months, his family – along with the other Aboriginal families from the Island – were dispossessed from their land and shifted to nearby Bellwood Reserve, where Gary's mother still lives. Gary did the rest of his primary schooling on the Reserve, in a school of about twenty students, where he found the classes easy. His family attended the Catholic church situated on the edge of the Reserve, and he even admits with half a grin that there is a photo of him as an altar boy.

The language spoken at Nambucca was Gumbaynggirr. All the Elders spoke it, and the children 'understood a few words'. There was no prohibition on the language as such, but vocabulary and fluency had been lost.

GUMBAYNGGIRR ... He spells it out with pride, sitting there in the coffee shop in Nambucca, knowing that he has been the major player in bringing this language back into its spoken form and, importantly, in having it acknowledged by the neighbouring white community as the significant language of the area.

Gary stops and laughs. He tells us that one of his influences was an uncle who was into crosswords. He remembers this uncle saying to him and the other kids who were mucking around and chiacking each other on the Reserve, 'if you're going to speak their language [English] you might as well learn it properly'.

Gary did learn it properly ... those early TV interviews

in the Sixties show him diffident and almost shy, but well-spoken and clear of thought.

LIFE ON THE RESERVE WAS FUN. IT WAS FISHING AND swimming, and rowing old people over to the local ocean beach, known simply as 'the beach'.

From sixth class through to second-year high school, he attended what he refers to as 'the convent', St Patrick's School at Macksville. At the end of his second year of high school, in 1960, he won a bursary to go to St John's College (known as Woodlawn College) in Lismore for his third year. Woodlawn College was a boarding school run by the Marist Fathers. The bursary took him through to his Leaving Certificate in 1962.

Of his time at Woodlawn, he says quite matter-of-factly: 'It was a good education'.

What was it like being a boarder in a Catholic boys' school, and an Aboriginal kid at that? He says there had been an Aboriginal student there before him – but he wasn't from 'the Reserve', which was obviously an important distinction. Gary's cousin, Michael Bryant, also attended the school, and was still there when Gary arrived. This was a great comfort. He was a year ahead of Gary but was two years older. Michael was a good athlete, which always helps.

Surprisingly, Gary reports that there was no hassle about racism at the school. There were Colombo Plan students there, 'well-to-do kids from the Pacific islands and also wealthy kids from Malaya'. Then he adds, 'Anyway, Nambucca was not as racist as Bowraville'.

I can't help comparing Gary's journey with that of his

cousin, Gary Foley, who had such a difficult and frankly racist time in his high school in the same area.

But this talk triggers something in Gary's memory – 'one thing stays in my mind' – and he goes on to recount a deeply painful experience.

'In 1957, when I was twelve, the Aboriginal Welfare Board was going to move a black family into Nambucca at a place called Newville, and there was a big campaign launched [by the white community] against moving them into this area and people talked about it a lot.

'The husband was a sawyer in the sawmill and he drank in the pub and he was a first-grade footballer, and yet still they didn't want this family in the basically white living area … it stays in my mind.'

Gary says that he thought to himself, 'They're my cousins', and repeats 'it stays in my mind'. He flutters his hands in the way he does when he's disturbed.

In 1962, he sat for the Leaving Certificate. He can even remember what he got. 'A's in agriculture, general maths and modern history and 'B's in English, physics and French. On the strength of this excellent pass he was offered a scholarship to Armidale Teachers' College.

But then the teachers at Woodlawn told him he could get an Abschol scholarship to Sydney University. Gary had heard nothing about the first stirrings of black activism in Sydney. However, he made a momentous decision and opted for university.

Perhaps the first of his sliding doors moments.

IN EARLY 1963, YOUNG GARY SET OFF FOR THE BIG SMOKE, and almost immediately met an older Aboriginal radical through a non-Aboriginal friend from Woodlawn College.

Gary Williams

His new black friend's name was Charlie Perkins.

At this rather crucial point in our interview Gary struggles with Duuwaa, who has become entangled with his lead under our table. Another regular at the coffee shop helps out.

Gary started university at the same time as Charlie Perkins. There is a newspaper photo of them on that day, a young and grinning Gary listening intently to an obviously older and wiser Charlie. The occasion was also recorded on the front cover of *Dawn* (May 1963), the Assimilationist magazine produced by the Aborigines Protection Board. Seated in the middle of the Quadrangle the two young men look impossibly out of place. Charlie was ten years older than Gary, and an important influence – although Gary explains that, in his first year at university, Charlie did not talk to him much about Aboriginal issues. Gary was doing an Arts degree and can remember that one of his subjects was anthropology, but seems a bit vague about the others.

In his first year, Gary lived in St John's College, one of the four traditional, conservative men's colleges attached to Sydney University. He was the only Aboriginal student there, although there were some students from Papua New Guinea.

He began to look up relatives in Redfern. His father's brother, Clive Williams, was living in Rozelle, and he began to visit him on a semi-regular basis.

Gary emphasises the importance of his Uncle Clive in his political development. Clive was a fluent Bandjalung speaker, and later helped start an Aboriginal section at the Northern Rivers College of Advanced Education.

It was his Uncle Clive who introduced him to the Aborigines Progressive Association, which had been founded in 1937 by William Ferguson and Jack Patten, and after a period of dormancy was resurrected by Bert Groves and Pearl Gibbs in the mid-1960s. Gary started attending meetings in 1963 and 1964, and met significant black activists Dulcie Flower, Bert Groves and Charlie Leon.

Clive also brought Gary to his first FCAATSI (Federal Council for the Advancement of Aborigines and Torres Strait Islanders) meeting, and took him to Tranby Co-operative College in Glebe to meet its legendary founder, renegade Anglican priest Alf Clint. Tranby was just beginning its trailblazing path towards providing further education for Aboriginal community activists.

GIVEN HIS MANY OTHER COMMITMENTS, GARY PREDICTABLY failed his Arts course, and in early 1964 he moved out of St John's College and in with Charlie Perkins, his wife Eileen and baby daughter Hetti, in a house in Arundel Street, down near the famous student pub, the Forest Lodge. He sees this move as pivotal.

He says he met a lot of people he would not otherwise have met, and he sees these connections as crucial to his thinking. Charlie was so much older and had travelled around the world – and for Gary this international view of the Indigenous struggle was new ground.

Gary watched how Charlie interacted with people and how he was involved with organisations like his soccer club, PanHellenic. Gary even attended a few matches. When I mentioned that PanHellenic was basically a Greek club, he sounded surprised and said, 'Yes, I think it was'.

Charlie Perkins was very active even this early in the black awakening. Gary admits his 'own head was somewhere else', but Charlie talked him into coming to meetings held by different Aboriginal-focused organisations, among them Student Action for Aborigines (SAFA), which had just been formed by Sydney University students. It was SAFA that eventually organised the famous 1965 Freedom Ride to towns in western New South Wales. Apart from Charlie, Gary remembers only one other Aboriginal participant on the trip – Gerry Mason, a non-student friend of Charlie's.

At the start of the Freedom Ride he remembers drinking with later lifelong mates, anarchist songster Paddy Dawson and Communist Party member Brian Aarons, in the Sussex Hotel in the city. Photos were taken of him and Charlie and others all ready to go. Then Gary received a message that he was needed in Nambucca for family reasons. So he had to abandon the first stage of the Freedom Ride. But he joined the others in Bowraville and Kempsey for the latter part.

In his customary deprecating manner, Gary says this section of the ride 'was not as heavy duty as out near Walgett where the locals tried to kill the bus riders'.

He recalls members of the public shouting at them, but in Kempsey it was 'not a hassle – it was just the issue about the swimming pool'. It is typical of Gary's rather laidback attitude to the world that Kempsey and its ban on black kids using the pool after school hours (adults were banned absolutely) is considered 'not a hassle'.

The pub in Bowraville did become an issue, though. Black and white drinkers, including Gary, were pictured in the media breaking the colour bar. An indignant letter-writer to the *Sydney Morning Herald* said it was a pity that the Freedom Riders were teaching Aboriginal people to drink. Gary recounts this story with a grin. 'I was nineteen and I was not a drinker at this stage. *I was just Aboriginal.*'

I ask him, was he aware at the time how important the Freedom Ride was, and he says, 'In one sense I was very aware of how important it was'. Then he refers back to the incident of the black family not being allowed to live in the white area of Nambucca that happened when he was twelve.

THE FREEDOM RIDE AND THE ENSUING PUBLICITY surrounding Charlie Perkins and the new young black activists had created its own vibe. 'Mobs started coming into Sydney from Moree and Walgett and places like that. They were inspired by Charlie and the Freedom Ride.'

One of the places where these youngsters started to meet was the Foundation for Aboriginal Affairs, in George Street in the city, which had been established as a 'welcoming social centre' in 1964 by a group including Charlie, Aboriginal community leader Ken Brindle and Methodist minister and social activist Ted Noffs. By 1965, Charlie had become the manager.

Gary frequented the Foundation, soaking up the social life and, inevitably, the angry black politics of the period. He went to concerts held there and also played bass guitar in the Foundation's band, which often featured Jimmy Miller. For a short while he was even the fill-in bass player for singer Jimmy Little. There would be about 200 people at the dance held at the Foundation every Saturday night, which would be followed by a concert on the Sunday night.

Lots of Kooris coming to the Foundation were also involved with FCAATSI. The young activists like Gary were asked to hand out leaflets and even speak at rallies. 'There was a real hope that we would deliver change and I just wanted to help out the people that I saw as doing stuff ...

doing good stuff.' One of these activists 'doing good stuff' was Faith Bandler, whose FCAATSI shop in Bathurst Street Gary remembers well.

AT THIS STAGE, GARY WAS NOT DOING THAT MUCH drinking. However, pubs were the important social and political meeting places for the young Kooris, so he used to go over Redfern way and meet up with friends at the Empress Hotel in Regent Street, Redfern, or the other Aboriginal pub, the Clifton, in Botany Street, Waterloo.

By the late Sixties, the Foundation was still operating but people were 'moving a bit towards setting up services in Redfern and concentrating on the police actions in Redfern'. He had got to know Gary Foley at the Foundation, although he had known him vaguely from Nambucca because they were distant cousins.

In 1967 or 1968, he met Paul Coe, an angry and charismatic young Wiradjuri man from Cowra, and an important relationship was established. The two Garys and Paul, along with Billy Craigie from Moree and Tony Coorey from Tweed Heads, began hanging out together. After FCAATSI ceased to be active, they started concentrating on what was happening in Redfern.

Inner-city Redfern had been a traditional living area for the Aboriginal community since the 1930s. But from the early 1960s it had been alive and jumping, with young Aboriginal activists arriving from North Coast and western NSW towns, inspired by American civil rights struggles and a bitter understanding of their own history.

The Aboriginal pubs, particularly the Empress and the Clifton, were regularly raided by police. Aboriginal patrons were arrested and often beaten for little more reason than just being there.

I ask, did he drink at the Empress, and he answers dismissively, 'everybody drank at the Empress'. But then he adds that the real flashpoint was the Clifton. When the police carried out their raids at the Clifton, most of the patrons would be in the lounge area at the back of the hotel, where the band would be playing. At the end of the night, the hotel guests would all come out the side door into a narrow lane, and the police made it into a 'race', like cattle in single file. 'The police cars would be up against the doors and everyone was forced to go out single file so they could grab you anytime and chuck you in the wagons.'

They did not necessarily target the leaders, 'just who they wanted to take'.

In describing the police raids, he recalls the groundbreaking work of senior University of New South Wales academic Hal Wootten and young junior staff from the UNSW Faculty of Law, particularly John Basten and George Zdenkowski, who would come to the hotel to drink and keep an eye on the often tense atmosphere between the clientele and the constabulary. He remembers Gordon Samuels (later NSW governor), academic Garth Nettheim and (later federal Cabinet minister) 'Diamond Jim' McClelland also coming to the hotel to socialise and observe police behaviour towards the Indigenous patrons.

GARY HAD MADE DO WITH VARIOUS HOLIDAY JOBS, BUT by 1965 he was seriously looking for paid work. When a progressive Supreme Court judge, Ken Jacobs, made it public that he was interested in having an Aboriginal tipstaff (judge's assistant), Gary was chosen for the position. Once again, *Dawn* (June 1965) reported on this important breakthrough.

Ken Jacobs was an interesting character. A self-described 'liberal' with an impeccable academic and legal background, he was later appointed to the High Court in 1974 by Gough Whitlam and Attorney-General Lionel Murphy, the first Labor appointment since 1946.

Gary liked Ken Jacobs, and remained in the position for five or six years. In fact, when I met Gary in 1968, he was working for Jacobs.

Gary, employed by a judge and with a working knowledge of the law, was particularly involved in the beginnings of what is now the Aboriginal Legal Service (ALS), but both he and Gary Foley always acknowledge the role of Paul Coe in getting the momentum going.

He expands on Coe's role with a snippet of memory. He was in Glebe one day and bumped into student activist Warwick Neilley and young lawyer Peter Tobin. They told him that Paul was calling a meeting in his place at Eveleigh Street in Redfern and asked if he wanted to come along. Gary went to that meeting and the rest is history. Among others, he met Hal Wootten there.

Late in 1969, this fledgling group managed to get some funding from the Federal Minister for Aboriginal Affairs, WC Wentworth. Until the funding arrived, the nascent ALS was run out of the UNSW Law School; their new office was opened in Regent Street, almost opposite the Clifton.

There was a further influx of radicalised young lawyers into Redfern, mainly from UNSW. Gary refers to this period with a light in his eye and proclaims himself as 'blooded in Redfern'.

He was not fully aware at the time of the importance of these activities and the fact that he was front and centre in one of the most important chapters in Aboriginal political struggle. It is so often the case that when people are in the thick of something momentous and historically significant they don't know it at the time.

GARY THEN SHEERS OFF ON ANOTHER TACK AND STARTS TO talk about the Black Panther group founded in Melbourne in 1972 and led by Queensland activist Denis Walker, Wiradjuri Melbourne-based Bruce McGuinness and Queensland-born Redfern-based Sol Bellear. The group tried to sponsor American Black Panther writer and organiser Stokely Carmichael out to Australia, but he was refused a visa. During this campaign they came up to Sydney and held a meeting in a pub in St Johns Road in Glebe, probably the Nag's Head.

Gary never became part of the Australian Black Panther Party, but he was certainly involved with the Black Power movement in Redfern. I always felt that this small secretive group was set up to intrigue the media and bamboozle ASIO. It was certainly successful on both counts.

Even white 'allies' like Nadia and me were caught up in the spirit of the times. The excitement in the air was palpable. Young black men and women in jeans and afros were invading the traditional inner-city space of white students. They lectured us about 'terra nullius' and the evils of Captain Cook. Paul Coe in particular was angry about police shootings, with several of his relatives having been killed by police – one at Redfern train station.

Paul and Gary started Law degrees in 1971. Gary quickly

decided it wasn't for him, but Paul soldiered on to an eventual degree.

WHAT DID GARY THINK ABOUT VIETNAM? HE SAYS HE ONLY participated as an onlooker at the demonstrations. He never actually took part. 'I still kind of thought of it as a whitefellas' war.' This is an interesting take from a thoughtful and politicised young man.

We then reminisce about Paul Coe's Moratorium speech at the old Sydney Stadium at Rushcutters Bay, in 1970, where Paul basically said, 'why are you fighting this racism in Vietnam and not concerned about the racism towards us?' (Nobody who heard his so-called 'mother fuckers speech' has forgotten it.) Paul also shouted to the captive audience that racism was so rampant in Australia that people did not even know they were racist. 'Look on either side of you, yes you are the racist.'

Judge Jacobs talked about the Vietnam War issue with Gary and gave him things to read. Gary says he would have been on the side of the protesters, but still he remained a spectator.

He registered for national service, even though an Aboriginal person, living as an Aboriginal person, did not need to register. But the judge had said to him, 'you're not actually living as an Aboriginal person'. When I ask what would he have done if he had been called up, he says in typical Gary fashion, 'Who knows?'

We then talk a little about Catholicism and Gary's favourite quote: *There are no atheists in foxholes*. He still has some form of Catholic faith, and he adds, 'Up in Nambucca the Catholics have services for Gurris'. He says, 'So it means I don't have to talk about the other stuff'.

A lot of stuff just happens ...

While Gary may have believed that Vietnam was 'a whitefellas' war' he was certainly an important part of the radical Aboriginal involvement in the anti-apartheid movement, and particularly the campaign against the racially selected Springbok rugby union team. Vietnam may not have resonated, but the blatant racism of apartheid certainly did.

IN 1971, HE WAS LIVING IN A HOUSE IN EBLEY STREET, BONDI Junction, with his then wife Norma Ingram, as well as Gary Foley, Bronwyn Penrith and Paul's sister Isabel Coe. Quite coincidentally, the house was just down the road from the Squire Inn Motel where the Springboks were staying during their controversial tour of Australia in the winter of that year.

At this stage in our coffee morning I get quite a shock. I ask Gary how the small group of Aboriginal activists got so heavily involved with the 'Stop the Tours' campaign. He tells me that I was the 'halfway person' who dragged him along to meetings and got him involved in the anti-apartheid movement. He says it just seemed logical to get involved, as some sort of extension of the fight. I am quietly chuffed about my role in his political education.

And then he laughs and says, 'Anyway ... apartheid was based on the Queensland Act' – the infamous legislation that decreed Queensland Aboriginal lives to be totally controlled by the manager of the reserve from which they came.

He remembers going to the Criterion, the famous left-wing pub in Sussex Street in Sydney, and meeting the 'Stop the Tours' campaign leaders who regularly drank there. He encountered prominent black Zimbabwean anti-apartheid activist Sekai Holland at about this time too.

Gary Williams

Gary mentions meeting Jim Boyce, one of the seven Wallabies who refused to play the Springboks, and having 'really good conversations' with him about the situation in South Africa. In fact, it was Jim who gave Gary the Springbok jerseys that the group used to great effect in the demonstrations. Photos of Paul Coe, Billy Craigie, Gary Foley and Gary Williams wearing the Springbok jerseys were flashed around the world, with the accompanying explanation that South African President Vorster had proudly boasted 'A black man will never wear the Springbok jersey'.

Did he get stimulation from the white student activists they were meeting, or was that an unrealistic question to put to him? Gary replies that the experience wasn't one-way and that he enjoyed the interaction. He says he still has friends from that period, mentioning Brian Aarons and Paddy Dawson in particular.

I ask him what he remembers about the anti-apartheid arrests, and once again he bowls me over. He totally surprises me by saying he remembers me being arrested at Manuka Oval in Canberra for supposedly cutting the barbed-wire fence and trying to fight my way through – when in actual fact, on that occasion, he and Gary Foley were the culprits and it was me who got arrested while standing there totally innocently with my mother. I am once again quietly chuffed, but also a little bit cranky that I had to go through all the tedious court processes while the two Garys got off scot-free.

WE THEN MOVE ON TO TALK ABOUT HIS INVOLVEMENT with the green bans in the early seventies. He says that he got involved in that through friendship with Bob Pringle, the

A lot of stuff just happens ...

president of the Builders Labourers' Federation (BLF), who had a number of close Aboriginal friends.

Gary uses the expression 'shared battles'. 'It was about keeping the working class in the inner city.' And then he says, 'These guys had supported us and we were going to support them'.

The BLF had instigated what was happily referred to as the first land rights claim in Australia, when in 1972 they put a ban on demolition of a row of houses in Redfern now known as 'The Block'. Bob Pringle had also become personally involved in defence of the Tent Embassy outside Parliament House in Canberra.

How did that period of intense political activity change Gary's life? He says it gave him a wider view. He started reading books, and he particularly remembers reading Franz Fanon on Black American agitator Malcolm X and writings by Malcolm X himself. But then there is that laugh again and he confesses that he had 'a bit of a problem getting through more than the first chapter of Paulo Freire's *Pedagogy of the Oppressed*'. I had a similar problem with the revolutionary Brazilian educator.

Another work that stuck in his brain was Black American Communist Angela Davis's *If They Come in the Morning*, with the title borrowed from James Baldwin's 1970 open letter to Davis, which had the closing lines: '*If they take you in the morning, they will be coming for us that night*'.

Gary describes how the recent introduction of the cashless welfare card to predominantly Aboriginal communities inspired him to refer to Baldwin's statement, to warn whites, 'If they come for us in the morning, they'll come for you at night'.

Gary Williams

WE LEAVE THE BOOKSHOP CAFE AND MOVE UP THE ROAD to 'Muurrbay', a wooden cottage in a more rural area of Nambucca, which is the former Catholic church where Gary's family used to worship. Gary now refers to it lovingly as the Language Centre. It is where he has spent the last few years working tirelessly on his language projects.

As he shows us around the centre, I notice the colourful mosaic work indicating the toilets – *Nyami*, 'Ladies' in Gumbaynggirr. Then I see THE POSTER, squeezed in between the sliding door and a bare IKEA bookcase.

Gary is pretty pleased that we've noticed it. In the mid-seventies, he tells us, he had come down to Sydney from Nambucca for a court case and was in need of money. Gary Foley said there was a guy taking political photos in Glebe – but he wanted a bloke without a beard – and as Foley had a beard, he suggested the gig to Gary. That's how iconic images happen.

As he sits there on the back verandah of Muurrbay, with Duuwaa restless at his feet, among the raucous bird conversations and bats shrieking in the background, he says thoughtfully, 'I'm the only one who came back'.

This is a really interesting thing for him to have said. Nadia asks, 'Do you mean that your trajectory was a full circle?'

And he says, 'I don't know about a trajectory. It was certainly a circle. There are so many unplanned things in life ... a lot of stuff just happens'.

In 1991, he came up to Nambucca and stayed. In 1997, he did the first language course run by Brother Steve, a white man who had been a driver for legendary community activist Mum Shirl in Redfern.

A lot of stuff just happens ...

'We started in Nambucca, and we got in at the beginning of the Indigenous language projects and the language programs have mushroomed into language revitalisation.'

He says he would like to mentor someone to continue his work here at the centre. He explains that it is a regional Language Centre. There are seven languages taught and studied – languages from Queensland through to the Hawkesbury – the old ATSIC 'Many Rivers' region. It was the only ATSIC region to get involved in endangered language study.

AT THIS STAGE WE NOTICE A TINY FIGURE WALKING DOWN the road from the Bellwood Reserve. Gary surprises us when he mentions quite casually that it is his mother – she is ninety-five and is walking 'for her exercise'. Jessie Williams is small and frail, but looks in very good spirits.

He's strangely diffident about seeing his mum, in that Gary way, but we are delighted to meet her. When we predictably enquire about her recipe for long life, she says, 'Eating millet meal in the morning'. Gary sort of rolls his eyes and says, 'Oh she always says that', but I vow to try millet meal if I can end up looking as good as she does at ninety-five.

So, Gary's narrative might have come full circle, but along the way he became an important part of that extraordinary story of radical Redfern in the 1960s and 1970s. Like the man himself, Gary's radicalisation was a gentle one – born not out of anger or resentment but out of place and happenstance. As he says, 'A lot of stuff just happens ...'

PETER BATCHELOR
Don't mourn but organise

Meredith Burgmann

I thought it might be quite hard interviewing Peter, as he is my brother-in-law and I have known him for over forty years. However, it made for fascinating conversation, as I'd never bothered to ask him all those questions that are so obvious once out there. His radicalisation by way of the BBB Mattress Factory had always been family mythology, but it actually turns out to be true!

Peter is tall and vaguely distinguished-looking, neatly dressed in a blue-and-white checked shirt and still with a youthful glint in his eyes. Years of a bureaucratic life (including six years as Victorian transport minister) have made him deliberate in his thought and speech, and you can actually see the gears clicking over in his brain as he puts his mind to even the most minor problems.

Peter was born in the working-class Sydney suburb of Guildford in 1950. His father, Garnet Batchelor, was transferred to Melbourne in 1958 and the family then lived in Beaumaris, a more middle-class bayside suburb, full of young families and nature lovers. His parents 'liked gardens and plenty of bush'.

Peter was the oldest of five children: four boys and a girl. His mother, Nea, was from a Catholic background; she maintained religious beliefs, but did not go to church. Peter believes her non-attendance was an understanding with his father, who came from a Methodist family. The compromise was that the children were brought up Anglican.

Anyway, religion was not a big issue in their lives. The children were sent to state schools, but they were also sent to Sunday school. Even though their parents did not attend church, all the children were duly baptised.

Peter's father was employed in hardware distribution, and worked his way up through the ranks to become general manager of a big hardware company. Before she was married, Nea had been employed as a clerk. She was also 'Miss Parramatta 1948', and the family have the sash and the photographs to prove it (frequently). After her marriage she did not work again in the waged work force.

As Peter was growing up, he was aware of his parents' political views, but nothing was overtly discussed. His father was a 'conservative thinker because of his managerial post' and liked Bob Menzies. Nea 'did not have much of a personal opinion' and tended to accept the world outlook that was brought into the home by her husband.

But the political allegiances of the extended family unit were another kettle of fish. Each year, when they travelled to Sydney for Christmas, Peter can remember his maternal grandmother, Mary Isabel Gwynne, having heated arguments with his mother, because his grandma disapproved of the conservative Batchelor family views.

'Ma' sold newspapers at the kiosk on Guildford train station. From a deeply Catholic Labor family, in the 1950s she was heavily involved in organisational support in the Guildford area for left-wing NSW Deputy Premier Jack Ferguson.

Peter went to the local primary schools and eventually landed at Beaumaris High. He tells me with a grin that he had 'mixed results at school'.

Beaumaris High was a very constraining environment. Peter was repelled by 'the conservative atmosphere and all the rules'. There was constant inspection of shoes and 'the girls had the length of their dresses monitored'. He remembers that in 1968, which was a crucial year for him, the students were all expected to wear full school uniform – against the tide of youth rebellion. The students adopted their own version of student revolt by altering the coloured stripes in their school ties.

But a couple of young teachers also could not stand this conservative regime. They were the English teacher, Elizabeth Courtney, and a maths teacher named Glen. Elizabeth Courtney liked to raise issues for the students to contemplate, and on one occasion she naively asked them for their ideas on what to talk about at these sessions. Peter and his friend suggested homosexuality, abortion and conscription. He grins. 'I think we were trying to be provocative.'

The teacher pointed out that 'we can't discuss any of these things in the staff room', but then said, 'let's see what we can do after school' – and so she started a drama group.

This was in 1968. And the first play they decided to do was Brecht's *Mother Courage*. No roles had actually been allocated before the headmistress heard about this project, banned it and 'shut it right down'.

Peter sighs. 'The whole atmosphere at school was one of constraint, containment, conformity and no ability to be different.' This produced a seething resentment.

He became friends with the two young teachers, who took on a type of mentoring role. Maths teacher Glen also took some of the students to plays out of school hours. It was at a party after one of these theatre visits that Glen told Peter, 'You know, I'm homosexual'. Peter says, 'We all suspected it anyway'. He also remembers Glen wanting to play Red Army songs on the gramophone. It was not a popular choice.

He sees the friendship of Elizabeth and Glen as crucial in his journey. 'Really, they were two people trying to get us through and survive the stultifying regime. The friendship allowed me as a young person to think beyond the constraints of the school.' Indeed, he regards his awakening as coming from these two teachers, rather than from his family.

A friend of the English teacher had just come back from Britain with an early copy of *Sgt. Pepper's Lonely Hearts Club Band*. Glen hand-wrote the lyrics, then reproduced them on a duplicating machine and handed the sheets out in maths class. The tune Peter can remember was 'A Day in the Life'. Glen played the record all lesson. 'Our class was the envy of the whole school.'

Peter had a Canadian friend called Stephen who was slightly more politically aware than he was. Steve's father played music from overseas to the boys, and one record he remembers clearly was by Pete Seeger. Steve's father had a collection of Folkways Records LPs from Canada, which he lent to Peter.

He vividly remembers attending the infamous US Consulate demonstration on 5 July 1968 with Steve. Peter describes himself as having 'gone along as a naive school kid

... It was a shocking thing ... there was rioting and there were beatings'.

The Age recorded the occasion with a typical flourish. The headline was 'Troopers Ride Down Anti-War Rioters', and the article went on to describe the protesters being left 'bloody and dazed'.

Peter, ever the well-prepared lad, had organised a note from his mother saying that he would be absent for the day. He didn't hand in the note, however, and when the school hierarchy began to suspect that he and Steve had gone to the demonstration they conducted a roll call and discovered that the boys were absent. The school rang the fathers (because that was who they considered were in charge), but when Peter eventually produced the note from his mother, it took the wind out of their sails. His father was embarrassed that Peter had done such a radical thing, but stuck up for his wife in giving Peter permission.

Nea was not into limiting or challenging her son's activities. In fact, politics was simply not discussed in the home. Peter lived with his family at Beaumaris without arguments until 1973, when he moved out totally amicably.

I ask about other expressions of opinion. Peter remembers another friend, who was hostile to the monarchy: at some gathering at which there were parents present, this friend refused to stand up for the then national anthem 'God Save the Queen', which created havoc. Peter thought his action was appropriate and brave.

In their last years at school, Peter and his friends began thinking more about Vietnam. Unsurprisingly, at this stage conscription was looming very large in their thoughts. Peter had come to a position of opposing conscription and had decided that the role of the Americans in Vietnam was evil.

Like many Australians, he lived the war every night through the TV coverage, which was significant in forming his view about what was happening. He particularly remembers the ghastly photos of the My Lai massacre (the murder of unarmed villagers by US troops) in March 1968. High school students in the main cities were beginning to organise. One of Peter's friends had a brother at the University of Melbourne, so they produced a magazine which SDS (Students for a Democratic Society) ran off for them, and they distributed it outside the gates of schools in the area.

Final exams called, and in the wash-up Peter was among a small number from his school who achieved university admission. He was also the first in his extended family to go to university.

He chose to go to Monash University because of the subjects that he wanted to study and also because it had a reputation for political activism – he still didn't see himself as a radical at this stage, but rather as 'ready to engage'. He was 'politically neutral or naive' and was very much looking for something different from the stifling school experience.

In 1970, Peter started an Economics degree, which included politics as well as economics subjects. He was interested in the political debates on campus, but seems to have resisted the relentless campaigns to get the students – the new students in particular – to commit to a particular ideology. Monash was not known as a hotbed of radicalism for nothing. The Maoists were in the ascendancy, and Peter remembers the key political activists at Monash at that period were Albert Langer, Mike Hyde, Kerry Miller and Jim Bacon – all firmly in the extreme Left or Maoist categories. He felt the atmosphere on campus was 'very sectarian, very ideological'.

He participated in campus activities as an individual, not as a member of any of the groups, and he had friends in all the various clubs. Along with many others he helped organise the Moratorium movement from the university.

Despite his opposition to the war, in mid-1970, when he turned twenty, Peter registered for national service. He was not intending to, but his mother persuaded him. She said, 'If you don't register, you'll end up in gaol'. Really, though, his mum's reasoning was about respectability and acceptance of the prevailing culture. In her view, non-registration was not a possibility.

However, Peter took steps to avoid the draft. He had been told that if you fell outside a certain weight and height you would not be accepted. So, he reduced his weight considerably – and he also obtained a passport in case he needed to make a speedy exit from the country.

At this point in Peter's story I find myself wondering: if he had been more involved with the university student culture, would he have taken the next step and refused to register? Peter was shortly to become totally absorbed by industrial militancy, which – although heady and engrossing at that time – was probably less obsessed with conscription and Vietnam than was the student body.

DURING UNIVERSITY VACATIONS, PETER HAD A VARIETY OF jobs. One involved shovelling chicken poo, and then there was a short-lived job on a building site. He realised he had been underpaid at the building job, and tried to talk to others on the site about it. He rang the Builders Labourers' Federation, and 'BL official Norm Wallace came out from the union and corrected my situation and all the others on the site'. Peter had thought this underpayment was an isolated incident, but it was clearly common practice to dud the workers. 'I felt very pleased that the union took notice of what I had to say. They quickly fixed it and corrected it for everybody else.'

That was Peter's first contact with the union movement.

Over the summer break of 1970–71, he went to work at the BBB Mattress Factory. He joined the Furnishing Trades Union immediately on arrival. Peter worked at the beginning of the production line in the unskilled and poorly paid 'wadding' section. This job was the 'sliding doors' moment that changed his entire life.

The following year he went back to the mattress factory, which had moved from a ramshackle old industrial building in South Melbourne to the outer suburbs in Clayton. On arriving, he found a modern workplace with modern production techniques and efficiencies.

The wadding for the mattresses was made in a closed area of the factory. Peter describes 'big machines with little hooks that would load and add material into the hopper which would scrunch it all up'. It was the second-worst place in the factory to work, but they did get an extra two dollars a week for working there.

There were three workers in the wadding section (who were called 'process workers in the fabric-teasing operations'), plus the supervisor. As well as Peter, there was a Greek Cypriot and a Chilean refugee, and the boss was Yugoslav. They had no common language, except for a little English, with which to communicate. Peter believes this was a deliberate tactic – but because they all knew enough English, they did manage to communicate through him.

We then talk a bit about the effect on Australian radical

politics of the left-wing refugees who came to Australia in the early 1970s, like the Chileans and the Greek Cypriots. This is a fascinating topic, but probably one for another day.

After the move to Clayton, there was huge discontent in the mattress factory. The new processes and techniques had created problems. But the thing that upset the workers most was the fact that – seemingly out of nowhere – an elevated office had appeared in the middle of the work floor. It was like a watchtower in a prison. The workers felt they were being spied on, and there was great resentment.

One night, a worker crept into the factory and painted over the windows of this raised supervision tower so that the bosses couldn't watch them. Peter laughs at this point – a happy memory. There was outrage from management, but they never discovered who had done it, although they did point the finger at a particular worker. Because the workers had to clock on and clock off, this process showed that they had all supposedly left the factory at the end of the day. This incident made the newspapers and was the beginning of a very hostile relationship between the workers and management. The shop steward took the full brunt of this bad relationship.

When Peter arrived there as usual for his holiday job in the summer of 1972–73, the atmosphere inside the factory was 'red hot'. The stage was set for the series of events that changed Peter's life forever.

He began summer working with the wadding machine as usual, and by the time he was meant to return to his university studies in March he had decided to stay at the factory because of his developing engagement with the workers and their intensifying struggle.

Peter describes his disengagement from the university

context. He felt that his academic topics didn't relate to the real world – they weren't relevant to the factory or to the wider industrial sector that was increasingly grabbing his attention.

He ended up staying at BBB for almost a year.

In Peter's part of the factory, the speed of work was guided by the machine, not by the workers. If he filled up the hopper as quickly as he could, the wadding would then work its way through the process at its usual regular pace, allowing him time to walk out onto the factory floor to chat with the workers – before darting back to his position. He became a more and more important part of the social and industrial network of the factory.

Eventually the union asked him whether he would become the assistant shop steward, a roaming brief that suited Peter perfectly. After taking on the role, he started going to the union's management committee meetings in town and was very much welcomed – because he was young, and because he was passionately committed to seeing that the workers would receive their due benefits.

There was an industry-wide campaign in 1973 focused on increased wages, four weeks annual leave, leave loadings, 'make-up pay' (compelling the boss to make up the difference in pay between the pitiful 'worker's comp' and the actual wage) and equal pay for women.

The Furnishing Trades, which was one of the smaller, less militant unions, usually had to wait as various benefits flowed through the system, but Peter was keen that the workers in his factory – particularly the women workers, most of whom were on the lower rates – gained these increased benefits as soon as he could organise it.

Peter had long been concerned by the fact that the

sewing machinists, who were women, were equated with process workers, rather than with more skilled workers who were better paid. There were lots of women in the factory, mainly in these poorly paid sewing positions. Because Peter's wadding machine dictated the pace for the workers further down the line, these workers could not make production move at a higher rate, and so wage rises were not possible in their part of the factory. You can hear Peter's voice soften as he talks about these mostly migrant, mostly women, process workers. In other sections of the factory, skill and speed could make a difference and pay rises could occur.

During one of the ongoing disputes, the shop steward was sacked and peremptorily marched out of the factory. The boss came out to talk to the workers gathered outside. Peter thought to himself, 'I'm not putting up with this – you can't sack the shop steward', and argued in the steward's defence. He too was promptly sacked. The union sent out an organiser, who managed to get both Peter and the shop steward reinstated.

Throughout that year, the union chose the situation at the mattress factory to head their industry-wide campaign. There was an ongoing battle for wages and conditions, and eventually 'our unit went out on strike'. Mattress factory workers downing tools attracted considerable publicity. Even in the heightened atmosphere of militancy in the late 1960s and early 1970s, it was unusual for a bunch of unskilled process workers, including many women, to take strike action. It was big news in the papers. The mattress workers made industrial gains and achieved huge wage rises.

Peter was not at this stage thinking of a union job as a career but, in November 1973, he was approached to become an organiser for the union. He regarded it as a dream job –

'a job I would have done for free'. In that era, it was unusual to have a young person employed as a union official. And although Peter had certainly 'come up from the shop floor', traditionally union officials had at least been tradesmen.

But unions were modernising and beginning to change their way of operating, and they were also starting to use the media effectively. There was a new, articulate, youngish union leadership, who were prepared to battle out their ideas – Peter particularly remembers John Halfpenny, the militant Communist official from the Metal Workers' Union. The new-broom union activists 'stood around at late-night parties singing "There Is Power in the Union" and the greatest favourite of all, "I Dreamed I Saw Joe Hill Last Night"', while making plans for wages breakthroughs and campaigns against stifling industrial legislation. Peter found himself in the middle of the battle between the Old and the New.

The 'Old' was exemplified by the day-to-day activity at the Trades Hall. Men ran the traditional union movement. The right-wingers called each other 'Mr' and the Old Left called each other 'Brother'. The Trades Hall 'was filled with dodgy unions such as the Coopers' Union and the Felt Hatters' Union and the Taxi Drivers' Union' (which was actually an organisation for the bosses, not the workers).

Militancy in Victoria was triggered by a split in the Trades Hall Council and the setting up of a breakaway group of rebel unions, which came to be known as the twenty-six 'Rebel Unions'. They developed their own structure. The state secretary of the Furnishing Trades Union was Left Labor Party stalwart, Ken Carr. He was also secretary of the Rebel Unions and was heavily involved in the union movement's increasingly radical political activity.

This militant unionism in Melbourne mirrored the rise of the Jack Mundey-led Builders Labourers' Federation and the green bans, which were happening in Sydney at this time. The economy was also enjoying a boom period, which of course made militant activity easier to encourage.

The New Left belief in the 'worker-student alliance' was not just a rallying cry. This was the beginning of the era in which progressive students and young workers deliberately chose to be part of the union movement and to express their radical views through the unions. In 1968, the Communist Party of Australia had been liberated from old Stalinist ideology by the split with Moscow-liners, and many articulate and committed CPA union officials were among the trade union leadership.

Peter's union participated in ongoing community campaigns. The one that he remembers clearly was the Fraser Island sand-mining issue in 1975. An American company, Dillingham's, which was involved in the destruction of Fraser Island, was constructing a building in Bourke Street in the city. Work was nearing completion, and the building's windows required glazing. Because glazing was furnishing trades work, the union put a ban on it, and Dillingham's could not finish the project. This sort of targeted industrial action was very effective at the time.

BUT PETER'S RADICAL ACTIVISM WASN'T LIMITED TO industrial issues.

In 1971, he took part in the mass demonstrations against the racially selected South African rugby team. He had become concerned about oppression in South Africa, and he remembers vividly the death of 'Black consciousness' campaigner Steve Biko. Peter really liked the trade unions' involvement in the anti-Springbok campaign, and he generally approved of 'the broad church' that was the anti-apartheid movement.

He protested at the Springbok game at Olympic Park. He recalls: 'We were on the embankment standing there … the game was about to start, there was great tension'. Seeing the police picking out and arresting people at random, he called out 'fascist pigs'.

The police took that as a pretext to arrest him. He didn't even see the start of the match. His young lawyer, Trevor Monti (later QC), from the trade unions group, tried to challenge his arrest in court, but Peter was found guilty. 'The police didn't lie, but we failed because evidently saying "fascist pigs" was offensive behaviour.'

Another political issue that captured the attention of Peter's union concerned the Newport Power Station. The environmental argument was that this gas-fired power station would cause pollution, and a widespread union campaign was mounted against its construction.

Showing the broad scope of union activities at the time, the Furnishing Trades also became involved in CARP, the Campaign Against Rising Prices, which was run by CPA stalwart Phyllis Johnson.

Eventually the twenty-six Rebel Unions rejoined the conservative unions in Melbourne Trades Hall. The Furnishing Trades Union was one of the last to rejoin. Peter remembers walking into a room full of old blokes in suits and waistcoats – some were even wearing hats (a very Melbourne thing). He describes himself as 'not a snappy dresser', mainly denim and a duffle coat, and his long hair in a ponytail. I wonder how the old stalwarts of Trades Hall viewed him at the time.

Because the Furnishing Trades was a small craft union it also had to deal with new industrialisation, machine automation and the beginning of prefab furniture companies such as IKEA. This in turn affected how the union was structured. Trade skills were being designed out of the process. There was downward pressure on margins and also the beginning of cheap imports. All of this was an explosive mixture in explosive times.

Peter worked at the Furnishing Trades union until 1983, when he left to work at the Labor Party. He had joined the party in 1973 and, like other young radicals, was very involved, mainly because of the rise of Whitlam. The union valued its affiliation with the Labor Party, and this included sending Peter off to work on election campaigns.

FINALLY, I ASK PETER TO REFLECT ON HOW HE HAD BEEN caught up in the spirit of the times.

His final years at school, his time at university and working in the mattress factory were life-changing experiences for him.

He lived in share houses with those of a similar world view. His political and industrial life got mixed up with his love for the music of the time. Even the way he dressed was seen by him as an act of defiance.

'When I was at school, the school determined everything. They constrained us. We were not allowed to think for ourselves and everything was kept in good order. They were turbulent times. Music, dress, sexual mores were changing. The school fought against this. Outside the school environment, you could see it all happening.'

However, Peter quickly draws the discussion back to his own unique radicalisation process. 'Watching things at university – the internal student politics. I was not excited by it because I was more interested in what the trade unions were doing at that time. Hawke and the ACTU [Australian Council of Trade Unions] took up leadership on so many critical issues.' He stops and ponders.

Once again, I realise how strange it is that it was not student life at 'Red Monash' that caught Peter's radical imagination. The most militant university campus in Australia had failed to achieve what the BBB Mattress Factory had done so successfully – turned Peter Batchelor into a lifelong leftie.

HELEN VOYSEY
The kid from the sticks

Nadia Wheatley

I first encountered Helen on YouTube, when a Google search for the 1970 Sydney Moratorium turned up a clip of a young woman addressing the crowd from the steps of the Town Hall. Of course, everyone was young in the Sixties, but this speaker was very young indeed. Representing the organisation called High School Students Against the War in Vietnam, Helen was in Year 12, but she had already been an activist for three years. She describes herself at that time as being 'the kid from the sticks'.

Born in 1952, Helen was three years old when her parents made the move from Sydney's eastern suburbs to the suburb of Castle Hill, an area of scrubby bushland, market gardens and chook farms on the city's north-west fringe. Patrick White, who lived there in this era, depicted the place in his play, *The Season at Sarsaparilla*, as the epitome of lower middle-class suburbia. But for Helen and her three brothers, the family's three-and-a-half-acre block and the timber bungalow their dad had built on it was a great place to grow up. With its open-plan architecture (unusual at the time), the Voysey home welcomed visitors, young and old, but Helen was always aware that her parents were 'very different' from many of their WASP Bible-Belt neighbours.

Lew Voysey was an industrial chemist who had his own business supplying feed and medicines to the local chicken farmers. That sounds dull, but Lew wasn't. When he was only seventeen, he had built himself a shack at Era Beach, between Sydney and Wollongong, where other shackholders included workers from the nearby coalmines and the remnants of a community of unemployed workers who had been made homeless by the Great Depression. The radicalism of the South Coast miners and unemployed was legendary, and must surely have rubbed off on the young man.

Helen's mother, Eva Spielman, had been born in 1922 in Vienna, where her family was part of the city's large and prosperous community of assimilated Jews. Indeed, Eva's father's sense of Austrian identity was so strong that he'd even fought for the Austro-Hungarian Army in the First World War. Later becoming one of Vienna's leading engineers, George Spielman travelled extensively, including to England, where some his professional colleagues were Quakers. After the *Anschluss* of March 1938, however, his wealth and social standing were no guarantee of safety, and he was taken to Nazi headquarters for questioning. His status as a war veteran allowed him to leave the country under a Nazi dispensation for veterans. Taking his two teenage daughters with him, George Spielman fled to England, where his Quaker friends acted as guarantors until he could get a visa for Australia.

Helen Voysey

Eva was seventeen years old when she arrived in Sydney in 1939. With Australia at war with Germany, the Spielmans were enemy aliens. But it wasn't only Eva's country of origin that drew her to the attention of the Australian security service. Enrolled as an evening student in a chemistry course at Sydney Technical College, Eva met fellow student Lew Voysey. A shared commitment to social justice caused both to join a radical association of science students, which in turn led them to the Communist Party of Australia. In 1943, Eva was interviewed at Police Headquarters by Military Police Intelligence. Helen, who has her mother's ASIO file, comments that it 'refers to her as "the alien" all the way through the interview'. Both Eva and Lew would leave the Party in 1956, in the wake of Krushchev's speech exposing Stalin's purges, but they retained a commitment to peace and internationalism.

The couple also got in and did things in their local community. In the intellectual backwater of Castle Hill, they sought like-minded people in the local amateur theatre group. One night, when Helen was about eight years old, she came out to the lounge room where the theatre group was rehearsing. 'And I stood at the glass doors listening to them play-reading this play, workshopping this play. And it was *The Crucible*, by Arthur Miller.'

Witch hunts, McCarthyism, Communism and paranoid conspiracy: it was a heady brew for any Australian suburban lounge room, but Eva Spielman's family history adds a further dimension to the enactment of this political fable.

For Helen, being 'exposed to' this Spielman history was a crucial influence. 'I was aware of the Jewish heritage', she recalls. 'I was aware of the flight from Austria.' The tale was passed on not only by her mother but also by her grandfather, who lived at the Voysey home until he died in 1964. Described by Helen as 'a grand European man', George Spielman did not regularly practise Judaism. Nevertheless, he lit lamps on the anniversary of his wife's death, and on one occasion he took Helen and her brother Peter (two years older) to a service at the Sydney Synagogue. In 1961, when he received a sum of money from the Austrian government as reparation for his confiscated property, he used it for a kind of memorial journey. Nine-year-old Helen accompanied her grandfather (then aged about seventy-five), her parents, her three brothers and other members of the extended family to Europe, where they spent six weeks in Vienna over the winter of 1961–62. This trip confirmed the dual identity that Helen felt.

'I've always felt this duality of being part European and yet very Australian', she explains. 'I've always felt that from my mother's side I had the European heritage and from my father's side I had the Australian heritage, associated with Era and the shack and with being in the bush.'

While for many urban Australians the Voysey home would have seemed remote enough, on summer weekends and holidays the family threw off all the trappings of suburbia. Essentially one room, their second home had no electricity or running water, and the family had to hike in. When I joined Helen at the shack for lunch one day, the visit began with a 45-minute trek in from the car park: easy enough, with just swimmers and a towel in my bag, and the view was breathtaking. But I can't imagine carting in young children and enough supplies for a week, let alone building materials or a kerosene fridge.

This combination of bush and beach seems to add up to an archetypical Australian childhood, but the global political tensions of the Cold War meant that Helen Voysey grew up with a 'childhood nightmare' in which she and her family were 'fried' in a nuclear holocaust. Initially evoked by a Campaign for Nuclear Disarmament (CND) 'Ban the Bomb' march to which her parents took her, this fear was reinforced by television news broadcasts and adult political discussions. The idea of nuclear holocaust was coloured, too, by the sense of the other Holocaust, which her mother and grandfather had escaped.

A second, and more specific, moment of awakening for Helen was the Cuban Missile Crisis of 1962. Of course, for many baby boomers, the final hours of this stand-off between the United States and the Soviet Union was the most memorable benchmark of the Cold War. Helen Voysey went to bed that night thinking: 'We're not going to wake up tomorrow. We are going to be fried'.

These were scary thoughts for a ten-year-old. And even living in 'the sticks', among the riding schools and chicken farms, would offer no protection from acid rain.

When the Missile Crisis ended, Helen's fear did not dissipate. She continued to go to sleep at night thinking that she and her family 'would not wake up the next morning'. In describing this belief, she connects it with her later leap into radical activism.

Meredith, whose family life was as loving as Helen's, asks the natural question. 'Did your parents ever try to allay these fears? Did they ever say "Oh, don't worry, it'll be all right" or anything?'

No. Typically, for Eva and Lew Voysey, the solution was not platitudes but action, to change the world.

'I think their attitude was that you try to do something about it. You go to CND marches. You be active in your community. You advocate your views. You try to convince others that there's another way.'

This model of activism and advocacy was something that Helen would follow.

CASTLE HILL WAS STILL SO LACKING IN SERVICES THAT IN 1966, when it came time for Helen to begin secondary school, the local high school was only three years old. However, the area was growing quickly, and over the time she was there, the school would expand to 1200 students.

Happy, motivated and mature, Helen 'did rather well' at school. 'I liked my teachers, and I think they liked me. I was one of those students who put her hand up and said things and was engaged.' This wasn't a recipe for popularity. 'You had to not be too bright to be part of the mob.' There were other reasons why Helen 'always felt a bit different'. She explains that her father was the president of the P & C for many years. 'So that was embarrassing.' Her mother 'had a strong accent' – unusual in those white Australian suburbs. 'And I was short', Helen adds. 'Only five foot. Most other people were quite a bit taller.'

Many of us suffer at school from a sense of not fitting in, but Helen Voysey's alienation is interesting, given the leadership role she would soon take – and not just among students in her own school.

Nevertheless, while she didn't belong to any of the gangs (especially not to the top girls' gang, in which everyone was named Robyn), at school there was one girl with whom Helen ended up in a 'best friend duo'. Outside school, there was Lenore, who lived on the North Shore and attended the prestigious North Sydney Girls' High. The daughter of

Eva's best friend, Lenore was 'like a sort of sister cousin'. Helen thinks it was probably through her that, at the age of fourteen, she started going to meetings of a youth group run by the Humanist Society.

A bit like a church fellowship without the church, this group met on Sunday mornings in a house in Crown Street in the inner city. For Helen, even getting there was an adventure, involving a train trip to Central, then 'a walk through back lanes and alleys where the women of the night were emerging from their houses'. The other regulars at these meetings were a few years older than Helen and were from the North Shore and eastern suburbs: a different demographic from the kids with whom Helen went to school. As well as discussions about current events and moral issues, there were social gatherings and outings to the theatre – all held in the daytime, so there was no problem about getting back to Castle Hill – and on one occasion there was a camp at Kangaroo Valley. A photograph from this weekend shows Helen at the front of the line of hikers, a sleeping bag and pack on her back, her dark hair in thick plaits, a determined look on her face. It is clear that wherever she is heading, she is going to get there.

In July 1968, at one of these Sunday meetings, Helen picked up a flyer for what was called a 'teach-in' about the Vietnam War for high school students. Then aged sixteen and in Year 10, Helen went along with several others from the Humanist Society; all up, there were a few hundred young people in the auditorium that afternoon. Helen recalls: 'And of course being the person who asked questions in school and stuff, I stuck my hand up and asked questions'.

Although Helen was not aware of it, this meeting was convened by Resistance, a Trotskyist organisation based at

The kid from the sticks

Bob Gould's Third World Bookshop in Goulburn Street, in Sydney's CBD. Gould himself wasn't at the event, but brothers John and Jim Percy, the two leading Resistance organisers, were among the speakers to whom Helen listened. At the time, she 'knew nothing about the Percys', but with hindsight, she is able to see that 'They had a plan, to form a high school organisation'. Although to the high school kids they came across as adults, Jim at this time was only nineteen and John was twenty-one.

When the decision was made to set up a committee, Helen 'got kind of singled out'. She remembers that 'one of the older guys' on the platform pointed down into the crowded auditorium. 'What about you?' he said. 'You asked a question.'

The next moment, Helen found herself head-hunted into the organising group of the fledgling High School Students Against the War in Vietnam (HSSAWV). From now on, her Sunday morning outings to the Humanist meetings were exchanged for after-school commutes to the Goulburn Street bookshop, where she joined a team of young activists who mostly came from high schools closer to the CBD. This 'committee', which met at least once a week, was 'a fairly fluid thing – no formal structure, just a core group to call on'. Although the Percys and other members of Resistance clearly had an ongoing role in HSSAWV, Helen insists that the secondary students themselves set the agenda. 'We tried to keep separate from Resistance. We had our own meetings, produced our own newsletter.'

No matter how autonomous the students were, they were dependent on the Goulburn Street bookshop both for a place to meet and the resources to publish material. By September, the first edition of *Student Underground* was ready for the Resistance Gestetner. All that was needed was someone to meet the legal requirement of authorising it. Because Helen's parents were sympathetic, she again put her hand up: and so the name 'H Voysey', followed by her parents' address, could be found in the small print at the bottom of the single-page publication, which appeared on 9 September 1968.

The news-sheet criticised the recent Russian invasion of Czechoslovakia as well as the American invasion of Vietnam but, to the reactionary forces of society, the actual content was less important than the fact that school students were getting together and voicing their opinions. The day after publication, the *Sydney Morning Herald* condemned it, citing Helen's name and address. Although this news item was small, it was on the front page. Helen recalls, 'That's when the shit hit the fan'.

'Someone wrote the word "COMMO" in enormous letters on the roadway outside our house – we lived on Pennant Hills Road, which is a fairly main artery. My father spotted it and went out in the early hours of the morning and tried to obliterate it.'

Most fathers of the 1960s would have hit the roof, but Lew Voysey took it in his stride. The reaction was very different when Helen turned up at school.

'Of course I'm called down to the headmaster's office: "What's all this about?"'

Helen reflects that the principal was 'a fair man. He just basically sort of said, '"You're not to bring this into the school. We don't like politics in the school."'

But the very fact of 'being hauled up' by the authorities had a 'radicalising effect' on Helen. She found herself 'thrown in the deep end, defending what we'd done'.

'The thing that was thrown at us most was "You're too young to think about politics."' As she voices her response to this, Helen puts the argument that she would put many a time in public.

'There's a war going on, we're seeing it on television every night. And we've grown up with this childhood fear of imminent death through nuclear holocaust. And it is 1968 – things are changing around the world. There is a big impact of that, even on Castle Hill High School. And *you* are telling us not to think about things, not to discuss politics!'

The 'you' in this rhetoric is not a single school principal (fair or otherwise) but the whole system of schooling; indeed, the system of society. Overall, Helen says, the public condemnation that she received for authorising the pamphlet 'made my commitment stronger'.

The front-page publicity was good for the cause. As principals and politicians called for the banning of *Student Underground*, demand increased. More editions of the newspaper were written and published, tackling more issues. Although opposition to conscription and the Vietnam War remained the main focus, the radical students challenged the schooling system itself when they put out information about students' rights in regard to detention and punishment. Parental authority was confronted in articles about hair length – a critical issue in the 1960s, when for many boys the first act of rebellion was to abandon the short-back-and-sides style of their fathers.

As the organisation took off, students in a number of high schools set up their own activist committees and brought out their own news-sheets. At Castle Hill, Helen's brother Peter (who was in Year 12) and fellow student Chips Mackinolty (in Year 9) helped produce the school's paper.

But despite their efforts, 'there was never really a serious group of students at Castle Hill High School'. It was 'too far out in the sticks' for many kids to be politically conscious. Activism 'was just seen as "that weird thing that Helen does."' When she was in Year 11, she was part of a group boycotting the prefect system; again, their numbers were too small for them to be effective. But if Helen Voysey, like all prophets, was despised in her 'home town', she was soon to be thrust onto a national stage.

BY THE END OF 1968, GROUPS OF RADICAL HIGH SCHOOL students were getting together in Melbourne as well as in Sydney. In Brisbane, a group called Students for Revolutionary Action produced a pamphlet urging students to seize weapons used by school cadet units. The Sydney network of students ran a conference with the title, *Is Your School Revolting?* To kids, this pun seemed hilarious; to certain grown-ups, it was frightening.

Towards the middle of the following year, ASIO was so concerned about the nationwide agitation that it produced a secret paper on the 'Programme for Revolution in High Schools'. In this document, High School Students Against the War in Vietnam was specifically named.

Among the strident voices questioning secondary students' right to discuss politics at school was that of Peter Coleman, editor of the CIA-funded *Quadrant* magazine, and a Liberal member of the NSW Parliament. Within weeks of the restricted circulation of the ASIO paper, he produced a pamphlet titled *School Power* and subtitled *Is your child being manipulated by political operators?* According to historian David McKnight, there are 'extraordinarily close parallels' between the ASIO document and the Coleman pamphlet, which was widely sold through newsagents.

Responding to this controversy, the ABC TV current affairs program, *This Day Tonight*, invited Helen Voysey onto the show to debate Peter Coleman. She was seventeen. He was forty.

'How did it go?' I ask Helen.

'Great', is all she says. 'I gave him a run for his money. I just gave him a run for his money.'

Again, the publicity value was fantastic. The circulation of *Student Underground* spread to about a hundred Sydney high schools. Kids started ringing up the Third World Bookshop, complaining that they were being discriminated against because the news-sheet hadn't reached their school.

Helen joined in the groups going around at night pasting up posters at schools. 'That was exciting', she recalls. 'You'd try to put them in some secret places where the authorities might not see them, but the kids would.'

Although the isolation of Castle Hill and the lack of public transport were hardly conducive to revolutionary action, she sometimes used to go out in the van with some of the older Resistance activists, including her brother Peter. Now having a gap year between school and university, he was working and living at the Third World Bookshop.

Peter and Helen's parents were strongly supportive of their activism. However, the Voysey household wasn't immune from the generational disputes of the 1960s. For Eva and Lew, the issue was the particular theoretical line that their radical offspring were following. Although Helen stresses that the issue of opposition to the Vietnam War was paramount for her, the ideological discussions that took place at the Third World Bookshop struck a chord.

'When I read what Trotsky wrote about Germany in 1931, 1932 – his warnings about Hitler – that was very meaningful to me because it made sense in my personal history.'

But for people such as Helen's parents, who had been Communists in the 1940s, Trotsky was the arch traitor. Although Eva and Lew had left the Party when they had learnt of Stalin's excesses, it was difficult to accept the ideology that Peter and Helen were voicing – no doubt with all the sanctimony of youth.

'I remember having arguments from a Trotskyist point of view with my parents', Helen recalls. 'We had these arguments within the family over where Stalinism had gone [wrong], and arguing the Trotskyist position of what Stalin had done to the Soviet Union and to the international Left.'

Nevertheless, in January 1969, Eva and Lew Voysey allowed their shack at Era Beach to be the hub for a weekend camp of about forty members of HSSAWV and some older Goulburn Street activists. The group jokingly described this as a guerrilla training camp, but the ASIO spy who infiltrated the camp sadly reported that nothing subversive had happened, and that there was not even any marijuana or promiscuity! Just sun and surf and long earnest discussions about the Fourth International.

By early 1970, anti-war groups around the country were coming together to organise the first Moratorium, scheduled to take place in May. In the broad-based (and often inharmonious) alliance planning the Sydney event, there were seasoned campaigners from the Communist Party, from the Labor Party, from the trade unions, from university groups, from a proliferation of peace groups. And there was the sole representative of HSSAWV, who arrived in school uniform after coming into town on the train.

Now in Year 12, Helen was doing Level 1 maths and science, and German, which she studied by correspondence. She was also doing English and history, at Level 2. Because of her activism, there was a great deal of pressure on her academically.

'I used to do my maths homework on the train journey – you know, calculus and integers and stuff. It was a three-quarter-of-an hour journey and that was a good period of time – about the same time as a school period – so I could get through a lot of stuff.

'So I was keeping up my studies to do well at school, because that was really important. I was the only girl at the school doing Level 1 maths with six blokes. After being singled out [for radical activities], it was really important that I stayed top of the grade.'

AND SO 8 MAY 1970 ARRIVED. HAVING BEEN INVITED TO speak on behalf of her organisation as part of the official Moratorium program, Helen felt 'incredibly nervous'.

In telling us about this, she divulges that she'd had a lisp as a child, so her mother had sent her to elocution lessons and got her involved with the local theatre group. Helen had recited poetry at eisteddfods, and acted in plays. In Year 10, she'd been part of a performance at school – a satirical review which the students themselves had written. Despite developing a certain confidence in public speaking through all of this, it was a different thing altogether to stand on the steps of the Sydney Town Hall and address 20 000 people. But there is no trace of nervousness in the young woman in the film footage of this event.

Helen Voysey

Wearing a dark coat adorned with a Moratorium badge, and with her hair in two long plaits, she looks directly at the assembled crowd as she speaks clearly and confidently into the microphone.

The high school administration don't like it when we take the Moratorium into the schools.

It bugs them to see the kids that they are training for *their* society turn around and question the values of that society. Not only do they not like it – they tried to suppress it. They tried their hardest to stop us from exercising our democratic rights, like discussion, like wearing a Moratorium badge into the school.

We're here in numbers. We want to stop this rotten war in Vietnam.

And we're doing our best within our schools to talk about this, to show other kids what *we* think is the truth about Vietnam.

Support us!

We need your support in fighting against the administration that is trying to keep discussion and debate out of the schools.

As Helen stepped away from the microphone, there were rousing cheers, for her, and for her fellow students.

The kid from the sticks

EVEN TODAY, AS I SIT AT MY DESK WATCHING THE YOUTUBE clip of this eighteen-year-old speaking so clearly and movingly against the war and for the political rights of young people, I feel like cheering. This is the same articulacy and passion that young people around the world are showing as they speak out about climate change.

Although I had previously met Helen a few times and even visited the Era shack, it was on 31 October 2018 that Meredith and I conducted the interview for this book. The first thing Helen did as she arrived was to remark on the strike of Australian high school students that was going on that very day. In that morning's *Sydney Morning Herald*, there was a letter signed by two fourteen-year-olds, explaining '*Why we're striking from school over climate change inaction*':

> It seems ridiculous that children have got to the point where they realise that the adults who are supposed to be in charge aren't doing enough to protect our futures from dangerous climate change.
>
> We have decided to go on strike from school to show our leaders that, right now, tackling climate change feels more important than our education.
>
> Please don't say that because we are children we can't think for ourselves and that we've been brainwashed. This is an excuse adults use to ignore kids. Being children may mean that we are less mature, less educated and less articulate, but it doesn't mean that we can't think for ourselves and make our own decisions.

Helen Voysey

It is a statement expressed with the same sincerity and simplicity as Helen Voysey's Moratorium speech. Today's students may have Instagram and TikTok instead of a Gestetner, but they know that direct action is the best way to get the attention of the mainstream media.

JOHN DERUM
We were mad 'Milligan anarchic'

Meredith Burgmann

Catching up with John Derum is always fun. Nadia and I have arranged to meet him at a local Glebe cafe, and after discussion about whether we will have a glass of chardy we all agree that it's not a good idea at lunchtime. And also John's come on his scooter, and doesn't want to have an accident. Gosh we're old.

These days, Derum is looking very distinguished – a shock of white hair, those well-known piercing blue eyes and classic sharp features. I'm sure he'd prefer to be described as 'hot', but distinguished will have to do him.

John Derum is the actor's actor who rose to fame as the narrator in 1970s cult TV show *Aunty Jack* and played important character roles in Australian theatre and TV over the next five decades. I, however, have always thought of John as Catholic powerbroker BA Santamaria – that wonderful role he played in the 1988 miniseries *True Believers*. Like soapie stars who get typecast as Toadie or Dax, he must hate it.

John Derum

It's quite ironic that he is about to embark on a description of his Catholic Melbourne childhood, straight out of Santamaria country. As John points out, the Mannix/Santamaria hegemony meant that Catholicism in Melbourne was very different from Catholicism in Sydney.

BORN IN 1946, JOHN WAS THE MIDDLE CHILD OF THREE boys. He describes himself as coming from 'a conventional Catholic family'. It was in fact Irish Catholic on both sides, and young John was taught Irish dancing and a lot of Irish music, including, of course, Irish rebel songs. ('My mother would have been a real bomb thrower', he says.) The Derums were also 'footy mad' – John's uncle and cousin both played for the 'Bloods' (South Melbourne, later the Swans). The family politics was Labor working class and 'whatever Mannix said'.

By Mannix, John means the Catholic archbishop of Melbourne, whom he goes on to describe as being 'six foot four with flowing white hair'. A dominating personality: 'when he wrote a letter saying "The Russians are coming" and it was read out in every church in Melbourne, then that is what was believed', John explains. It was holy gospel in more ways than one. 'At least he wasn't one of those terrible Brits', he adds, by way of justification.

But while Melbourne's archbishop held sway over all the faithful, he looms surprisingly large in John's story, through the personal role he played in the life of John's mother, Jean.

The only girl among six children, Jean was three years old when her mother died. After making a will stipulating that the children be kept together in Melbourne, or be returned to relatives in Ireland, their father proceeded to go off to the Great War. When he subsequently was killed in France, Dr Mannix became a kind of guardian for the six orphans. Little wonder that John's mother accepted whatever he said.

John's father was much quieter than his mother, and John never really knew whether he 'went along with the whole Catholic thing' or not. His father, in fact, had a sneaking admiration for left-wing ALP leader Jim Cairns, but did not actually create a family row by defending him.

(This reminds me of my own family, where my father was very quiet but had secret Labor views, while my mother fiercely handed out for the Liberal Party on election day. Perhaps in the 1950s, in the pre-social media soul-baring days, many families dealt with their political differences in this way.)

Still relating his family's Catholic credentials, John tells us that his paternal grandfather got more politically strident as the years went on, and was eventually involved with the Knights of the Southern Cross, a secretive right-wing Labor-oriented Catholic group.

Suddenly John drops a bombshell. He tells us that his (paternal) grandmother was matron-of-honour at John Wren's wedding. What a hoot. This really is life imitating art. Or perhaps it is art imitating life.

John Wren was the corrupt Melbourne businessman and political powerbroker who became the fictional John West in Communist author Frank Hardy's iconic 1950 novel *Power Without Glory*. It was his wife, Ellen Wren, who was the complainant in Hardy's trial for criminal libel. Perhaps the women in his circle knew nothing about Wren's illegal gambling activities and were shocked by the revelations that came out during the court case. 'They didn't know that Wren had been up to this stuff.' But the men certainly knew.

John Derum

Not only is John Derum confused in my mind with BA Santamaria, but now he also becomes somehow involved with Frank Hardy and *Power Without Glory* – another great television show (1976) about working-class Melbourne, political power and Catholicism.

When I ask him how he felt about playing Santamaria, his face visibly brightens and he says it was a great part. It obviously came to him easily: he proceeds to outline the weekly ritual whereby a young John watched 'Santa' on television every Sunday. He patiently explains that Santamaria's program, *Point of View*, had a brilliant slot, 11.45 on a Sunday morning, 'straight after Mass and just before *World of Sport*. So even if people didn't catch the whole program, Santamaria got a massive rating for the last five minutes of his weekly tirade.

'We were told at our school to watch *Point of View*, so in fact any kid in my class could have done that Santamaria accent', he modestly concludes.

But my unvoiced query is, could they have got the staring eyes and the steely glance quite as right as John did?

His school was a Marist Brothers day school where, by the time he was in upper primary, John was starting to question his faith. 'We thought the Brothers were idiots, and they mostly were, but some were probably all right.' He adds wryly, 'Apart from the intimidation and bullying, there was no actual sexual assault'.

AND SO TO THE QUESTION OF WAR AND PEACE. HOW DID this play out in the Derum family?

John begins by saying, 'Mum and Dad's contemporaries had been in Korea, and there was absolute contempt for that one'. John himself seems puzzled by that forgotten war:

We were mad 'Milligan anarchic'

'What the hell was that about?'

Vietnam was hotly discussed within the family.

When conscription was introduced, 'Mum and Dad got very suspicious – especially Mum. Here she was, she had three boys, and she'd lost her father to the First World War, and had a brother killed in Ambon in the Second World War ...' He ponders his mother's feelings.

Turning twenty in January 1966, John was in the second tranche of young men with marbles in the barrel of the 'lottery of death'. His friend, Aarne Neeme (later a well-known theatre director), had been in the first batch. Although Aarne had ticked the box on the registration form that asked 'Are you a conscientious objector?', he had been called up. John embarks on a long story about how Aarne's life was dominated by this decision for a decade and it bred in John a suspicion that 'ticking the box' was inadvisable.

At the time, there were other stories along these lines. Whether any of them are true is irrelevant. Everyone believed them and everyone had their own sure-fire version of how to get out of the call-up. As I put to John, there was a lot of judicious 'disappearing' of the names of those who would have been considered troublesome recruits.

When the time came for John to register, he wasn't a student, which would have delivered him automatic deferral, so he had to decide what to do. Someone, somewhere, had told him that even if you didn't tick the 'conscientious objector' box you could change your mind later on. John didn't trust 'them', as he calls the authorities. In fact, he believed that 'they' were going to call up everyone who ticked that box and make an example of them. Aarne Neeme had ticked the box and he was called up. John therefore left that square vacant.

He concludes, 'So this was the gamble I took'.

To his surprise, he received notification that his birth date had not been chosen. But as he mumbles, 'I still don't believe that birthday bullshit'.

BY 1966, WHEN HE DODGED THE BULLET OF THE CALL-UP, John was already heavily involved in the theatre life of Melbourne.

John had known from the age of thirteen or fourteen that he wanted to be an actor or producer, and after leaving school had begun to do the rounds of the theatres, looking for an opportunity. The third place he approached was 'terrific'. This was the Emerald Hill Theatre, under the inspired stewardship of Wal Cherry and George Whaley. The seventeen-year-old had found his home.

Founded in 1961, the Emerald Hill Theatre in South Melbourne was the centre of new drama in Australia. In its programming it managed to combine the grim working-class British theatre tradition and new anti-war satires from around the world. Theatre historian Julian Meyrick writes of the 'two generations' in the theatre, contrasting the generation of the 1950s and 1960s who 'consciously borrowed their working methods from the British theatre of the time' with the 'Australian-born New Wave generation who came into their maturity during the Vietnam war and worked through the late 1960s and '70s with an alternative sensibility'. John had landed slap-bang in the middle of this change.

'People were coming out of the fifties', John explains, but he hesitates before saying any more. He is strangely kind to the fifties. 'It really was a drawing of breath ... of coming out of the war and the Depression.'

We were mad 'Milligan anarchic'

By the time John arrived at Emerald Hill, they were 'doing shows that were anti-Vietnam, anti-war in general, stuff by Bertolt Brecht and John Arden'.

English playwright Arden was particularly important, because he came out to Australia. John describes how one day Wal Cherry said, 'We've got this John Arden coming out, a wonderful man, and nobody knows any of his plays. We'll have to do one'. Arden's iconic 1959 anti-war drama, *Serjeant Musgrave's Dance*, was the one they chose. Although there had been an earlier production of this play at Sydney University's Union Theatre, this was the first Melbourne production of the gloomy and even macabre tale of four deserters from a foreign imperialist war who bring chaos and tragedy to a quiet English village. For an aspiring actor – only eighteen years old – to get a role in this play and actually meet the playwright was an astonishing experience.

That was September 1964.

Over the next few years, Emerald Hill provided much of the intelligentsia's ammunition in opposition to the war. It presented ensemble revues: *The Thin Line* in October 1966; *A Funny Thing Happened on the Way to the Front* in November 1966; *On Stage Vietnam* in November 1967; and Jean-Claude van Itallie's *America Hurrah* in August 1968. John muses, 'We did the sketches and the folk singers did their songs and we went to the pub furious that conscription and the war still hadn't stopped.'

John was on stage in many of these shows, but whether or not he was in these productions, John avidly lapped up the prevailing atmosphere.

'I don't think it could happen now', he reflects, as he considers a theatre milieu that was much more flexible than in later years.

John Derum

In 1966, John Sumner, long-time director of the Melbourne Theatre Company, commissioned a play from local actor and writer Alan Hopgood called *Private Yuk Objects*, about a country yokel being conscripted and finishing up in Vietnam. In a parallel story within the play, an older Australian soldier is in conversation with his Vietcong captor. In the play, which John describes as 'the first play in the world to be based on the Vietnam War', he had the role of an anti-war demonstrator. On several occasions during the play's run, he and the other actors who performed in the demonstration scenes 'would be going to demonstrations on our way to the theatre and the play we were doing was about the demonstrations'. John points out, 'It would take forever to get that play up and running now'.

'Can you remember a moment when you suddenly decided that you were against the Vietnam War?' I ask him.

Sounding a bit hesitant, John says he thinks it was merely a process of hearing people say things around the theatre, like '"That's wrong!" or "Why's that happening?"' Surrounded by people in their twenties and thirties, who seemed so much older than he was, John was very much influenced by their comments and their questioning.

Rather than deliberately reading anti-war material, John says he was shaped by the work of 'the English playwrights'. He names John Osborne, Harold Pinter and, again, John Arden. He is firm that his political conversion came not only from acting in their plays, but also from reading them, and reading about them in publications like *Plays and Players* magazine, which came from England.

'When you're doing a Spike Milligan play, you're also reading the books about it', he goes on to explain. 'And when you're doing John Arden, you're also reading his other plays and what people are saying about his other plays. The same with Pinter's and Osborne's works, and when other people are doing an Osborne, you go to watch that too ... and all of those English plays.'

I realise that, unlike our other interviewees, John's radicalisation has stemmed from the 1960s British playwrights rather than from any American sources. John defensively mentions US writer Arthur Miller and I quibble, saying that Miller's plays were not really about Vietnam, they were about the American dream. But John points out the radicalising effect of anything that 'wasn't that staid conservatism of the fifties'.

As we talk about the major influences on his life, I tell John that he's mentioned Wal Cherry several times. John says that actually the co-leader of the Emerald Hill Theatre, George Whaley, was probably a greater influence on him. He says that George was more influential because he was more articulate. And, as John adds, 'more angry about what was going on. George was a great teacher'.

Whaley, who was about ten years older than John, had been a fine fencer, but had given up the sport for drama. John and I joke that he would have been very good in Shakespearean sword fights.

At this stage, the chops arrive and our attention is diverted.

SOME TIME AFTER OUR CONVERSATION RESUMES, JOHN suddenly tells the story of his radicalisation moment, without realising it. This happens when, out of the blue, he starts to talk about capital punishment and the hanging of Ronald Ryan, even citing the exact date (3 February 1967) when this occurred.

John Derum

Ryan had been found guilty of shooting a warder during an attempt to escape from Pentridge Prison. Victorian Premier Henry Bolte was determined to have him executed as part of his law and order agenda.

The event occasioned widespread protest, especially in the days leading up to it. John Derum, then aged twenty-one, was still living at the family home, a short walk from the gaol.

'It was the weekend before the execution ...' He begins his account. 'We lived in Coburg and there was all sorts of madness going on. People were saying they were going to break into the gaol and free Ronald Ryan. The night before the execution, there was going to be a vigil outside the gaol and I thought, "I'm not going to do that."'

But eventually, at about four in the morning, John walked up Sydney Road to the gaol and joined the crowd of people standing outside. He later realised, 'We actually walked the same route as where the shooting happened'.

He continues, 'It was quite extraordinary, that demonstration, because where we were standing, on the corner, outside the main entrance of Pentridge Gaol, that was the door that Ryan escaped out of and it was the same door the press would walk out of after the execution.

'It was really weird because it was eight o'clock in the morning on a Friday. Trams were going by and people were reading newspapers about what was happening.

'The only thing we heard was suddenly this flock of birds took off! Pigeons took off, right on eight o'clock, and later we were told by journalists Patrick Tennison and Ron Saw, who were official observers, that when the trapdoor clanged it scared everyone, including the birds.'

We are all quiet for little while. Then I ask, 'Did that have a huge influence on you?'

'That morning did', John says. 'That morning did.' He explains, 'Because it was ridiculous, hanging people ... and they just did it'.

I share that it had a huge influence on me, and I was far away in Sydney.

John finishes, 'You just thought to yourself "They're not listening."'

Years later, John talked to prisoner-cum-playwright Jim McNeil. Jim revealed that he had taught Ryan to read and, as Jim put it, Ryan taught him about sums. John comments, 'That sort of reinforced the human-ness of the man'. He adds that, fifty years on from the execution, it appears 'there's quite a plausible case to be put that the warder was shot accidentally by another warder'.

After an uncomfortable moment, we get back to the matter of John's political awakening. I ask if Ryan's hanging left him with contempt for the people who did it.

'Yes, of course', he replies. 'It was ridiculous, hanging people in the Sixties.' He adds, 'But I couldn't have had much more contempt for Bolte and [Chief Secretary] Rylah than I already did'.

He continues this train of thought with a run-down on one of the infamous Victorian politicians of the time, Sir Arthur Rylah.

'We were doing a revue and the title that was suggested was *Mr Rylah's Teenage Daughter*.' This was a commentary on Rylah's famous remark about American feminist Mary McCarthy's novel *The Group*: 'I wouldn't want my teenage daughter to be reading that'.

They didn't actually use that title but, John says, maybe he should lie and say that they did.

John Derum

IN 1967, NOT LONG AFTER RYAN'S EXECUTION, JOHN moved to Sydney to do a show at the Astor Theatre at Woolloomooloo. Although it was to be for ten weeks, it ran for ten months, and by then Sydney was his home.

Early on in his Sydney 'visit', John met up again with Aarne Neeme and actor/producer Michael Boddy. They got John involved in Arts Vietnam, a group of actors, artists and musicians who staged anti-war shows and exhibitions during the 1960s and early 1970s, often at the New Theatre in Newtown.

In 1968, John was part of an Arts Vietnam show at the Teachers' Federation building, where Margret RoadKnight and Jeannie Lewis were on the program. Michael Boddy had the idea for the song they sang for the finale. As he recalls this, John breaks into a very melodic version of the famous advertising jingle, '*I like Aeroplane Jelly, Aeroplane Jelly for me ...*'

His voice falters as he continues: 'And then the scene changes to an Asian girl in pyjamas writhing as she's burning from napalm jelly'.

I remember that chilling scene as John recreates it. 'By this stage did you feel that Vietnam had somehow taken over your life?' I ask.

John considers for a moment before agreeing. Then he moves on to remember that, 'Of course in Sydney, there was R&R'. This was the US Army's 'rest and recuperation' leave, which had thousands of uniformed servicemen swarming into bars and public venues in the city. At the time, John was appearing in shows at some of these places. Speaking of the American soldiers, he says, 'They were just ordinary people when you talked to them. They didn't know what they were doing in Vietnam. Even in revue at the Chevron we were doing Nixon jokes. That sort of continual anti-war humour seeps into your skin'.

When we ask John, did he identify with any groups, such as Trotskyists or anarchists, he is quite frank, 'No, I didn't know enough'. But as Nadia snidely comments, that hasn't stopped anyone else being a Trot.

What happened when he went back to Melbourne? Were his politics taking him to the left of his parents? John says that his dad's politics were shifting and he was opening up. His mum was drifting towards the left, but she still thought that the Johnsons (US President Lyndon and his wife 'Lady Bird') 'seemed very nice people'. His mother was still going to Mass, his father 'probably not'.

John suddenly mentions the influence of folk music on his political development – Pete Seeger in particular. Nadia enquires whether he just listened to Pete Seeger records or whether he went to 'dark places on Friday nights to listen to folk singers playing Pete Seeger songs'. John admits to a bit of both. I realise again that Pete Seeger is the first American influence that John has mentioned without prompting; in my own political radicalisation, Americans were everything.

As well as listening to American folk music, John went to live folk concerts at the Emerald Hill Theatre. He mentions Marian Henderson and a very young Margret RoadKnight as stars of these occasions. It's John who suggests that we should interview Margret for this book.

Was free speech a big issue for John, in his area of the arts?

He replies by talking about performing in John Antrobus and Spike Milligan's post-apocalyptic comedy *The Bedsitting Room* in 1965. 'A marvellous anti-war play', says John. In England, the Lord Chancellor still had the role of reading and approving each play to be performed, so in the Melbourne performances they actually included the Lord Chancellor as a character reading out his censorial comments. Spike Milligan had become quite involved in the Melbourne production and sent the producers extra jokes, replacing (former UK prime minister) Harold Macmillan gags with Robert Menzies ones.

The companion piece to *The Bedsitting Room* was a play by John Antrobus called *You'll Come to Love Your Sperm Test*. The Melbourne *Herald* would not run ads for it, as they considered the title unseemly. The play was directed by George Whaley, who changed the ads to read: '*You'll Come to Love Your Whale Test* directed by George Spermly'. 'We got marvellous mileage from that', John says smugly. 'We were mad "Milligan anarchic", very anti-war, very anti-something or other.'

He then proudly recounts a Milligan story from about 1973. John had been cast in a Bobby Limb comedic production featuring Spike in one of the skits. Spike was a frequent visitor to the NSW Central Coast, where his mother lived. In his role as 'the journalist' in the comedy, John drove up to Woy Woy, to find Milligan conducting a hunger strike on the steps of the 'town hall', except of course there was no Woy Woy Town Hall, so he had to conduct the protest on the courthouse steps. Spike's 'protest' was because the last bus from Woy Woy to Patonga had been discontinued and Spike couldn't get home after the pub had shut. For some reason, during gaps in the filming of this archetypal Milligan nonsense, John found himself spending some hours in the back seat of a car with Spike while they reminisced about the Melbourne production of *The Bedsitting Room*. What an opportunity to finetune his Milligan anarchism! Although

John does offer that Spike had a terrible hangover, because he'd just returned from meeting up with his old army mates in New Zealand.

I PUT TO HIM THAT HIS POLITICAL IDEOLOGY HAD COME about almost entirely through the arts, and he agrees.

John says, 'When my son, Oliver, was having a demonstration at Penrith High one day, I said to him, "But everything we demonstrated against, we lost." And Oliver came back to me a few days later and said, "But Dad, they didn't bring back conscription, and we haven't had another Vietnam and they haven't hanged anyone else." It was great that he spotted that'.

What were the social issues that were also important? We talk about women and gay people in the acting community, and John believes that those were not high-priority issues in the Australian theatre context – which, compared to the rest of Australian society, was probably true.

So then we ask about Aboriginal activism, and John brings up the story of Jack Charles, the Indigenous actor with the archetypical background of discrimination, forced Assimilation, Stolen Childhood and prison. John also mentions Bob Maza and Gary Foley, and then the plays by Jack Davis and Gerry Bostock. It is a rich vein, but we are running out of time.

As he heads off to find his scooter, we are still immersed in Catholic Melbourne and 'mad Milligan anarchism'.

ROBBIE SWAN
Fun along the way

Meredith Burgmann

I feel a bit icky about interviewing Australia's best-known pornographer – yes, that's how I feel about talking about sex in public – but I needn't have worried. When we ask Robbie Swan to nominate his radicalising influence, he immediately responds 'drugs'. I'm totally relieved, but also a bit surprised, as no other interviewee has mentioned drugs as an important influence. But of course it was bound to be. By the late 1960s, baby boomers were consuming drugs in great quantities – and different sorts of drugs from previous generations, especially LSD and other psychotropics.

The first thing I need to say about Robbie is that he had emailed us earlier in the day, saying, 'I'm not much of a lunch eater, really, and would be much happier just having a cuppa if that's okay'. How the mighty have fallen.

Robbie arrives, cheerful, ebullient and sort of fluffy. I remember now why I had liked him the minute I met him: which was during a friend's quixotic 2016 election campaign for Robbie's amazingly successful Sex Party. Co-founded by Robbie and Victorian MLC Fiona Patten, the Sex Party has morphed into the Reason Party (leaving politically ignorant eighteen-year-old boys around Australia with no one to vote for). Robbie has spent the latter part of his entertaining life as an advocate and defender of adult Australians' right to view non-violent erotica.

ROBBIE WAS BORN IN SYDNEY INTO A HAPPY FAMILY OF four children. He moved to Canberra in 1953 at the age of two. His father was from Queanbeyan and had been a fighter pilot in the Second World War; by the 1950s, he had risen through the public service to become director of the Australian Trade Commission Service.

His mother came from abject poverty in the NSW Hunter region and was a strong Liberal supporter. His father was also a Menzies man and a stalwart Liberal Party supporter well into the 1970s. In fact – and here's the kicker – Robbie was named Robert after Robert Gordon Menzies. He grins with delight. I wonder what that old Tory would have felt about his namesake.

Robbie was the oldest of four: three boys and a girl. After they moved to Canberra he attended Narrabundah High. My memory of Narrabundah at that time was that it was caught between rolling green hills and suburban development – half horse-mad and half faux-bikie gangs.

I am not surprised to discover that Robbie was a bit of a rebel at school. He was voted in as a prefect by the other students, but then the teachers, who had the final say, 'weeded him out' and said no – he was too much of a radical. Even then, he was anti-authoritarian. He explains matter-of-factly that he wanted to react against people who 'would not let him do stuff'.

At high school, Robbie's streak of anti-authoritarianism led him to have various battles. About grooming, for example. He was always very hairy and could grow a beard at twelve (he looks half embarrassed and half proud at this admission), so when long hair was banned he grew his sideburns as long as he could. 'So in 1967 or 1968 I had long sideburns and lime-green socks.' Wow.

We have been talking for some time before I remember to ask him about his family's religious background. It turns out his parents were Church of England, from an Irish Protestant background. I find it very interesting that interviewees from Catholic backgrounds refer to it very early in their reminiscences, but for those with a C of E background it hardly rates. Maybe it's because as a religion it is so much less all-consuming.

Then Robbie mentions something really surprising. He says that his parents 'didn't go to church and they loved pornography'. He was always able to find pornographic books and magazines under his parents' bed. How interesting, these lovers of dear Sir Robert ensconced in leafy Red Hill with their *Canberra Times* and their subversive taste in porn. Then he mentions finding Mary McCarthy's iconic erotic novel *The Group* in the house. This is very different from the experience of some of our other interviewees, who remember having to go out and search for it.

We query Robbie about whether any teachers had been important to him, and at this stage he seems quite surprised to remember that he had as his English teacher Geoff Page, the well-known Australian poet, who taught him about literature in such a way that it resonated. Robbie was introduced to TS Eliot and, he says, 'It opened me up inside'. The three of us then self-indulgently carry on quite a conversation about how TS Eliot was a great conservative, but – as Nadia points out – he was also a modernist. So I assume it was the way in which Eliot put his words together, rather than what he actually said, that would have had an effect on Robbie. Although I've always felt that all that high church Anglicanism 'bells and smells' stuff was tailor-made for druggie culture.

Robbie did his Higher School Certificate in 1968 and matriculated on the strength of his excellent English result. However, before he could start university, a remark from a school friend that there were labourers' jobs up on the Gove Peninsula in the Northern Territory inspired him to fly there. He ended up working at Gove for nine months.

There he met some young American surveyors, who were quite heavily into LSD. He also came across the music of Jimi Hendrix and, as he remembers, 'There was an explosion of creativity'. In this strangely beautiful but dry and isolated land he took LSD and smoked dope. Robbie, as we now know him, was beginning to emerge.

It was the young US surveyors who supplied the acid, and they were very upfront in talking about the Vietnam War. When I ask Robbie, were they draft dodgers, it was as though he'd never really thought about it, but he agreed they may well have been.

These chats with the young Americans represented the first time Robbie had really talked about Vietnam. This was also the first time he had taken drugs. I query whether it was Vietnam that was the flashpoint for his conversion. 'No', he repeats, with that cheeky grin, 'it was drugs'. He adds: 'There was a character called Hamburger Joe from Glebe who brought in the hash. He used to smuggle it up north in the soles of his sandals'.

As Robbie raves about Gove, he struggles for the right word. 'It was *pristine*, Aboriginal people there had never seen a white person, there were beautiful orchids trailing down from the trees and there were pythons. It had never been touched.'

Robbie found the music of the time transformative, and he believes that his radicalisation was cultural and not political. He keeps mentioning Jimi Hendrix, but also the Beatles and Cream. And we talk a little bit about how even the Beatles had a soft-core anti-war message. He describes his time in Gove as a real awakening.

He casually mentions an incident he witnessed when some Aboriginal locals were locked up for being drunk on a Friday night. Robbie started taking photographs of them being detained, shooting three or four rolls of film. He was going to send these down to his friend Jack Waterford, who was a cadet at the *Canberra Times*, but security guys from the company he was working for saw him taking the photographs and all of his film was confiscated.

Security then searched Robbie's living quarters, a demountable 'donga', presumably trying to find subversive material, and he was expelled from Gove for having taken the photographs. Robbie says that this did not have any real effect on him, as he'd already decided he wanted to move on. He wanted to buy a big bike and take off, because *Easy Rider* had just hit the movie screens. The young Robbie was predictable.

He was ready for another adventure. But there was always this niggle at the back of his mind about the war. The young American guys had said to him, 'You'll have to go to war or go to gaol'.

Fun along the way

RETURNING TO CANBERRA IN 1970, ROBBIE STARTED A creative writing course at the Canberra College of Advanced Education. One of the students he befriended was (later children's book author) Morris Gleitzman, who he says was 'switched on but didn't do drugs'. But Robbie was obviously very friendly with him.

While at the CAE, he felt a little bit of an outsider. The other students were committed to doing the course and really wanted to become serious writers – whereas Robbie saw the college more as a place where he could sell drugs.

Robbie has written about this stage of his life in an essay, 'Riders on the Storm'. He describes his 'annus criminalus':

> I'd never consciously broken a law before in my life.
> Like most young teenage boys, I'd raided the parent's
> booze cabinet and ridden my noisy BSA 'Bantam'
> without a license. But not until the Autumn of 1970,
> had I ever thought about purposefully breaking a law.

The politics of the war were such that all the students he was mixing with were caught up in it. The draft was looming large for all young men, and Robbie's marble was to be included in the lottery of September 1971. He didn't register – and made it clear that he was not registering. 'I had already decided that this war was nothing like the world wars of the European dictators that my father and grandfather had fought in.'

This created some havoc at home. His mother never said anything about the war, but Robbie tells us he knew she didn't want him to go. Like mothers the world over, she just wanted him not to be killed. However, his father, a Second World War veteran, and his grandfather, a First World War vet who had been in the Imperial Camel Corps in Palestine, saw this as cowardice, and thought that Robbie was not prepared to fight for his country. This led to arguments. Though 'there was no smashing of plates', life at home became strained. As it happened, his marble was not drawn.

Leaving home seemed like an inevitable next step. Robbie's lifestyle was simply too 'out there' for his conservative parents. He admits that he sometimes used to wear a dress home after a night out on the town. He also adds, almost as an afterthought, that at this stage he 'had a couple of male lovers'.

Robbie does concede that he might have been doing all of this a bit on purpose to test his parents. He says this behaviour infuriated his father.

Nadia asks whether his father was worried about Communists taking over the country, and whether he ever made those sorts of arguments. Robbie says it was true for his father, but not for his mother. He says, 'Dad was part of the establishment at that point, and the same for Grandfather'. We ask him about his closest brother, and he says, 'Col was supportive of me, but he had started a trade, smoked a joint or two, but never took acid'.

The small campus of the Canberra CAE was out at Belconnen, the Canberra equivalent of being sent to the gulag, and after some months Robbie moved to the more centrally located Australian National University. As he explains, he wasn't attending ANU, he was just squatting in Lennox House, one of the university halls. But moving into the centre of town where ANU was situated was 'better to sell drugs'. At this time, Robbie says, there were three or four major dealers at the university. He became a grower for the drug trade.

Fun along the way

Robbie has written about this part of his life.

I lived off campus between a group house in O'Connor and occasionally with a girlfriend at Canning Street in Ainslie. This house was better known at the time as 'Ho Chi Minh House'. It was a staging post for student radicals in Canberra in 1971, and a haven for draft dodgers. It had a flagpole in the front yard and a granny flat underneath ... The North Vietnamese flag was often hoisted up the flagpole and collection plates were frequently passed around to raise funds for the North Vietnamese freedom fighters. The house was also home to a number of radical feminists, and was the birthplace of the Women's Electoral Lobby.

There were political meetings in this house almost every day, and on one occasion housemate Jack Waterford said, 'You'll never make a revolutionary, because real revolutionaries don't take drugs'. Robbie describes Jack as 'the guy with the microphone, he was capable and politically astute'. This memory of what Jack said to him seems to be seared into his brain. Robbie recalls that the Trotskyists and Maoists in the various share houses were happy to smoke dope and drink, but they were not into the hallucinogens. He thinks that Jack was wrong and that 'a lot of those guys would have done better if they'd taken a few serious pills'. As he says, 'you've got to have a bit of fun along the way'. He saw taking drugs, particularly the hallucinogens, as a really revolutionary thing to do.

For Robbie, politics was not the prime motivator – it was 'consciousness' that was the important element. He saw psychotropic drugs as the lever to push consciousness into action. He says that when you took these drugs, you saw patterns emerge.

Recent research has in fact described this process. The LSD affects the thalamus, the part of the brain that filters information to the cerebral cortex, the highly developed area handling sensory awareness. LSD opens this filter and the cortex gets hit with 'cognitive overload', which causes strong visual hallucinations and distorted or imaginary sights and sounds.

When he talks about drugs such as mescaline, Robbie describes how Picasso (who took this drug) saw something in the patterns ... 'you just see things differently'. He says with a sense of urgency that good revolutionaries need to see things differently.

Nadia asks him if he has read Castaneda. I feel a bit ignorant here, but the name rings a bell through the mists of time, so I google him. Carlos Castaneda was an American anthropologist, who was inspired to write about shamanism after living for a time among the descendants of the Toltec peoples of Mexico. He encouraged American youth to have 'awareness of energies, beings, and worlds which lie outside the perceptual paradigm of the vast majority of human beings on this planet'. Well, there you have it.

Robbie says yes, that he found Castaneda was pretty important. However, he also experienced this change of consciousness through TS Eliot's poetry. Some trip!

At this time, he and up to half-a-dozen carloads of 'heads' would drive out into the pine forests around Canberra with high-quality LSD and spend the day reading from spiritual texts, playing music and making love. LSD had only been added to the illegal drug schedule a few years before. The demonising of this 'sacrament' was strongly resented, and taking it was seen not only as a genuine spiritual activity, but also as a 'form of protest at the state's interference in our lives'.

Robbie then segues to the iconic Canberra Aquarius Arts Festival of 1971. This was the third of the student-organised flower-power rock festivals that became known as Australia's Woodstock, and which culminated at Nimbin in New South Wales in 1973. He describes it in 'Riders on the Storm' as 'an event I thought might really change things in Australia'.

> The first Aquarius Arts Festival at the Australian National University, was an inspired blend of rock and roll, academia and student politics. After a few days of sex, drugs and rock and roll, we all began to believe our own rhetoric. Things were changing. The arts festival had started to infect ordinary people like bank tellers and bus drivers, who seemed to show genuine interest in what was happening on campus.
>
> Bands such as Daddy Cool and Spectrum played in a big marquee erected outside the Chifley Library. Thousands arrived from interstate and the University surrounds were filled with curious students, hippies and onlookers. On the third day, as students were lounging around on the lawns outside the library, 'smoking pot and digging the music', a large number of riot police arrived in full SWAT gear.
>
> They waded into the crowds, bashing and batting people with truncheons and shields. People ran screaming, with blood flowing through their long hair and beards, with the police giving chase. Many of the most badly

> beaten appeared to be women. The police arrested
> over a hundred people that day on the most spurious
> of charges. I was numb with fear and rage. With the
> US Kent State University shootings (May 1970) still
> fresh in my memory, I joined a large group of students
> who looked like they knew what they were doing. We
> barricaded ourselves in the old union building and drew
> up plans for the next day, the *Day of Rage*. I remember
> sleeping in the downstairs music room that night, which
> just happened to be the place to transact psychedelic
> business on campus. It was a broken sleep to say the
> least. The next day, was the *Day of Rage*.

Being reminded of these incidents, I suddenly remember that I too was arrested at that brutal event known as the Day of Rage. It also becomes clear to me that I must have driven down to Canberra from Sydney on hearing of the arrests and bashings the day before. I've often wondered why I ended up in Canberra.

In his essay, Robbie ponders the Aquarius Festival.

> Who ordered this brutal action and why? This was never
> explained. The sense of utter betrayal stayed with me
> like a terrible nightmare. These people were employed to
> protect us, not to attack us. It was totally unprovoked
> and unjustified. The sense of outrage that I felt from that
> day on began to dominate the major decisions of my life.

Robbie wasn't the only person to be radicalised that day. He remembers a young Commonwealth Police officer who took the microphone on the grassy slopes to the east of the Union building and addressed the crowd.

Fun along the way

> He flung off his hat and coat and publicly resigned from
> the police force in protest at the events of the last few
> days. In front of a cheering and adoring crowd he vowed
> to fight in future for freedom and against oppression.

IN 'RIDERS ON THE STORM', ROBBIE MOVES ON TO DESCRIBE the 1971 campaign against the South African Springboks' disastrous tour of Australia. In July they played a match at Manuka Oval in Canberra. But once again, politics and the Beat generation collided.

> It was a transparent attempt by the racist regime to
> make them look like good sporting citizens and I would
> have none of it. I joined a protest group at the university
> and plans were drawn up to disrupt the Canberra
> game. And then – the unthinkable! Jim Morrison, lead
> singer of The Doors, beat poet and hip philosopher to
> a generation, was found dead in a bathtub in France.
> We were gutted. How could he do this on the eve of the
> Springbok tour?

Before the Day of Rage, did Robbie think of police as benign beings? His description of his first serious run-in with the coercive forces of the state is telling. In late 1971, Robbie was living in an old rented farmhouse in the Brindabella Valley:

> A surfing mate of mine arrived from Broulee on the
> south coast for a visit. He'd brought some new mescaline
> from California with him, and we took it together
> while we harvested peas and lettuce from the garden.

> I asked him if he'd like to see a crop of marijuana, which of course he did. I picked up a .22 rifle in case I saw a rabbit for the dog, and together we walked up to the crop. On arrival, we started watering it with buckets until three large and uncoordinated men blundered into the clearing from upstream. As the first one stopped upon seeing us, his two colleagues ran into him from behind. I recognised them instantly as police. Panic and laughter at their slapstick entry both invaded my consciousness. They ordered me to put the rifle down, which I promptly did. In my spun out state I remember thinking at the time that one bloke was a dead ringer for Robert Plant from Led Zeppelin.

The police kept asking him about his 'Italian mates' and were convinced that somehow the young druggie students were tied up with the so-called Italian mafia in Griffith, in southern New South Wales.

Robbie was arrested, charged with growing 600 marijuana plants and thrown into the Queanbeyan watch house.

> My cell mate was an old drunk who'd been picked up at the Royal Hotel earlier in the day. Being still under the considerable effect of high quality Californian mescaline, the whole episode was surreal to say the least.

We ask him, was he scared about facing a probable long prison sentence? He replies with a grin that he was still tripping for a couple of weeks on the mescaline, and it didn't really sink in. He talks sadly, however, about his mate who was charged with him – even though he was found not guilty, he later suicided. Robbie doesn't seem to want this pushed further, so we don't.

His parents rallied around and were supportive. 'They took the position of putting one foot in front of the other.' His mother used to pull the curtains so that people couldn't see that they were home. But, of course, they lost friends. Robbie is reflective: 'My parents were amazing'. This reminds me sharply of my mother's reaction to my own arrests, and the fact that she was receiving poison-pen letters while I remained pretty unscathed as a result of my political activity.

Nadia pulls Robbie back to the central question. Were these changes to his views – brought about by conscription, police aggression, drugs and the times – profound and long-lasting? Were they life-changing?

Robbie agrees that his sense of outrage was strong. Seeing it all up close, he understood how society was beginning to break down and how things had to change. He says that it all pushed him towards meditation and an understanding that 'there needed to be societal change, not politics as the be-all-and-end-all. People had to change their attitudes'. He goes on to say that he became 'more into the spiritual side of things'.

This is where Robbie totally loses me. I have always suspected that I was the least spiritual person in our cohort. I was an activist and never one for meditation. However, perhaps as a result of the drugs – Robbie certainly seems to think that they were important – he became involved with transcendental meditation.

In this new, more self-focused period of his life, he met an Australian academic, Dr John Price, 'an Einstein figure, but gentle', who in order to teach Robbie about transcendental meditation told him that he wasn't allowed to smoke pot for fifteen days. When we ask if he did this, Robbie is honest enough to confess that he stopped for about three days. However, he rather defiantly maintains that, overall, what he learnt about transcendental meditation 'had a real effect' on his life.

He then reveals that he taught his father to meditate. He says that his father 'changed his view on the Vietnam War and on Robert Menzies in about 1974' and even apologised to Robbie. His father had been treasurer of the RSL at Manuka and had observed the Vietnam vets who came back shattered – like the veterans of the First World War.

In 1971, as part of Robbie's journey towards things of the mind, he met in Canberra an old Polish mystic, Dr Kasimir Zakswiez, the head of the Rosicrucian Order in Australia, who 'looked like the first Doctor Who, tall with hair flying away and with a long droopy scarf'. Robbie's mentor John Price gave him the money to travel to Seelisberg in Switzerland, where he worked at an ashram teaching meditation for four or five years. Robbie says that he still meditates and does yoga every day. However, the quiet life was not for him, and eventually he and the Swiss group parted ways. He had begun writing political articles for *Penthouse* and *Playboy*, so the transcendental meditation movement threw him out.

Finally, I ask the biggie. How did he become involved with the adult entertainment industry? Was this the result of his experiences in the 1960s and 1970s?

Robbie's reply is quite matter of fact. He was propelled into the defence of the pornography business in the late 1980s, when Attorney-General Lionel Bowen tried to bring in an X rating for films. Robbie was working as a journalist at the time and was approached by the pornography industry to defend them. He regarded it as a freedom of speech issue, because in the pornographic films that he was defending, 'there were no illegal acts. And I simply couldn't see why pictures of legal acts could in fact be outlawed'. Strangely, he makes a lot of sense.

We seem to have come full circle, and I now know a lot more about drugs, transcendental meditation and even spirituality than I did before we started. Strangely, not much more about the sex business – thank goodness.

As Robbie wanders off down the street towards Gleebooks, I wonder what Sir Robert would make of his druggie Sex Party namesake.

JOZEFA SOBSKI
Opening doors to other worlds

Nadia Wheatley

In the early 1970s, Glebe Point Road was a very different place from today's trendy strip. Although hundreds of Sydney University students (myself among them) walked along the road every day on the way to their cockroach-infested share houses, there wasn't a bookshop or a cafe to be seen, and many of the shops were empty. Number 67, however, was different. Beyond a shopfront window draped with dusty red hessian curtains (left over from an earlier incarnation as the premises of the Labor Club), the front room was the meeting room of Women's Liberation. Although I used to go on Women's Liberation marches, and I read the local feminist publications *Mejane* and *Refractory Girl*, the women at the organisation's Sydney headquarters seemed so intimidating that, after a single venture inside, I was too scared ever to go back. If I'd done so, I would surely have met Jozefa Sobski.

When I ask Jozefa what she was like as a little girl, she replies, 'Bossy and confident'. At this, she laughs her enormous laugh, which always seems surprisingly big to have come from someone with such a tiny frame.

Bossy and confident was how everyone at 67 Glebe Point Road seemed to me, but Jozefa had needed more than that to get there. While the members of Women's Liberation were often typified as being privileged Anglo-Australians, Jozefa's parents had come to Australia as refugees in the aftermath of the Second World War. Jozefa herself spent the first nine years of her life in a succession of migrant hostels, and she didn't speak English until she went to school.

THE MEMORIAL LEAFLET THAT JOZEFA PRODUCED IN 2016 on the occasion of her mother's funeral includes a poignant wedding photograph of a very serious-looking young couple. The 22-year-old bride wears what seems to be a traditional white gown, but it was actually made from a lace curtain. The groom's coat conceals the fact that his 'shirt' is really only a collar. The newlyweds were part of a job lot of half a dozen couples married in January 1946 in a Catholic wedding ceremony held at a Displaced Persons camp in Germany.

Maria Kazimierska and Wojciech Sobski were Polish citizens – the former of Ukrainian heritage and the latter of Polish heritage. When the Second World War broke out, their families' villages were occupied in turn by the Russians and the Germans. Maria left an unhappy home for a job on a dairy farm in Germany when she was only eighteen. At around the age of sixteen, Wojciech was captured and imprisoned by Russians; after making his escape, he was captured by Germans and transported to the Third Reich as a *Zwangsarbeiter* (forced labourer).

'They were both captives, really', Jozefa says. She goes on to relate the romantic story of their first meeting. 'They just happened to be on adjoining farms. And my father had this wonderful baritone voice – he'd sing all these Ukrainian and Polish folk songs and hymns, he loved singing. My mother also loved to sing, and had been in a church choir – singing was almost her favourite thing. And so, one day she heard him singing, and that's how they met.'

From then until the war's end, the two teenagers spent their one free day a month together. After the Allied victory, thousands of Poles were repatriated, but neither Maria nor Wojciech wished to return to their homeland, which was now a part of the Soviet Union. On Maria's part, there was no attachment to what had been a complicated and miserable family situation. Wojciech did not want to live under Communism. As well, he believed his family to be dead. With no home or employment prospects in Germany, the couple lived in a succession of Displaced Persons camps until Australia's post-war immigration scheme offered a chance of a new life. By the time they boarded the migrant ship in October 1948, Maria was pregnant, but she had to conceal the fact or she would have been refused transport.

Arriving at Sydney's Circular Quay, the Sobskis were given a sandwich and a banana, and were then sent on a steam train to Bathurst Migrant Reception and Training Centre, where their first daughter was born. Called Bronia (short for her middle name, Bronislawa) by her parents, she would come to use her first name, Jozefa, for her 'Australian life'.

Within a short time, Wojciech Sobski was obliged to leave his wife and child, in order to begin two years of indentured labour for Sydney's Metropolitan Water Sewerage and

Drainage Board. Maria and baby Bronia were later moved to migrant camps at Nelson Bay (where another daughter, Janina, was born) and Greta, in the Hunter Valley. After a separation of five years, the family was finally reunited in 1953, when Wojciech – by then an overseer for the Water Board – managed to find a place for them in Villawood Migrant Hostel, in Sydney's south-west. The family home there was half a Nissen hut, partitioned into three rooms. There was a communal ablutions and laundry block and a communal kitchen, where Maria worked from 4 am, making breakfast for shifts of workers and school students.

Jozefa, now about four years old, joined the cohort of 150 or so children of pre-school age, who 'all played together, irrespective of the language they spoke' and 'got up to all sorts of pranks'. A weekly class run by an order of Polish-American nuns was provided for the migrant centre's Polish children. Jozefa really enjoyed this first introduction to education, and remembers that they learnt the alphabet. One of the nuns was 'so lovely' that Jozefa used to follow her around, 'like a little lamb' trailing after its mother.

For Poles like the Sobskis, Catholicism was as much a cultural as a religious force; it was a link with the homeland. When it was time for school, Jozefa was enrolled at St Patrick's, Guildford, run by the order of Josephite nuns known as the 'Brown Joeys'. Like most Catholic systemic schools of the era, St Pat's was so crowded that classes had a hundred or more children crammed into a dilapidated room, with a single nun (probably with no teaching qualifications) in charge. Girls and boys were taught together until the end of third class, at which time the boys were siphoned off to a different school. Although the children from Villawood were called 'camp kids' by the other students, it helped that they weren't alone. Jozefa was one of a group of five children, united by the fact that none of them understood English.

Despite the initial language difficulty, she 'became good at school quite quickly'. As well as being bossy and self-confident, she was articulate.

'And I loved school', she declares. 'I just loved it. I loved the learning, I loved the interaction with other kids. The nuns weren't always benign, they were pretty strict disciplinarians, there was a lot of caning that went on, but I remember most of the nuns quite fondly. There were some very good women there.'

In 1957, when Jozefa was nine, her parents' third daughter, Jadwiga, was born. The next year, the family moved to Miowera Road, a short walk from the migrant hostel, where Jozefa's father had bought a block of land and built a two-bedroom brick-veneer house. In this area, where most of the dwellings belonged to the Housing Commission, the 'Australians resented migrants for building their own homes'.

'There was a strong initial resentment against everybody who moved into the community from the hostel', Jozefa recalls. 'The kids sat on fences and called us names – such as "dagoes" and "camp kids" – and they used to set on us. And my mother too would be harassed by the kids.'

Despite the racism of their neighbours, in that same year, Maria and Wojciech Sobski celebrated their new status as home-owners by becoming Australian citizens. But a certificate could not bestow a sense of belonging. In an email she sent to me, Jozefa wrote of her parents:

> No matter how long they were here, their love of the
> country where they spent their childhoods never left

them. Part of their heart was always elsewhere yearning. There was always a sense of something lost.

At Miowera Road, the Sobskis' community continued to include many people from the migrant camp, who came to their house for parties.

'Did your parents and their friends talk about their experiences during the war and in the DP camps?' I ask.

'*Endlessly!*' Jozefa groans. 'They talked about the war endlessly and they talked endlessly about Communism as an evil, because the fact that Poland was Communist, Ukraine was Communist, meant they could never go back home to visit.'

Jozefa's mother wasn't interested in Australian politics, but her father transferred the politics of his homeland to his new country. Although he was grateful to Labor leader Arthur Calwell for inaugurating Australia's post-war immigration scheme, Wojciech Sobski gave his political allegiance to Robert Menzies, whom he regarded as 'a wonderful godlike figure'. Jozefa adds: 'My father was Liberal, through and through'.

This wasn't the only difference between Jozefa's parents. An autodidact who loved to read – history books, especially – Wojciech was better educated than his wife, who'd had to leave her village school at the age of twelve. Jozefa could see the long-term effect that this educational disadvantage had, even within the home: 'My mother didn't have any of the knowledge that would give her strength and empower her to be able to enter an argument with my father. She had to argue from quite a different point of view, or she was silenced, and then she would just withdraw'.

Like many of the war-damaged men who arrived in the

migrant camps, Wojciech sometimes took refuge in alcohol. But although his anger was 'so ferocious it would frighten the shit out of us', he was never physically violent to his family, 'apart from the spankings that were then commonplace'.

While Wojciech was the 'dominant personality' in the household, Jozefa describes Maria as 'the best of mothers', with whom 'you always felt safe'. She 'had social strengths. She made friends easily, loved to dance, to sing. She was the best of homemakers'.

Jozefa shares many of these same strengths. In an email inviting me to her house for lunch – this was before we had actually met in person – Jozefa wrote, 'I enjoy entertaining. Inherited from my dear mother who loved cooking for others'. And in the photographs in Maria's memorial leaflet, I can see her eldest daughter in Maria Sobski's wide cheekbones and broad smile.

JOZEFA'S STORY IS ONE OF EDUCATION, SO IT IS NEAT THAT in 1962, when she went into secondary school, she was one of the 'guinea pigs' in the first year of the new Wyndham Scheme of education, which replaced five years of secondary schooling with six. Schools across New South Wales were suddenly faced with the need for more buildings and more teachers; in this time before State Aid to non-government schools, the poorer Catholic schools particularly struggled. Jozefa stayed at St Pat's for her first year of high school, then moved to Holy Trinity, Granville, also run by the Josephites.

Meanwhile, Catholicism was changing under the influence of Pope John XXIII. Jozefa remembers that 'Vatican II had a huge impact on me, as a believer. The church was opening up, reforming'. A particular and 'quite profound' influence on her was a Czech priest, Father Mika, who had embraced the new liberation theology. He and Jozefa 'spent a lot of time talking about the implications of Vatican II, and how the Church needed to reach out to people and stop simply hounding them as sinners, and taking money from them'. Jozefa describes herself at that time as 'a devout church-goer, a very devout Catholic'. Indeed, she was so pious that Father Mika told her she was 'too serious a Catholic'. And when she was in third-year high school, one of the nuns, believing Jozefa 'would never lose her faith', recommended she sit for a bursary and switch to Birrong Girls' High, which would provide more opportunities than her Catholic school could offer.

Jozefa passed the exam with flying colours, and made the move. She believes that, if she hadn't got the bursary, she would have left school at the age of fifteen, as most of the other girls in her peer group did. Even with the little bit of extra money, her parents found it difficult to pay for uniforms and textbooks, as well as the upkeep of a daughter who could have been at work and contributing to the family income. But her father, who valued education, supported her ambition.

At the state high school, Jozefa met girls from a different social class. She laughs: 'Some even did their debut!' Dressing up in a long white frock and being presented to a local dignitary was not one of Jozefa Sobski's ambitions. Already, she was 'aspiring to *do* something'. She explains: 'I wanted to make a contribution. I don't know where that came from, but I think it came partly from the Catholicism, the talk of missions'. Another powerful influence was 'all the saint books' – the little hagiographies of women saints that had been the only books available in the St Pat's library. Although these stories were didactic in purpose, they provided models of empowered girls and women, who often stood up to their fathers and refused to marry. Jozefa, too, 'didn't want to get married'.

'I already knew that. I didn't know why – I don't know whether it was because of my mother's experience, or my observation of how women were treated.

'I already had a sense of women's rights, and I don't know where that came from, except I remember an English teacher at Birrong Girls' High saying to me, "Oh, you're a bit of a feminist."

'And I thought *Oh, gosh*, and I had to look that up because I hadn't any idea what that was. And then I thought, "Yes, I am. I probably am." At first I'd thought it was something bad.'

SINCE THE TIME OF HER CHILDHOOD ADORATION OF THE Polish nun, Jozefa had been aware of feeling attracted to women. At Birrong Girls' High, she met someone who reciprocated her feelings. Although 'the sexual element was almost non-existent', this was nevertheless a 'deeply passionate and fulfilling relationship' that continued through Jozefa's final two years of schooling.

At the end of 1967, Jozefa – now aged eighteen – sat for the first-ever Higher School Certificate (HSC) examinations. Once school was over, her friend wanted Jozefa to live with her. Not wishing to be 'trapped', Jozefa broke off the attachment.

Soon afterwards, she went to Confession at a church where she wasn't known, and told the priest about the relationship she had been in. As she left the confession booth that day, she thought, *What does this mean?* Jozefa explains: 'I didn't feel I could say three Hail Marys and it would all go away, because [the experience] was now part of my life'.

With Confession playing such a central role in the religion in which Jozefa had been raised, this realisation undermined her Catholicism. But the culture of the Church was so ingrained that it couldn't easily be shaken off.

When I raise this incident with Jozefa in a follow-up to our first interview, she explains that while it represented the emotional rejection of her faith, the intellectual rejection would take longer. The final marker on this journey came four years later, when Jozefa decided not to go to Confession after having an abortion.

'So those two events in my personal life really tore me away from the Church – not because I had transgressed, but *because I didn't feel guilty* about either of them.' To make this completely clear, Jozefa repeats: 'I should have felt guilt and I should have felt regret and I should have sought forgiveness, I should have bent my knee to God, but I didn't'.

Jozefa's trajectory was very different from that of many Catholics, who recoil from the Church because they can't bear the burden of guilt. Jozefa's issue was that she could not see herself as having committed a mortal sin.

'Once I'd done the Confession, I thought to myself, "Why would God condemn this?" and I decided "*He*" wouldn't.' Jozefa laughs uproariously, as if at her young self who had even imagined God as a male being.

Jozefa Sobski

IN THE HSC EXAMS, JOZEFA HAD DONE SO WELL THAT SHE gained both a Commonwealth Scholarship (covering only university fees) and a Teachers' College Scholarship, which provided a living allowance as well, but bonded the recipient to work for the Department of Education for a number of years after graduation. For Jozefa, the choice was clear. Her father had been questioning why she needed to go on to university but, once she was able to pay her own way, he even converted the garage into a bedroom and study for her. To save money, she would continue to live in this 'refuge' until she was twenty-seven.

Choosing the University of New South Wales because it allowed her to combine science with her favourite subject, English literature, she arrived there in the crucible year of 1968. Already, UNSW students were protesting on campus against the authoritarian structures of the university, and were joining other students on the city streets in demonstrations against conscription and the Vietnam War. For Jozefa, it was enough during this first year to take in the sudden expansion of her world through both the diversity of the other students she was meeting, and through the literature on the syllabus.

Her first-year results in English gave Jozefa entry to the honours course, and the other dozen or so honours students would become her core group of university friends. In her second year, Jozefa 'got involved in quite a revolt' when radical tutors and students took on the conservative head of department and demanded the inclusion of contemporary Australian and American literature in the course. Jozefa herself was enjoying the traditional course, but she supported the campaign on principle: 'I have always felt that citizens have to be empowered to impact on the system or the society if it is impacting on their lives in an adverse way'. Although 'the battle was not won', radicalisation in one area flowed into another. Through the history she was studying, Jozefa developed 'a totally different perspective on the Vietnam War'. This was different indeed from the fear and loathing of Communism that had been part of her upbringing.

In 1971, while Jozefa was doing her final honours year in English, one of her tutors gave her a copy of *The Female Eunuch* (first published twelve months earlier). This book changed the mindset of a lot of women, but for 22-year-old Jozefa, it was a complete revelation. While Germaine Greer's analysis led her 'suddenly to realise that the world was a patriarchal place run by men, to serve their interests, and women were the handmaidens', it was as if she saw this paradigm played out every evening when she went home to Villawood.

'I suddenly saw my mother in such a different light. And while in the past I wouldn't have, I now sprang to her defence on so many occasions with my father, because I felt he'd had the best of her. She had given her life for him and he took her for granted.

'Suddenly the whole world looked different to me – and I realised why I sometimes got so angry. And [*The Female Eunuch*] also assured me that my anger was justified.'

Although Jozefa again laughs as she says that, she goes on to describe how, when she and her father were arguing, 'sometimes the lights would shake with the thunder of our voices'.

But the battle wasn't only over women's rights. Wojciech Sobski could see that his daughter 'had shifted politically on so many issues'.

Jozefa recalls: 'I was starting to talk positively about

Communism, which was anathema to him. He thought I was being *ruined* by university'.

Finally there came a point where Jozefa realised, 'I'm not going to change his mind, and he's not going to change mine'. And the two combatants agreed 'to move to our respective camps and shut up, because it just distressed the rest of the family'.

At the end of that final year, Jozefa's results would have enabled her to continue academic study, but her scholarship obliged her to do a Diploma of Education. In this new course, one of her tutors was Daniela Torsh (then known as Dany Humphreys), a 26-year-old feminist, whose tutorials provided a critical analysis of sexism both in the school curriculum and in the way schools were administered. This was another eye-opener, after which Jozefa 'didn't look back'.

IT WAS EARLY IN THIS SAME YEAR OF 1972 THAT JOZEFA found her way to the Glebe headquarters of Women's Liberation.

'*You* were terrified?' she demands when Meredith and I both say how scared we were of the women there. 'You think *I* wasn't terrified?'

But unlike us, Jozefa kept going back.

She carefully draws a distinction between what she saw as the political side of Women's Liberation and her own personal liberation as a lesbian. Although she'd had a few heterosexual relationships at university, by now she was 'settled' in her sexual identity. However, she 'didn't want the personal to intrude on the political to such a degree that it distorted what I really cared about and what I wanted to do'.

In May 1972, when the Glebe premises became the meeting place of a radical lesbian group, Jozefa made the move to the new Women's Liberation headquarters at 25 Alberta Street, Surry Hills. There, her 'volunteer duty' meant hours of secretarial work – 'opening letters, responding to letters, sending material out, contributing to the newsletter, putting that together, mailing it out'.

But though the headquarters of Women's Liberation had shifted, a lot of the movement's radical activism remained in Glebe, notably at the Derwent Street home of septuagenarian feminist Bessie Guthrie, whose parlour became the workplace of the *Mejane* collective, which Jozefa joined for the last two issues of the newspaper.

In a talk given at a 2019 seminar about Radical Glebe, Jozefa spoke warmly about Bessie, and the campaign for reform of the penal provisions of the child welfare system that she had run for many years. Jozefa recalled joining a rally at the Parramatta Girls' Home in December 1973, and another at Bidura Girls' Shelter on International Women's Day in March 1974 – both rallies inspired by Bessie Guthrie.

Again in March 1974, there was 'the glorious sunny morning' when Jozefa and other members of the *Mejane* collective 'went to Westmoreland Street where a group of women led by Anne Summers was preparing to break down the door of one of the vacant houses in the Glebe Estate'. The house, which had the sweet old-fashioned name of Elsie, was part of the area that the Whitlam government had purchased from the Church of England in 1970, with the idea of converting it to public housing. After Anne's efforts with a hammer failed, an unlocked window was discovered. Climbing in, the women proceeded to establish Elsie Women's

Refuge. 'It was the start of the women's refuge movement and eventual government funding', Jozefa points out.

Another campaign was directed against the discriminatory ban on women drinking in public bars. In early 1973, Jozefa and fifteen other women went across the harbour to Manly, where there was a hotel that was known for refusing to serve women.

'Off we went', she recalls, 'no plan, no fall-back position, no nothing. We all walked into the public bar, and they refused to serve us. They said, "There's another place for ladies out the back."'

After 'the most god-awful verbal brawl', the women moved down the road to another pub, where the proprietor, warned by his colleague, had called the police before they arrived. Quickly the whole thing degenerated into 'a circus'. Unable to get the sixteen protestors into a single police car, the police walked the women to the cop shop, where the officer at the desk asked: 'Who wants to be arrested?' Four volunteers were duly lumbered, but the case was eventually thrown out of court.

HAVING COMPLETED HER TEACHING COURSE AT THE END of 1972, when the new school year began the 23-year-old novice was appointed to Lurnea High School, where she was tossed headlong into the most difficult General Ability (GA) class.

Although Lurnea was in the same south-western area of Sydney where Jozefa herself lived, she encountered there a completely unfamiliar kind of economic and social disadvantage. Many of the school's 1300 students were 'damaged kids', the product of 'damaged parents'. A number were second-generation Australians of Italian and Maltese backgrounds, but whereas the migrant kids with whom Jozefa had grown up were keen to get an education, these students 'were totally off the rails and very unhappy'. To this turbulent mix was added a tyrannical male principal, a male deputy who was ex air force, and a staffroom dominated by a right-wing Catholic maths master.

Fortunately, there was 'a small feminist enclave' of teachers in the school, who helped Jozefa learn how to manage a classroom. But the kids weren't the only challenge. One day, the young teacher arrived at work to find that an anti-abortion petition had been put on top of the staff sign-in book. When Jozefa brought in a pro-abortion petition the following day, she 'got into a whole heap of trouble'. Her introduction to the trade union movement came when the Teachers' Federation supported her over her stand. Unionism was a crucial piece in Jozefa's personal political jigsaw.

While most students at Lurnea faced problems of economic disadvantage, Jozefa was acutely aware of the particular lack of opportunities suffered by the girls in the school. Looking back to this time, she recalls, 'There was no way I wasn't going to be an activist around the issues of education and girls'. While she gives credit for this to the influence both of the women's movement and Daniela Torsh's seminars, I think there was also the lasting effect of having gone to all-girls schools from middle primary onwards. In her own education, Jozefa had not had to battle sexism in the classroom.

By now, Sydney Women's Liberation was so strong that the organisation was forming specialist groups in a number of key areas. Along with Joan Bielski, Wendy McCarthy and other activists, Jozefa was a member of the inaugural group calling itself NSW Women in Education. Making common cause with activists in the Teachers' Federation, such as Jennie George and Cathy Bloch, the group lobbied government about the need for special support for the education of girls, and they opened a resource centre that teachers could go to for non-sexist classroom materials. The network that was established during a national conference on curriculum development, held in Melbourne in 1975, resulted in state groups being formed across the country. This was the basis for the Australian Women's Education Coalition, which for over a decade produced the newsletter, *Bluestocking*.

In 1978, Jozefa left the classroom for a job in a new unit set up in the state Ministry of Education, under the Wran Labor government. From this time, almost until her retirement in 2003, Jozefa Sobski's professional life was devoted to furthering education for girls and women.

When I ask her about the long-term effect of her political commitment and activity in the Sixties, her answer is unequivocal: 'Well, it defined me really. It defined me. It defined all the directions I have taken'.

Jozefa goes on to explain: '"Career" was not even a word in my vocabulary. You did work, and you tried to do the kind of work that would make a contribution. So teaching was the starting point for me. And then I went into the Social Development Unit of the Ministry of Education, because that was going to change policy around girls' schooling. I went from there to TAFE because it offered all sorts of opportunities for meeting the needs of mature age women who had missed out on getting a further education'.

She concludes by reiterating that the radicalism formed in the Sixties has 'defined' her. 'Every step I have taken.'

But again I think the forces that shaped Jozefa's choices run deeper than the feminist activism she encountered at university and in Women's Liberation. In shrugging off many of the common attractions of a 'career' (such as salary, security, and social mobility) she follows the lead of her father, who saw commitment to public service as the proper human goal. Just as Wojciech Sobski worked for the Water Board throughout his life, to repay the country that provided a new home, for Jozefa as well there is a circle of reciprocity and responsibility. She explains: 'Education gave you the key to open doors to other worlds and to help you to become more socially mobile. And then in turn to give back to society'. In her commitment to working for others, there is also the influence of the Catholic sense of mission, and the example of vocation given by the nuns who taught her.

But as well, and crucially, there is the influence of her mother. While Wojciech Sobski, with his dominant personality, grabbed the spotlight in the family, it is Maria, whose education only went to sixth class, who really brought home to Jozefa the importance of education for girls.

PETER MANNING
Taking a stand

Nadia Wheatley

In November 1956, as Soviet tanks were poised for the invasion of Hungary, a Christian Brother in a Sydney primary school gave his students a terrifying demonstration of the fate that Hungary's Cardinal Mindszenty might endure if Communists took over his country. After placing his hands around his throat and pretending to strangle himself, the teacher urged the boys to pray for the anti-Communist cardinal. One child did more than pray. His imagination stirred by this performance, he 'sprang into action' and wrote a letter to his father's favourite newspaper, the *Daily Telegraph*, denouncing the Soviet invasion. When this was duly published under 'Peter Manning, Bondi, aged 11', Peter's father was proud, and the staff at Waverley College were impressed to see one of their students 'standing up for Catholics and the Church'. Peter reflects, 'I'd put my flag into the ground and said, "Here I stand", and that was seen as admirable'.

Taking a stand

This is a cute story about a boy who was a kind of anti-Communist prodigy, but the way Peter followed this up – without any prompting from his teachers – is the mark of the journalist he would later become. 'Intrigued by these Communists' that he kept hearing about at school, the boy 'wanted to understand more about why this party was such an ogre'. So he caught a tram into the city and went to the Communist Party of Australia bookshop, where he bought Marx and Engels' *Selected Works*, volumes 1 and 2. 'It was like pornography', he confesses as he describes the furtive thrill associated with making this purchase.

Peter Manning's account of 'going into the heart of evil' is like an episode from a story in the *Boy's Own Paper*, in which a common theme was that of a heroic schoolboy singlehandedly taking on the dastardly Bolsheviks. But his description of the 'dark, gloomy and grey' ambience of the CPA bookshop is mirrored by his account of a visit he made some twelve years later to a private gathering of the far right Australian Association for Cultural Freedom, which was meeting in a dark room of the Belvedere Hotel, Kings Cross. 'It was like an image of a coven', he says of his first sight of the inner circle of this CIA front. 'It felt like a cult.' Although he was being wooed to join the group, he fled the scene. This reaction was part of a broader rejection of the values instilled by Church and school. But this is to jump too far ahead in Peter Manning's story …

BORN IN 1945, PETER WAS AN ONLY CHILD OF CATHOLIC parents whose own parents were working class. Peter's father, however, had middle-class aspirations. Although Michael Manning was the sole employee as well as proprietor of a small laundry business, he saw himself as an entrepreneur. A classic example of Robert Menzies' 'Forgotten People', he was such a strong supporter of Ming that he even took his four-year-old son to hear him speak at the local Bondi Beach amphitheatre during the 1949 election campaign. Peter's mother was a very different sort of person. A pacifist and feminist – albeit one who was out of sync with her times – Rosemary Manning (née Weston) was an outgoing woman who sang along to the advertising jingles on commercial television. Her husband listened to ABC Radio.

By the time Peter was four or five, these differences of temperament and viewpoint had become so great that the marriage ended. Over the course of his childhood, Peter stayed with his father in Bondi, but spent his holidays in the western suburb of Parramatta, close to where his mother had found employment as personal assistant to the proprietor of a toy factory. (An enchanting workplace for a child to visit!)

Despite being aware of the 'great differences' between his two homes, Peter grew up in the assurance that he was dearly loved by both his parents, and he liked the new partners with whom they each settled down. However, divorce was forbidden by the Catholic Church, and in even the secular world of 1950s Australia it carried a huge social stigma. Peter 'felt the disapproval of [his] parents from the school', and his 'family life' made him the odd one out among his classmates, none of whom had step-parents or parents who lived apart. 'I was well aware that it was strange. I was well tuned to how different my experience was. There was a very narrow version of what was normal at Waverley College.' Even being an only child was highly unusual, in a Catholic environment.

In describing his estrangement from the social norms of his peers, Peter shows no sign of resentment. Rather, he sees a positive side to his outsider status. 'I think it gave me the ability to stand on my own two feet, emotionally, socially, politically', he says. 'I think I developed a shell – a strength, really – to deal with pejorative behaviour towards me, for any reason. I don't mean I was defensive, but I was just happy in my own skin.'

A thoughtful boy as well as an independent one, he used to ride his bike to nearby Rose Bay, where he spent hours watching the seaplanes taking off and landing. This was thinking time. 'I had my own world in my head.'

Despite this, Peter swallowed whole the ideology of Waverley College. 'I trusted the Brothers, I trusted the teachers, I trusted the school in general. I was very open to whatever the Brothers said was correct.' Reflecting on that experience, Peter adds that the school and the religion 'provided a sort of safe spot' in which he was able to define himself. 'It was like I was institutionalising myself, and quite enjoying it.'

It is not surprising that, from within this institutionalised world, Peter began to consider becoming a priest. Sensibly, his mother made him promise to spend a few years at university before committing himself. He had no other career plans, but he did think he'd like to be a writer – not of fiction, but about aspects of the world and current affairs. If this was in keeping with the precocious eleven-year-old who had fired off a letter about the invasion of Hungary, it was only natural that, when Peter wanted a job in the summer holidays between school and university, he found employment as a copy boy at the *Daily Telegraph*.

PETER HAD JUST TURNED SEVENTEEN WHEN HE ARRIVED AT Sydney University in the Orientation Week of 1962. In an essay about coming of age during the Cold War, he describes himself at that time as being 'a perfectly formed bullet out of conservative Pius XII and Cardinal Gilroy's Catholic Church'. It is interesting that Peter cites the pontiff who had issued the decree excommunicating Communists from the Christian faith. In fact, by the time Peter left school, Pius XII had been succeeded by the more liberal Pope John XXIII, who in 1962 would convene the Second Vatican Council, in order (as he said) to 'open the windows [of the Church] and let in some fresh air'. But the new Catholic liberalism that was part of the spirit of the Sixties hadn't yet reached most of Catholic Australia. And so, 'spring-loaded' as Peter was with his anti-Communist ideology, he had barely arrived on campus when he set about resurrecting the university's DLP Club, which had died some years before.

The Democratic Labor Party is now so moribund that this seems almost a student jape, like founding the Tiddlywinks Club or the Chocolate Lovers Society. But in 1962 that wasn't the case. Formed in 1955, when the Catholic and virulently anti-Communist right wing of the Australian Labor Party in Victoria split from the main body of the party, by the early 1960s the DLP held the balance of power in the Senate. As well, by directing its second preference votes for the Lower House to the Liberal Party, it was able to keep Labor out of office federally and Menzies in government.

Although Peter stresses that he never actually joined the Democratic Labor Party, for someone under the age of fifty to have anything to do with it was, at the very least, an act of eccentricity. Despite its tiny membership, the re-formed club attracted attention to itself on campus simply by its existence. And its energetic leader raised its profile even more by the articles and opinion pieces he began writing for the student newspaper, *Honi Soit*. All of this was while Peter was still in his first year – a time when most other freshers were still working out how to get to the pub.

In other ways, the anti-Communist activist was a normal student. When Meredith and I ask him how he felt during this initial burst of political activity, Peter laughs. 'I think it was too many hormones! Too much energy! I arrived at university as a virgin, and I was amazed at all the beautiful girls. It was seventh heaven after being in a boys' school.' Unsurprisingly, he quickly jettisoned his idea of becoming a priest. However, he continued to see himself 'as a good Catholic, and that meant keeping your virginity until you got married'. Despite 'the frustration and angst' that this caused – to various girlfriends as well as himself – he remained true to his beliefs, but 'it was very hard when you were trying to be a good Catholic boy and not give in'. Pointing out that the 1960s was 'a sexy period', he adds: 'A lot of the politics was hormonally driven, and the desire for revolution was partly sexually motivated'.

Of course it was. I remember a popular T-shirt that proclaimed: 'Every time I make love, I make revolution'. But although I was only too aware of how the so-called student leaders of the Left were able to attract girls, it never occurred to me that right-wing boys were sexy. Obviously, however, any sort of political activism can be charismatic. It was while Peter was on the DLP Club stall in the Orientation Week of his second year at university that he was 'blown away by the beauty and style' of an outspoken young woman named Maria Beswick. Although her father was in the National

Civic Council (a right-wing Catholic lobby group founded by BA Santamaria), she had a political will of her own. Within a few months, Peter and Maria were a couple.

Paradoxically, perhaps, the religious impulse that had initially steered Peter to the right now began to lead him towards the left. In the course of our conversation, he names a number of political mentors, but again and again he comes back to Father Ted Kennedy, the radical priest who in the 1960s was Sydney's University's Catholic chaplain. Ted's base, in a Church-owned terrace house opposite the campus, was the regular meeting place for the university branch of the Newman Society. This community of intellectuals, which included historians Bob Scribner and John Iremonger and philosopher Bill Ginnane, had an influence that went beyond Catholic students. Protestants such as Meredith's elder sister, Beverley Burgmann – and a few years later, Meredith herself – joined the free-ranging conversations about politics and religion. But for students who had been to Catholic schools, what was going on was far more profound.

The radicalism was twofold. Peter describes how 'The texts circulating at these meetings were redefining who God was, by putting the idea that people of other faiths were seeking God in their own way, and were not destined for Hell'. On a more concrete level, the old 'trinkets' of the Faith – 'the statues, the Rosary, the Catechism' – were being jettisoned and the liturgy was being changed to a much simpler style of worship, with a greater inclusion of the laity.

These reforms were, of course, part of the 'fresh air' that was being let into the Church by Pope John XXIII, but for Peter Manning it was Father Ted Kennedy – whom he describes as 'a great deconstructer' – who exemplified the new liberation theology.

'We all had to read the Bible – we had to read the New Testament – and we had to read Matthew's Gospel, in particular. That had the kind of Christian humanism that Ted was very much about. But the thing that was revolutionary for me was Ted saying, "Live your values of love and social justice in the world, don't hide in a church."'

As 'all these old ideas were coming crashing down', Peter discovered that 'this was opening up other ideological spaces that were fantastic and exciting'. Within a short time, he was actually living at the heart of all this excitement. When he left home after a row with his father, he was invited by Ted to move into one of the upstairs rooms in the terrace. This was despite the fact that Peter and Ted did not see eye to eye on the question of the war in Vietnam, and Australia's involvement in it.

Still holding firm to the anti-Communist views that had been instilled in him at school, Peter supported the foreign policy of the DLP – which at its crudest was that the people of Vietnam would be better off dead than red. In 1964, when he was in his third year at university, he wrote a background article for *Honi Soit*, titled 'War in Vietnam', in which he called for further Australian military and economic commitment to the anti-Communist regime in the South.

In the course of that year, however, Peter Manning underwent a political awakening. He explains, 'My brain was seeing the ridiculous nature of the argument that you have to bomb the hell out of Vietnam, in order to save it, for freedom'. While his 'earlier certainty was fast cracking under the pressure of US bombing', it was also cracking under the force of the arguments of his political opponents. In particular, the president of the DLP Club was having long earnest discussions with the Labor Club president, Brian

Aarons, scion of what was sometimes called the Royal Family of the Communist Party of Australia.

My own memory, from a slightly later time at Sydney University, is of a schism so great between Left and Right that the only exchanges were of jeers and rotten fruit – or, sometimes, of punches. I even remember accompanying a member of Students for a Democratic Society to hospital after he was bayoneted by a member of the University Regiment.

However, this affinity between the two student club presidents is not really so surprising. While some young members of the far Right were changing with the times, radical Communists were embracing the New Left ideology that was set against the Soviet-style Communism of the Old Left. Peter and Brian were both opposed to Stalinism, although they came to this position from different sides of the political spectrum. There was just the sticking point of whether it was better for the people of Vietnam to be dead or red.

As the US bombing campaign escalated through 1965 and the number of deaths kept growing, Peter came to agree with Brian, and with other influential friends. One was his old schoolmate, Ross Burns, who made it clear that he thought Peter's views on Vietnam were simplistic. Newer friends included radical Trotskyist, Hall Greenland, and the quietly spoken anarchist, Michael Matteson, who would soon become the country's most notorious draft resister. If some of the revolutionary impulse of the era was to do with sex, a lot of it had to do with mateship – a particular kind of mateship that flourished in the small pond of the Sydney University campus.

But once again, for Peter the greatest influence was Ted Kennedy. Although the radical chaplain never overtly challenged his views on Vietnam, he introduced Peter to the philosophy of American peace activist, Dorothy Day, whose belief in 'the power of conscience' had led her to take a stand even against the Second World War.

A secular take on these same values of peace and love and social justice could be found in the folk music that was seeping out of America and into the cafes and bars of Sydney. As well as listening to records by overseas stars such as Joan Baez and Bob Dylan, Peter and Maria often used to go out to listen to live folk music. They even saw Woody Guthrie when the legendary American folk singer came to Sydney. Although the anti-war message of folk songs was at odds with the DLP line, Peter 'enjoyed them all'.

Meanwhile, as all these influences were challenging Peter Manning to question his position on the Vietnam War, he was being confronted with an example of the famous Sixties adage that *the personal is political*. Due to turn twenty in February 1965, he was eligible for conscription, which had been introduced by the Menzies government a few months earlier. By this time, Peter was seeing himself as a conscientious objector to the war in Vietnam, but he filled in the registration papers. By some sort of terrible irony, when that month's lottery was picked, his birth date was one of the numbers that came out of the barrel.

What should he do? The situation was 'very confronting' for his family, as well as for Peter himself. On the one hand, there was what he calls 'the Manning men tradition of going to war'. His mother's father, Harold Weston, had survived Gallipoli, only to lose a leg on the Somme; it was this that had caused her to become a pacifist. Peter's father supported Australia's participation in the war in Indochina, but he didn't want to lose his beloved only son.

As the appointment for Peter's medical examination

and his induction into the army approached, he 'turned all this over' in his head. Should he evade the call-up, as some young men in the anti-war movement were starting to do? Or should he 'front up'? There was a third alternative: go to the military board, declare himself a conscientious objector, and ask for exemption.

Showing great integrity, Peter decided he couldn't take that option because of the public support that, until recently, he had given to Australia's military presence in Vietnam. Feeling he had no choice but to comply, he went to the medical examination.

Reprieve! It turned out that Peter had a protruding bone in his feet that would prevent him from undertaking long marches on jungle trails. Failed on the spot, Peter felt 'a fantastic sense of relief'.

This incident opened the way for him to go where his heart and mind were already taking him. Now, there were no doubts. 'I felt rock solid. I saw the absurdity of the argument that we have to destroy Vietnam in order to save it.' But again, it took courage to follow his convictions. Fortunately, Maria Beswick had been going through a political sea-change at the same time as Peter, but the other students in the DLP Club and older DLP powerbrokers, such as Senator Jack Kane and Terry Tobin QC, 'all saw [Peter] as a traitor to the right-wing cause'. Some of the Left would also doubt the sincerity of his turnaround; to this day, he is occasionally challenged about his DLP past, which he sees as a kind of albatross he is doomed to carry around his neck. This is particularly unfair because Peter Manning, more than most of the Left, was made to suffer for his opposition to the Vietnam War.

Taking a stand

RUNNING IN TANDEM WITH PETER'S CAREER IN UNIVERSITY politics was the beginning of his lifelong professional career. Ever since his initial holiday job at the *Daily Telegraph*, he had continued to earn an occasional bit of cash by working there from time to time as a copy boy. Indeed, he was there on the memorable night in October 1963 when the Cuban Missile Crisis came to a head.

Before relating this story, Peter sets the scene: the Telex machine clattering, the paper jolting out, people shouting even more than usual. 'The tension in the office was visceral. Everyone was thinking: "Will we all be dead tomorrow?"' Caught up in the hysteria, Peter considered walking off the job, in order to spend his last night on earth at home with his family. But, fired up with the noble ideal of the duty of the reporter to get the news out, no matter what, the copy boy decided he should stand by the Telex machine and deliver the incoming messages to the paper's editor. As a compromise, the eighteen-year-old rang his father and told him that he loved him. Mr Manning, on the other end of the phone line, 'seemed remarkably blasé' about the political situation. And sure enough, despite Peter's fears, by the end of the night shift the Third World War had not started.

This employment at the *Telegraph* was just a part-time job, not a cadetship. Increasingly, however, as his final university exams approached, Peter had in mind the idea of pursuing some sort of career in journalism. He had no plan for how to go about this, but again he struck it lucky. Out of the blue, he received a phone call from Peter Coleman, then editor of the conservative journal, the *Bulletin*. By that time, Peter Manning 'had long left the DLP behind and was writing all sorts of different things', but Coleman hadn't heard of his conversion. On the basis of Peter's early student journalism, the *Bulletin* editor believed that his writing 'had the sort of small-l liberal right bias' that he wanted for the magazine. So he gave Peter a job. A few months later, when Donald Horne took over the editorship, he realised that Peter had not had any training in professional journalism, and sent him off to the *Sydney Morning Herald* to do a cadetship.

By now, Peter and Maria had married. In 1968, the year when national and international protest exploded onto the streets, the young couple had their first child. Peter was only twenty-two, Maria twenty-one. Two years later, the couple's second child was born. Like many Catholics of their generation, Maria and Peter had settled into the responsibilities of married life and parenthood when their peers were revelling in all the freedoms of the Sexual Revolution. Peter found there to be 'a vast chasm' between himself and a lot of his male mates, 'who were having great fun', and he ended up 'pining a little bit for all that chaos and anarchy and pleasure that was out there'.

'I remember going to parties and thinking, "Oh my God, we're married, and look at this scene here!"' he reflects. 'Even though I was absolutely in love with Maria, it struck me pretty quickly that I had locked myself down.'

THIS DIFFERENCE IN PETER MANNING'S SITUATION – OF being a family breadwinner with what he calls 'a serious job' – would come to a head in 1970.

By now, opposition to Australia's military presence in Vietnam had become a groundswell. The Moratorium movement, organised by a broad alliance of left-wing organisations, aimed to demonstrate this opposition in a national day of protest under the slogan 'Stop Work to Stop the War'. In Sydney, campaign headquarters was the office of the Association for International Co-operation and Disarmament, run by Ken McLeod. Now back at the *Bulletin* after his cadetship with Fairfax, Peter was sent by his editor (Donald Horne's successor) to interview McLeod about the campaign.

Warned about Peter's earlier DLP associations, and unaware that he had changed his views, Ken McLeod was initially wary. He was soon reassured. At the end of the long and wide-ranging discussion, Peter told Ken that he'd like to be involved in the organisation of the anti-war stoppage. Over the coming weeks, he worked in his spare time on the Moratorium newspaper, *Out Now!*

Working behind the scenes was one thing, but Peter also 'wanted to publicly join the bandwagon to stop the war'. He explains, 'I wanted to send a signal that my four years of prominent advocacy for the US position was gone'. When the day of the Moratorium came, and the speeches from the top of the steps of Sydney Town Hall were due to start, Peter asked Ken McLeod (acting as MC) if he could speak. He had something he really wanted to say.

'In my short contribution I told 20 000 people that the Vietnamese National Liberation Front should be allowed to take over if they had the popular will behind them. *Better red than dead*. I said that this level of killing had to stop, even at the cost of a Communist future for most Vietnamese. I ended with a rousing shout of "Out now!"'

Standing behind Peter as he spoke was Tom Uren, a federal Labor politician and long-term anti-war activist. When Peter stepped back from the microphone, Tom tapped him on the back, said, 'Well done, comrade', and shook his hand. Nearly fifty years later, Peter still sounds very moved as he describes this 'extraordinary moment'. He adds, 'Tom asked me later to join the Labor Party but I thanked him and said I couldn't as a journalist'.

If taking a stand at the Moratorium was a very public coming out for the former anti-Communist, Peter was also soon 'out' in a different sense.

When he returned to the *Bulletin* the next day, still wearing his Moratorium badge, the editor came to him and said, 'We're not finding what you write of much interest any more'. The message was clear: pack up your desk and go. In shock, Peter went to the pub, where he was consoled by other members of what was known in the Australian Journalists' Association as 'the new journalists group' – friends such as David Dale, Michael Symons and Lindsay Foyle. This sacking wasn't just a temporary banishment; it led to a long time of exile before Peter got another 'serious job'. The experience served to reinforce the difference between him and his counter-culture mates.

For those of us who were students, the Moratorium's action-plan of 'stopping work to stop the war' required no sacrifice: none of us worked, anyway. It was just a case of another day, another march downtown. But for Peter Manning, with a wife and two young children, the months of trying to support a family on the irregular payments of a freelancer were 'traumatic'. If there was any penance required for what Peter calls the 'teenage treachery' of his DLP association, he certainly did it.

Of course, Peter Manning went on to have a distinguished career in journalism, which included being executive producer of *Four Corners*, general manager of the ABC's Radio National, and head of Current Affairs for the Seven

Network. In this career, he was well served by having gone through the process of seeing both sides of an issue. Summing up his 'conversion' over the question of the Vietnam War, Peter alludes to 'specific moments of change that brought my own certainties into question'. It was not a matter of a single epiphany on the road to the platform of Sydney Town Hall but, rather, a long and arduous journey. Among the 'wider influences at work' on him, he cites the way that Father Ted Kennedy, by dissolving the conception of the Church as 'a fortress against the world', had 'undermined the very basis' of the '"us and them" polarity'. Once that dichotomy was shown to be false, Peter was able to question other axioms of his upbringing.

Conclusion

Meredith Burgmann and Nadia Wheatley

When we began writing this book, we had no idea how the pieces would come together. That time we call the Sixties was made up of so many varied experiences.

As it turned out, however, the twenty people we chose to include had more in common than might be apparent at first sight.

Our characters really do span the political spectrum – Anarchism, Trotskyism, Maoism, Pragmatism, as well as Labor Party members, DLP supporters, the non-aligned, and those who just wanted to keep their noses clean. We also included three Peters – but hey, it was the Sixties.

Feminism threads through all the stories, particularly those of the women. Vivienne Binns embraces feminism and her lesbian identity. Jozefa Sobski, Bronwyn Penrith and Nadia all have their own struggles, and Margaret Reynolds and her friend Bobbi Sykes suffer sexism at its worst in Far North Queensland.

Like the changing patterns of a kaleidoscope, we shift in

Conclusion

and out of each other's stories. We find out through this book that Robbie Swan was bashed with Meredith at Canberra's 'Day of Rage'; and that Gary Foley and Gary Williams committed the offence that she was arrested for at Manuka Oval during the Springbok tour. And although the two of us have remained close friends since 1968, Meredith didn't even realise she was important in Nadia's radicalisation story until she read her chapter.

There are characters who pop in and out of narratives. Peter Duncan from Adelaide and Albert Langer from Melbourne both talk about radical journalist Darce Cassidy (famous for founding the South Gundagai Liberation Front). Dany Torsh is part of the stories of both Jozefa Sobski and Geoff Robertson. Glen Tomasetti is talked about by Margret RoadKnight and also, surprisingly, by Albert Langer. Margret RoadKnight, in turn, makes an appearance in John Derum's story, and David Marr worked at one stage as a research assistant for Peter Manning. Vivienne Binns and Roger Foley collaborated on the important Happening, *WOOM*.

It must sound like we all knew each other, but mostly we did not. Our characters lived in different cities around Australia and were in different organisations, or were active in different areas of the struggle. And in those days, living in a different state was a bit like living in a different country. Flights were expensive and we all had such bomby cars that they would never have survived an interstate trip. So we mostly didn't meet each other.

The interlinking themes are also interesting. When asking about our interviewees' childhoods, we were fascinated to discover that religion almost always cropped up in their stories.

Radicals

The great cleavage for our cohort growing up was the Catholic/Protestant divide. However, the importance of this divide was more commonly expressed by our Catholic participants – probably because Catholicism is so much more all-encompassing as a life experience. Often our participants could not move further along their chosen radical pathway until they had resolved their questions of faith. Once again this was most important for the Catholics.

Jozefa Sobski in particular struggled with her Catholicism. She was even told by her priest that she was 'too serious a Catholic'. For Peter Manning, Catholicism was the motivating force for his early support for the DLP, but Father Ted Kennedy, who talked about dissolving the conception of the Church as a 'fortress against the world', showed young Peter a way forward.

A number of the people we interviewed came from affluent families. The set-up of the Marr family firm of ironmongers sounds like something from nineteenth-century Manchester. Albert Langer came from a well-to-do Toorak family. Brian Laver's extended family were Queensland cattlemen and A-grade tennis players.

In complete contrast to these privileged backgrounds was the childhood environment of Jozefa Sobski, whose family lived in migrant hostels until she was ten. Our three Aboriginal participants also came from backgrounds that were economically poor, but loving and culturally rich.

Coming out of staid 1950s homes, with the emphasis on how things should be and how they should seem, many participants described their parents as 'fighting for middle-class respectability'.

Some parents were hostile to their children's new lives. David Marr and Roger Foley fought their fathers. Helen

Conclusion

Voysey and Meredith had supportive families. Robbie Swan's parents were antagonistic during the first stage of his rebellion, but the whole family pulled together when he was looking at serious gaol time. Nadia's relatives continually berated her for her politics, and to this day remain hostile to her views.

One topic that arises over and over again in the stories is Robert Menzies, who bestrode Australia like the proverbial Colossus. Our participants often described their parents' politics not by their allegiance to a party, but by what they thought of Menzies, and even when there were differences of opinion, he was still dominant. Almost unanimously he was considered, 'That nice Mr Menzies'. Margaret Reynolds didn't know for many years that 'Pig Iron Bob' was the same person as 'that lovely Mr Menzies'. Jozefa Sobski stresses the importance of Menzies to her immigrant father, who – having been imprisoned by both Germans and Russians – gave Menzies his total allegiance. But of all our characters, it is David Marr who expresses most vehemently the stifling tedium of growing up under 'Ming'.

Another giant in our 1960s existence was the conservative Catholic commentator and master of political intrigue, BA Santamaria. He and his regular Sunday morning television broadcast (strategically programmed between the end of Mass and the start of *World of Sport*) was watched not only in the Catholic households of Peter Manning, John Derum and Margret RoadKnight, but also in the Protestant home of Brian Laver's grandmother in Far North Queensland.

The importance of teachers in the life of our proto-revolutionaries also crops up regularly in conversation. Peter Batchelor, John Derum and Brian Laver, in particular, talk about the influence of teachers. Surprisingly, Gary

Foley mentions his helpful teacher in primary school before revealing the extraordinary racism of his high school headmaster, who ordered the bright student to leave school because 'We don't want your kind here'. David Marr talks about the influence of a particular liberal history teacher, and of the importance of progressive teachers in general.

Mentors and friends were also influential in the radical development of many of our characters. Vivienne Binns was fortunate enough to have two male lovers who played a significant role in her sexual and artistic liberation. Roger Foley's on-again/off-again friendship with Albie Thoms was very important to both.

For Gary Williams, when starting university in 1963, it was very helpful to have Charlie Perkins, ten years older, enrolling on the same day. However, it was Gary's Uncle Clive, from the next suburb, who guided his early political steps.

By unacknowledged consent, we excluded from our concerns the Jesus People, the passion for India and 'finding yourself'. Did we look sufficiently closely at the issues of religious groups, the hippies, and the influence of rock-and-roll? Perhaps that is for the next volume, but at least Robbie Swan talks about 'our Woodstock', the first Aquarius Festival. He also became a proponent of that wonderful Sixties preoccupation, transcendental meditation (even converting his father to it).

We did ask about our characters' drug use, but – far from being the 'turn on, tune in, drop out' generation – most of our activists smoked only occasionally, or didn't do drugs at all. Robbie Swan again is the exception – to the tune of being busted for growing a cash crop of six hundred plants. Psychotropic drugs, which are sometimes seen as synonymous with the Sixties, were really only indulged in by Roger Foley and Robbie.

Rather than just focusing on political culture, we made the decision early on to look at Australian culture more broadly. This of course included art, theatre, music and the counter-culture generally. Again there were connections. To raise awareness about Aboriginal issues, Bronwyn Penrith performed in street theatre, which was little different from the Happenings and performance art that were produced by Roger Foley and Vivienne Binns. Both John Derum and Margret RoadKnight took part in *Arts Vietnam* performances, and Albert Langer, at the age of fourteen, organised a folk concert in aid of the anti-apartheid movement. In Brisbane, there were rock bands as well as folk musicians at the regular concerts Brian Laver put on at Foco.

Overall, we not only learnt a lot from this broadening of the theme to include the arts, but it made this book about the Sixties far richer.

WHAT WERE THE ISSUES THAT TRIGGERED PEOPLE'S FIRST acts of rebellion?

Dress is often seen as a symbol of revolt. Peter Batchelor grew long hair and wore denim. Meredith's rebellion was short white boots and a miniskirt. And Robbie Swan came home in a woman's dress, to shock his parents. (It worked.)

Naturally, dress also arose as part of rebellion at school, but often the issue at stake seemed trivial. Peter Batchelor and his schoolfriends altered the stripes in their despised uniform ties. Peter Duncan revolted against caps instead of hats for the fourth form boys.

Sometimes, school issues were more weighty. For Geoff Robertson, the irritant was the censorship of his Leaving Certificate copy of *The Tempest*. Helen Voysey and her comrades in High School Students Against the War in Vietnam argued for the right of students to discuss controversial political issues and to distribute their own underground publications. They also opposed the prefect system.

The workplace, too, could be part of the radicalisation process. Over some years, Peter Batchelor's holiday jobs in a mattress factory led to his becoming a trade union activist. David Marr describes his political education occurring through his colleagues at the *Bulletin* ('secondary school') and the *National Times* ('university'). Jozefa Sobski acknowledges the importance of the support she received from feminist colleagues and the Teachers' Federation representative at her first high school job.

The industrial militancy and economic boom of the late 1960s helped create the scene for the environmental activism of the NSW Builders Labourers' Federation and the green bans. This brief flowering of the concept of socially responsible labour was particularly important for those of us in Sydney. For Meredith it was pivotal.

The economic boom also allowed students, in particular, to indulge in radical activity, knowing that they would still get a job.

BEFORE WE BEGAN INTERVIEWING PEOPLE FOR THIS BOOK, we imagined that Vietnam would be the radicalising issue for all our participants. But we were surprised to discover that there were also very particular local triggers. Australia was

Conclusion

on fire with radical causes. For instance, in South Australia, the problem of the conservative gerrymander loomed large for Peter Duncan. On many campuses, student rights were at least as important as Vietnam. And in Brisbane, the students had to battle about the right to march on the street, before they could protest about the war.

Overall, the twin issues of conscription and Vietnam created an atmosphere of demonstrations and chaos, but that alone wasn't what gripped many of us.

Opposition to capital punishment, racism and apartheid ... support for land rights, drug law reform, women's rights, gay rights ... there were so many issues that brought our participants out into the street. Censorship was a particularly big concern for Geoff Robertson, Robbie Swan and David Marr.

For some, their worries were more fifties than Sixties. Geoffrey Robertson continually referred back to the White Australia Policy. Helen Voysey was affected by the campaign for nuclear disarmament and her fear, as a terrified ten-year-old, that she was going to be fried by an atom bomb. John Derum was impelled to action by the execution of Ronald Ryan. Vivienne Binns struggled to find her personal and artistic truth in an art world stuck in the mindset and misogyny of the 1950s.

Sometimes, the trigger was immediate. Robbie Swan had a visceral response to violent police action during the 'Day of Rage'. Gary Foley was shocked at being bashed by police at Regent Street Police Station after being picked up for talking to a white girl in Railway Square. Meredith woke up one morning deciding she was a socialist. In rural Rockhampton, Brian Laver saw documentaries about Nazi concentration camps and Stalinist gulags and instantly became a self-declared anti-totalitarian, at the age of thirteen. Nadia went into her first sit-in completely ignorant about Vietnam; within an hour, she was ready to break the Crimes Act.

There are these blinding moments of realisation, but often there were a series of minor triggers to the process of radicalisation.

Margaret Reynolds was awakened to the racism of Townsville when she saw a young Indigenous man being violently thrown out of a pub. Later, she met activist trade unionists when calling into a bookshop for a glass of water. Her feminism erupted when her friend Bobbi Sykes was put down by a bureaucrat at a meeting. These were all important in her awakening. Was any one trigger more important than another?

Others moved gradually into their new radical lives. Margret RoadKnight, for instance, can't really put a finger on her process of radicalisation, and Gary Williams describes moving from the Freedom Ride to setting up the Aboriginal Legal Service in Redfern as if these were just a series of events, rather than actual decisions. For him, 'Stuff just happens'.

What are the books that flicked the switch?

For Meredith it was the straightforward history of class oppression in Cole and Postgate's *The Common People*. For Jozefa Sobski it was Germaine Greer's *The Female Eunuch*. For Gary Foley it was the *Autobiography of Malcolm X*. For Gary Williams it was Angela Davis's, *If They Come in the Morning*. Bronwyn Penrith mentions the importance of Eldridge Cleaver's *Soul on Ice*. But we white students were reading the same books as our Aboriginal comrades. We all read Malcolm X, Stokely Carmichael, James Baldwin and Eldridge Cleaver. The importance of the Black American experience can't be overestimated. It was what we were seeing every night on our TV screens, along with the Vietnam War. Sol Belair and Bob Maza, who crop up in a couple of accounts, actually met Jesse Jackson during a short visit to the States.

And was it always books? Not at all.

Margret RoadKnight was inspired by the words of Malvina Reynolds in her spine-chilling anti-nuclear song 'What Have They Done to the Rain?' John Derum soaked up the anti-war plays of the British realists. Roger Foley read weird stuff like the *Tulane Review*, which made sense to him at the time. David Marr emphasises the importance of the rise of independent left papers like *Nation Review* and the *National Times*.

Meanwhile, Albert Langer came to his Maoist ideology via many, many books in the state library as well as the propaganda sent to him by snail mail in response to his short-wave radio log-ins. These publications included Soviet and American pamphlets as well as (of course) copies of the colourful *Peking Review*.

Although the Australian Left was influenced by international ideologies, it was, on the whole, devoid of the violent aspects of the American and European movements. No Weather Underground, no Angry Brigade, no Baader-Meinhof Gang for us down under. Perhaps this can partly be explained by the fact there is almost no culture of political violence in modern Australia (as distinct from the violent massacres of colonial Australia). Also, we had a class-based party that was committed to bringing the troops home. American youth had no democratic road to peace – both parties were intent on pursuing the war.

Radicals

SO WHAT WAS THE EFFECT OF BEING PART OF THE RADICAL Sixties?

Did we change the world? How did we do it? We believed we had the ability to bring about change. We would 'pull up the daffodils of the bourgeoisie' until they stopped the war. We would stop the racist tours, we would win land rights, we would get rid of censorship and the White Australia Policy, stop executions, even get Whitlam elected. We believed.

Young activists of today often express regret that they were not around in the Sixties. They are envious of our sense of hope and our self-belief.

Where did this utter self-belief spring from – and why do young radicals not have it today?

Perhaps it is because twenty-first century issues are so much more complex. Our issues were stark. Young men were being conscripted to fight and die in a war most of us did not believe in. Football teams were playing racially selected all-white sides from a murderous regime. First Nations Australians had no right to any of their land. The death penalty was still being carried out. Simple and brutal issues.

Today, activists struggle with much more nuanced arguments. What are the scientific proofs of human-induced climate change? Why is the land rights process so cumbersome? What is the answer to refugees dying at sea?

But there IS still hope. We now have equal marriage in Australia. World poverty has been markedly reduced. There are more women in decision-making positions. We recycle. We are moving away from fossil fuels. Most countries now no longer execute their citizens. And we have numerous First Nations doctors and academics, as well as rock stars, artists and sportspeople.

Conclusion

WHAT WE FIND AMONG THE PARTICIPANTS IN THIS BOOK is that they all believe that their Sixties experience changed them forever. Some of us even changed our professions. David Marr and Peter Manning became journalists, believing that writing and reporting was the way to change the world. Meredith gave up English honours to study politics. Bronwyn managed to avoid the Assimilationist path laid out for her.

What did our characters do with their lives? Some were scarred by their experiences in the struggle, but all have continued to work for 'a better world' – some in public and sensational ways. Geoffrey Robertson battles tyrants and supports tarts and troublemakers at the Old Bailey. Peter Duncan introduced the first decriminalisation of homosexuality legislation in Australia. David Marr regularly fights the good fight on our screens and in our journals. Bronwyn Penrith is chair of Mudgin-Gal Aboriginal Women's Centre in Redfern.

Helen Voysey successfully lobbies to get the coastal cabins in the Royal National Park listed on the State Heritage Register. Margaret Reynolds chairs the Friends of the ABC. Gary Foley teaches the Aboriginal history of resistance to a new generation of activists, and Gary Williams does crucial work to preserve and promote the Gumbaynggirr language. Peter Manning is one of the leading supporters of the Palestinian cause in Australia. At the age of eighty, Vivienne Binns continues her daily search for Truth and Beauty and is soon to have two retrospective exhibitions.

SOMETIMES DURING OUR CONVERSATIONS WE HAD moments of insight. When Geoff Robertson referred to the previous generation of expats (Clive James, Barry

Humphries, Germaine Greer) leaving Australia because they were BORED, whereas our generation weren't bored, they were ANGRY, we suddenly realised that he was right.

Another such moment of clarity was when Aboriginal activist Gary Williams described his lack of interest in demonstrating against the Vietnam War was because he had always seen it as a 'whitefellas' war'. It was the first time we'd ever thought of it in that way, and once again he was right.

For all of us, the Sixties were about idealism, aspiration and determination. The settled verities of the fifties were being challenged in the streets and the lecture theatres. We were determined to change the world – and we did.

No book can ever really do justice to the hope and exhilaration of the radical Sixties. We like to think we have had a go ... anyway, we had fun along the way.

Biographies

Peter Batchelor

Peter Batchelor is a prominent Victorian left-wing Labor politician and community activist.

After his time working at the BBB Mattress Factory in the early 1970s, he was head-hunted for an organising job with the Furnishing Trades Union. He spent nine years there before starting work in 1982 as an organiser in the Victorian ALP head office, which at that time was controlled by the Left.

He was Victorian state secretary of the ALP until 1990, when he was elected to Victorian Parliament in the seat of Thomastown, which he represented until his retirement in 2010.

He spent eleven years as Government Leader of the House and held five portfolios in the Bracks and Brumby governments: Transport, Arts, Energy, Community Development and Major Projects.

It is his six years as Minister for Transport for which he is best remembered. During that time, he was responsible for overseeing the $750 million Regional Fast Rail Project, building Victoria's first fast-train services to rural Victorian centres like Bendigo, Ballarat and Geelong. He also exceeded the election commitment to cut the road toll by 20 per cent.

As Minister for Energy and Resources he introduced feed-in tariffs for domestic rooftop solar panels as part of a Climate Change initiative.

After leaving parliament, he served as chair of the Community Broadcasting Foundation, a charity distributing $20 million a year to community radio and TV stations.

He also oversaw the setting up of the National Rail Safety Regulator and served on its board for six years.

Vivienne Binns

Vivienne Binns OAM is acknowledged as one of the founders of the Women's Art Movement in Australia, and is recognised for her active advocacy within community arts, especially among women and regional artists.

In the five decades since her explosive 1967 show at Sydney's Watters Gallery, Vivienne has held thirty solo exhibitions at commercial galleries in Sydney, Melbourne, Brisbane and Hobart, and at a number of regional galleries.

Her awards include the Ros Bower Memorial Award for her visionary contribution to community art (1986) and the National Art School Fellowship (2016). She has been the Australia Council Artist-in-Residence in Tokyo (1991) and London (2001).

Known in the 1970s and 1980s for her work in a range of media, Vivienne Binns has focused on studio-based painting during the last thirty years. Her work explores what it means to be an artist in Australia with its combined Indigenous and European histories, and with its place in the Asia-Pacific region. Her travels have taken her to Burma, Malaysia, Thailand, Sumatra, Papua New Guinea, Western Samoa, the Cook Islands, Noumea and New Caledonia. She attended the sixth, seventh and eighth South Pacific Festival of Arts.

After teaching at various institutions, Vivienne developed an association with the Australian National University, Canberra, where she was head of Core Studies (1999–2007) and senior lecturer, Painting Workshop (2008–12). Although she retired from teaching in 2013, Vivienne is an Emeritus Fellow of ANU and continues her friendships and mentoring relationships with students.

Vivienne continues to work most days in her studio as well as collating and maintaining her comprehensive electronic archive. Her most recent solo exhibition was at Sutton Gallery, Melbourne, in 2018. Both the Museum of Contemporary Art, Sydney, and the Monash University Museum of Art will be holding retrospective exhibitions of her work in 2022. These will be a fitting tribute to a long and brilliant career.

Meredith Burgmann

Meredith Burgmann is a feminist, trade unionist, anti-racist activist and academic, and a former president of the NSW Legislative Council.

After Meredith's radicalisation at Sydney University during the Vietnam protests, she became a convenor of the anti-Springbok campaign of 1971, famously running onto the field and stopping play at the Sydney Cricket Ground.

She was an early member of Women's Liberation and active in land rights and green bans campaigns. She has been arrested on numerous occasions.

Meredith did her PhD on the Builders Labourers' Federation and was a senior lecturer in industrial relations at Macquarie University. In 1985, she was elected as the first woman president of the academics' union, now known as the National Tertiary Education Union (NTEU) in New South Wales. She was a founding member of the National Pay Equity Coalition and the Trade Union Committee on Aboriginal Rights.

She was elected to the NSW Upper House in 1991, and in 1999 became the first Labor woman president. As president, Meredith scaled back expensive and ostentatious traditions and opened the parliamentary precincts up to diverse community groups.

She founded and still organises the Ernie Awards for Sexism, now in their twenty-eighth year. This gives her expertise in dopey and shocking remarks by sportsmen, celebrity chefs, unionists and politicians. She is also a founding member of EMILY's List.

Since leaving parliament she has been elected president of the Australian Council for International Development (the peak body for NGO aid organisations), has worked as a consultant for the United Nations Development Programme, and has undertaken training programs for women candidates in the Pacific. She has continued her interest in Timor-Leste and in 2016 was awarded the Order of Timor-Leste by President Taur Matan Ruak. She worked on both Obama campaigns in New Hampshire and Texas.

Meredith has edited or co-authored three books: on misogyny, green bans and ASIO.

She is a life member of the ALP and the NTEU and is a foundation member (1982) and ambassador for the Sydney Swans (*Yaaay!*).

John Derum

John Derum AM is an actor and writer whose performance career has been mainly in comedy and Australian writing. He is happiest when it is both.

Since his Sixties experience in theatre at Emerald Hill in Melbourne, he has often appeared on television as well as continuing to work in his first love, the theatre.

His television work has included *The Mavis Bramston Show*, *The Aunty Jack Show*, *Australia A–Z*, *The True Blue Show* and *Ratbags*. He also wrote and performed satirical sketches for *This Day Tonight*, *7.30 Report* and *Willesee at Seven*.

John is probably best known for *More Than a Sentimental Bloke*, his tribute to the Australian poet CJ Dennis, which he wrote and produced. He performed this piece more than 500 times throughout Australia and in numerous radio and television spin-offs. The tribute led to other long-running productions, including ABC television's *That's Australia* and *The Oz Game*.

During 1983–85, John appeared in the epic stage production of *The Life and Adventures of Nicholas Nickleby*. Other theatre work has included the Arthur Miller classic, *The Crucible*, for the Sydney Theatre Company, and David Hare's *The Power of Yes*, at Belvoir.

In 2011, John and writer Pat Sheil combined to win the short play competition at the Short + Sweet Theatre Festival at the Seymour Centre with the hilarious solo performance, *A Safe Pair of Hands*.

John has also worked in theatre administration and company management.

He has continued to campaign around issues of concern for Australian performers through his membership of Actors' Equity/MEAA. He has also represented the wider community, through his election to the Blue Mountains City Council.

Easing into retirement, he found a new career recording some thirty audiobooks when he really should have been playing bowls.

Peter Duncan

Peter Duncan was a reforming Labor attorney-general in South Australia's Don Dunstan government, that later became a federal MP and minister.

Peter was elected to the South Australian House of Assembly in 1973 at the age of twenty-eight. As a private member he introduced a bill to decriminalise homosexuality which, after several attempts, was eventually passed. This was the first successful decriminalisation legislation in Australia.

In 1975, Peter became the Attorney-General and with the support of Don Dunstan passed a remarkable suite of progressive legislation, much of which became a template for other Australian jurisdictions and all of which still stands.

In a whirlwind period of four years, Peter legislated to abolish capital punishment and the crime of public drunkenness. He outlawed discrimination on the grounds of illegitimacy, regularised the situation of de facto couples before the law, reformed rape and sexual offence trial procedures, and legislated to criminalise rape in marriage.

Peter set up the administration to enforce action under the Sex Discrimination Act and appointed Mary Beasley as the first commissioner for Equal Opportunity.

He also introduced the first MPs disclosure of interests legislation in Australia.

On the financial side, new legislation was introduced to enable credit unions to more effectively compete with banks, and the Residential Tenancy Act established an inexpensive and speedy tribunal. He established the Legal Services Commission to make sure legal aid was available to all in need.

He set up an inquiry into the rights of persons with disabilities, but the South Australian Labor government fell in 1979 before its findings could be implemented.

Peter served in the federal parliament from 1984 to 1996 and was Minister for Land Transport and Infrastructure Support and Minister for Employment and Education Services in the Hawke government.

Ellis D Fogg (Roger Foley)

Ellis D Fogg was the pseudonym under which Roger Foley produced his lightshows in the Sixties. Now known as Roger Foley-Fogg, he has been described as Australia's most innovative lighting designer and lumino-kinetic sculptor.

Apart from his lightshow work, in 1967 Roger produced an early Happening (now known as performance art), *Destruction in Art*, at the University of New South

Wales with Jenni Nixon, and in 1971 exhibited an early environment/installation at Watters Gallery, *WOOM*, with Vivienne Binns. He was a member of the Yellow House artists' commune in Potts Point.

In conjunction with Peter Sculthorpe and John Hopkins, Roger produced lightshows for the ABC's 'Prom' concerts with the Sydney and Melbourne symphony orchestras.

He also presented an installation with Fujiko Nakaya, *FOG in FOGG*, for the 1978 Biennale of Sydney.

In the 1990s, he directed lumino-kinetic projections on the façade of the Museum of Contemporary Art in Sydney and also produced an installation for the Historic Houses Trust, *The Face of Luna Park on Hyde Park Barracks*.

In 1993, he was the producer and designer of 'Artists for Labor', a concert of Australian talent in support of the re-election of Prime Minister Paul Keating.

From 2000 to 2008, Roger worked with five Aboriginal communities in the Kimberley, Western Australia, producing lightshows for the Gija people, assisting them to tell their stories.

Roger has an ongoing project – permanent Sixties-style lighting of the heritage rainbow village of Nimbin in New South Wales. How fitting.

Roger has twice been a finalist in the Blake Prize for religious art and also won the Best Float Design Award for the 1989 Sydney Gay and Lesbian Mardi Gras. He has received two grants from the Australia Council for experimental theatre work.

Gary Foley

Gary Foley, from the Gumbaynggirr Nation of the NSW North Coast, is one of Australia's best-known Aboriginal activists and commentators. He is also a historian, an author, an actor and an inspirational teacher.

A decade after the Springbok demonstrations and the Aboriginal Embassy struggles (outlined in his chapter), Gary was involved in the Commonwealth Games protests in Brisbane (1982). He also took a vocal role in protests during the 1988 Bicentenary celebrations. One of the founders of Redfern's Aboriginal Legal Service and Aboriginal Health Service, he was also instrumental in the establishment of the Victorian Aboriginal Health Service in Melbourne.

In 1974, Gary was part of an Aboriginal delegation that toured China, and in 1979 he set up the Aboriginal Information Centre in London. Four years later, he became the first Aboriginal director of the Aboriginal Arts Board of the Australia Council.

Pursuing his love of acting, which had begun with the 1973 television comedy series *Basically Black*, in 1976 Gary co-wrote and acted in the classic Aboriginal road movie, *Back Roads*, directed by Phil Noyce. Together with other cast members, he toured the film to the Cannes Film Festival and on to Germany and London. Gary also appeared in the films *Going Down*, *Buckeye & Pinto*, *Pandemonium* and *Dogs in Space*. In 2011, he wrote the script for his autobiographical one-man show, which he performed at the Melbourne Arts Festival and at the Sydney Opera House, to great acclaim.

In 1994, Gary created the Koori History website <kooriweb.org>, which continues to be one of the most comprehensive Aboriginal education resources available.

After his return to formal education, Gary completed his Bachelor of Arts and in 2002 gained first class honours in history. Between 2005 and 2008, he was a tutor/lecturer at the University of Melbourne, where in 2012 he completed a PhD in history.

He is currently professor of history, Moondani Balluk Indigenous Academic Unit, at Victoria University.

Albert Langer (Arthur Dent)

Albert Langer is an Australian political activist who since the late 1990s has lived under the name of Arthur Dent.

After the events described in this book were over, Albert Langer failed to settle down as an unemployed revolutionary activist.

He worked as a teacher for a year and then as a Telecom linesman. Taking a year's leave without pay, he was a visiting research fellow at the Peace Research Institute Oslo, studying the strategic role of ballistic missile submarines and their navigation systems in nuclear warfare. Returning to Australia and to his former employment, he qualified as a Telecom cable-jointer.

With his customary turn of phrase, he explains that 'When Mao Tsetung died and the fascist regime took over in China', he was spokesperson for the Red Eureka Movement (REM) 'which supported continuing the revolution in China, a global united front against Soviet imperialism, and hostility to pseudo-leftism, in opposition to all other formerly

"Maoist" groups which lined up behind the Chinese or Albanian regimes and/or went nuts and/or green instead of red'.

When REM 'faded away along with the Sixties Left', Albert Langer turned his interest to opposing copyright law as a spokesperson for Software Liberation; liberating Iraq from fascism; and daily participation in the 'Occupy Melbourne' movement.

Becoming newly notorious during the 1990s over his advocacy of the so-called 'Langer Vote', he was imprisoned in 1996 after arguing before a full bench of the High Court that it was legal to vote against both major parties. Eight years later, the Electoral Commission tried to arrest him again, to force him to pay court costs. As he relates in his piece in this book, it was at this point that he assumed the name of the anti-hero of *The Hitchhiker's Guide to the Galaxy*.

Arthur Dent is currently researching Maksakovsky's Marxist theory of 'The Capitalist Cycle' in preparation for the next battle with the Vogon Constructor Fleet. He describes himself as 'still at large but incommunicado'.

Brian Laver

Brian Laver variously describes himself as a libertarian socialist, a revolutionary anarchist, and a social ecologist. He has also been described as the world's only Anarchist International Tennis Coach.

After completing his honours degree in history in 1967, and going on to run Foco and the Red and Black Bookshop, Brian spent some years of 'R&R' on a 25-acre macadamia farm on Brisbane's outer fringe, where he and his wife built an Edna Walling-style cottage.

This was followed by a job as editor at Brisbane's Jacaranda Press. After being drummed out of this position by right-wing ALP powerbroker Jack Egerton, Brian moved his family to Victoria. Even there, he was blacklisted from a number of jobs, ranging from teaching to building work, before he finally secured work at a Zionist college.

After returning north, through the latter half of the 1970s he had a series of appointments at Queensland and Griffith universities, teaching courses in imperialism, war and revolution.

Meanwhile, his brother Ian had established Laver's International Tennis Resort in Florida, USA, where Brian took on the job of head of marketing as well as head professional in 1979. While working there, Brian coached teams from China and Brazil and other countries.

Returning to Australia at the request of his parents in 1985, he ran the anarchist bookshops Maria Luisa Bookshop and Zapata's Bookshop, and continued his career as a tennis coach. He is a director of the Institute for Social Ecology in Australia.

Every year, Brian attends the Australian Open in Melbourne with cousin Rodney.

He is writing his memoir.

Peter Manning

Peter Manning is a well-known Australian journalist, author, broadcaster, commentator and academic. After beginning as a journalist at Fairfax, he was a reporter in print, radio and television and online for thirty years.

Biographies

In the 1980s, Peter was a field producer and then executive producer of *Four Corners*, during which time the program won numerous awards for its investigative journalism.

As head of TV News and Current Affairs at the ABC (1989–93), Peter began the network's very successful website <abc.net.au> and founded *Lateline*, *Foreign Correspondent* and *Landline*.

He was later the head of News and Current Affairs at the Seven Network (1996–2000).

After retiring from journalism, Peter began his career as an academic as adjunct professor of journalism at the University of Technology, Sydney (2000–2009). Over the next three years he was senior lecturer in journalism at Monash University. In 2014, Peter was awarded his Doctorate of Philosophy in the Faculty of Arts and Sciences at UTS. He is currently an adjunct professor in journalism at that university's School of Communication.

In addition to numerous publications in a range of journals and books, Peter is the author of *Janet Venn-Brown: A life in art* (2016), *Us and Them: A journalist's investigation of media, Muslims and the Middle East* (2006), *Dog Whistle Politics and Journalism* (2004) and *Green Bans* (1975).

Peter's most recent book is *Representing Palestine: Media and journalism in Australia since World War I* (2018).

A long-term campaigner for justice for the people of Palestine, in 2019 Peter stayed in Bethlehem while researching his current book, concerning the fifty-year history of Bethlehem University as Palestine's first university. It is due for publication in 2022.

David Marr

David Marr is one of Australia's best-known writers, journalists and commentators on politics and the arts.

Towards the end of the 1970s, David took time out from daily journalism to write a biography of Chief Justice Sir Garfield Barwick, one of the leading plotters in the coup against Whitlam. *Barwick* appeared in 1980 and won the NSW Premier's Literary Award that year.

After a couple of years editing the *National Times*, David spent over a decade working on books and in television and radio. In 1985, he began work on a biography of Patrick White. Published in 1991, *Patrick White: A life* won a number of literary prizes. After the White fuss died down, David had a second stint on ABC Television's *Four Corners* and in 1994 became the first presenter of ABC Radio National's *Arts Today*.

Though he had vowed never to return to newspapers, he was lured to the *Sydney Morning Herald* in 1996. He was based at the paper for the next sixteen years, writing on politics, law, LGBTI issues, censorship, refugees and race. In that time he published a couple of collections of his writings, and with his colleague Marian Wilkinson wrote *Dark Victory*, a forensic account of the Tampa refugee crisis.

For three years from 2002, David presented ABC Television's *Media Watch*. After his return to the *Herald*, he began to appear regularly on ABC Television's *Insiders*; wrote occasionally for *The Monthly*; and published essays on John Howard, Kevin Rudd, Tony Abbott, Bill Shorten and Pauline Hanson for the *Quarterly Essay* series.

David retired from the *Sydney Morning Herald* at sixty-five, but found himself writing at the *Guardian*. His little book, *The Prince: Faith, abuse and George Pell*, continued to be updated and reissued as that saga developed. In 2018, he published *My Country*, a collection of his reporting, speeches and essays from the last forty-five years.

Bronwyn Penrith

Bronwyn Penrith is a widely respected Aboriginal Elder, who has a lifelong commitment and engagement with her Community. She holds the family responsibilities of a mother, grandmother and great-grandmother, and is also a recognised kinship carer. A trained facilitator and mentor, experienced in running community education and cultural awareness workshops, Bronwyn does much of her work in a voluntary capacity.

Alongside her position as senior director, Burbangana Group (a private consulting company), she is chairperson of Mudgin-Gal Aboriginal Women's Centre and a director of the Redfern Foundation Ltd. She is registered with the Attorney-General's Department as a family dispute resolution practitioner, and is also a member of the Aboriginal Women's Consultative Network of the NSW Women's Legal Resource Centre.

Bronwyn is the NSW representative on the National Aboriginal and Torres Strait Islander Women's Alliance. This organisation has identified gendered violence and Aboriginal women in business as priorities.

In 2016, Bronwyn fulfilled the role of Elder at the Building Better Lives for Ourselves Conference, attended by a hundred Aboriginal and Torres Strait Islander women brought together by the Department of Prime Minister and Cabinet.

Recently at Mudgin-Gal, Bronwyn led the making of a possum skin cloak – the first sewn by local Aboriginal women in 200 years. She also initiated an invitation for Aboriginal women to reclaim their Corroboree – a preparation for Ceremony to which over sixty women from four generations responded.

Bronwyn is deeply connected to Country, and recently travelled to her home Country to witness the first traditional burn in that area since the coming of white people to Brungle.

Margaret Reynolds

Margaret Reynolds is a feminist, activist, educator and author and a former Labor senator and minister.

During her politicisation experiences in Townsville in the Sixties, Margaret joined the ALP because of Gough Whitlam's commitment to end conscription and support women's issues and land rights.

In 1979, she was elected to the Townsville City Council, where the progressive Labor team made important social and cultural policy gains in a difficult environment. A highlight of her time on council was when the Aboriginal community presented an Aboriginal flag to the Townsville community. Aboriginal Elder, Shorty O'Neill, and Margaret, representing the council, raised it in the city mall.

In 1983, she was unexpectedly elected to the federal Senate, becoming the first Labor woman from Queensland to be elected to the upper house. During sixteen years in the Senate she focused on a wide range of national and international issues, particularly those relating to women.

During the Hawke government, Margaret served terms

as Minister for Local Government and Minister for the Status of Women.

After leaving parliament, she lectured in human rights and international politics at the University of Queensland and headed the Tasmanian section of National Disability Services, the national peak body representing disability service providers.

She has served terms as president of the United Nations Association of Australia and is presently chair of the Friends of the ABC.

Her writings include *HERstory: Australian Labor women in Federal, State and Territory Parliaments* (co-editor); *The Last Bastion: Labor women working towards equality in the parliaments of Australia*; and her memoir *Living Politics*.

Margret RoadKnight

Margret RoadKnight is an Australian singer who performs in a wide variety of styles, including blues, jazz, gospel, cabaret and folk.

Emerging from the Melbourne folk music and anti-war protest scenes of the Sixties, Margret has had a successful music career spanning ten albums and almost six decades.

In the 1960s and 1970s, Margret appeared on numerous television shows, including *Folkmoot*, hosted by Leonard Teale; *Dave's Place*, hosted by the Kingston Trio's Dave Guard; and the ABC's *Open-End*.

In 1975, she released a cover version of Bob Hudson's 'Girls in Our Town', which became her most important hit and a bit of a feminist anthem.

She toured overseas extensively, often representing Australia, notably in China in 1978, and at the United Nations Special Session on Disarmament in 1982.

Margret has also promoted tours by international artists and produced shows focusing on her favoured artists, including Paul Robeson and Malvina Reynolds.

For three years, Margret broadcast radio shows on Black gospel music, and she has also worked on music programs in schools in conjunction with Musica Viva.

In her long career, she has been showered with honours and awards, including 'Artist of the Year' at the Port Fairy Folk Festival in 1998; 'Lifetime Achievement' at the National Folk Festival in 2014; and 'Lifetime Achievement' at the inaugural Australian Women in Music Awards in 2018. In 1991, she was the first singer added to the famous Montsalvat Jazz Festival Honour Roll.

Probably most significantly, her recording of 'Girls in Our Town' has been selected for the 'Sounds of Australia' collection in the National Film and Sound Archives.

Geoffrey Robertson

Geoffrey Robertson AO is an international human rights lawyer, writer and TV personality.

After Geoffrey's tumultuous time advocating for change and advising the revolutionary students of Sydney in the 1960s, he left for Oxford as the 1970 Rhodes Scholar. As a barrister in London he defended, among others, the *Oz* editors; Peter (now Lord) Hain; Salman Rushdie; Julian Assange; *Gay News*; and various anarchists and suspected IRA members. He was made a QC in 1988.

In 1990, he founded, and still leads, Doughty Street Chambers – the largest human rights practice in Europe.

Geoffrey appeared for many facing the death penalty in the Caribbean, and in 1994 won a case in the Privy Council which saved hundreds from the gallows. He has defended dissidents in Singapore, Africa and the Middle East. He was Amnesty International's observer in South Africa in the last years of apartheid.

Geoffrey worked with Václav Havel in Czechoslovakia during the 'Velvet Revolution' and he secured Yulia Tymoshenko's release from prison in the Ukraine in 2014. He investigated the Medellín Cartel; helped restore democracy in Fiji; and was involved in the prosecutions of Chile's General Pinochet and Malawi dictator Hastings Banda.

Geoffrey was the first president of the Special Court, the United Nations-backed war crimes court in Sierra Leone.

He received the New York State Bar Association Award for distinction in international law in 2011. He is a Master of the Middle Temple and a visiting professor at the New College of Humanities in London.

Geoffrey conducted his long-running television program, *Geoffrey Robertson's Hypotheticals*, for the ABC, and for other networks in Britain and the United States, from 1985 to 2014.

He is the author of many books, including *Crimes Against Humanity* and his autobiography, *Rather His Own Man: In court with tyrants, tarts and troublemakers*. His other publications of note are *The Tyrannicide Brief*, *Dreaming Too Loud*, *The Justice Game*, *The Case of the Pope* and *Who Owns History?*

Jozefa Sobski

Jozefa Sobski AM has been an active and committed feminist from the early seventies, when she joined Sydney Women's Liberation.

In her professional life she was a high school teacher of English and history, principal of a TAFE College, director of South Western Sydney Institute of TAFE and deputy director-general of Education and Training. Her early career in teaching and work as a policy adviser in the NSW Ministry of Education was devoted to ending sex discrimination in education at all levels and in all its forms.

Jozefa was an inaugural member of NSW Women in Education (1973–92) and the Australian Women's Education Coalition.

When retiring from paid public service in 2003, Jozefa reconnected with her activist origins and her commitment to migrant communities. She chaired the Community Languages Schools Board from 2009–18 and was a member of the Board of Rape and Domestic Violence Services Australia from 2006–16, as well as becoming convenor of the Women's Electoral Lobby (WEL) NSW.

Currently, she is an executive member of WEL NSW and a member of WEL Australia. She is also chair of the Board of Jessie Street National Women's Library and vice president of the Haberfield Association. She is active in the TAFE Community Alliance and is a member of the National Foundation for Australian Women, EMILY's List and Immigrant Women's Speakout Association.

Robbie Swan

Robbie Swan is a writer, editor and radio producer with a special interest in alternative lifestyles and environmentally sustainable living. He is best known as an anti-censorship campaigner.

Robbie survived his torrid encounters with the repressive state apparatus in the 1970s and escaped to a higher place (Switzerland), where he taught transcendental meditation.

In the 1980s, he edited *Simply Living*, an alternative/ environmental anti-nuclear magazine. He was the founder and editor of the satirical journal *Matilda*. He had a stint as Phillip Adams's producer on his radio show and researched material for Richard Neville's *Extra Dimensions* for the Ten Network.

The 1990s saw him remake himself as Caroline Sweetly, the founder and editor of *Ecstasy Magazine*. An even more remarkable remake resulted in him becoming the editor of rugby league magazine, *Raiders Country*. He co-edited with Phillip Adams the humour magazine, *Kookaburra*, and finished off the decade by editing *Eros*, the adult trade industry paper.

In 2000, he co-published the booklet, *Hypocrites*, which was the first time that a list of the names of paedophile priests was published in Australia.

In 2001, he co-founded the National Museum of Erotica in Canberra.

In 2009, he and his partner in life and politics, Fiona Patten, founded the Australian Sex Party, which gained immediate voter support and eventually won Fiona a seat in the Victorian Legislative Council.

Robbie and Fiona remain involved in environmental issues, particularly through their work with the Brindabella Wildlife and Wilderness Reserve in New South Wales.

Helen Voysey

Helen Voysey is a doctor and committed community activist. She believes that the organisational skills she learnt as a young activist gave her the skills she has needed in order to practise medicine.

After completing high school, she worked for nine months as a psychiatric nurse at Callan Park in Sydney in order to earn enough money to go overseas. By May 1971 she was in London, where she was employed as a graphic design assistant on the daily Trotskyist newspaper, the *Workers Press*. In her spare time, she co-ordinated a Young Socialist group in South London, working with disadvantaged youth.

In 1975, Helen returned to Australia and commenced a degree in Medicine, completing this in 1981.

While subsequently travelling around Australia, she found herself in 1985 at the handover of Uluru. This led her to work as the first female doctor at Anyinginyi Congress Aboriginal Corporation in Tennant Creek and later as a district medical officer for the Barkly region.

Suffering a cervical spinal injury in a vehicle rollover on an outback road in 1989, she was evacuated to the Royal Adelaide Hospital Spinal Unit. On recovery she returned to Tennant Creek as medical superintendent of the hospital. She left the Territory in 1990, but returned regularly as a locum to Anyinginyi Congress and the Royal Flying Doctor Service

Medical Clinic at Yulara. Co-author of a research paper on renal disease in the Barkly, she campaigned alongside Warumungu people for a renal unit to be established in Tennant Creek. This opened in 2005.

After her father's death in 2002, Helen became president of the Royal National Park Coastal Cabins Protection League and successfully lobbied to have the shack communities listed on the State Heritage Register.

Helen lives in the northern Illawarra with her husband and enjoys taking her grandchildren to the Era Beach shack, continuing the family heritage. She works part-time as a general practitioner in Wollongong.

Nadia Wheatley

Nadia Wheatley is an award-winning Australian writer, whose published works include picture books, novels, biography, memoir and history.

After not being sent down from university for the tomato (described in her piece for this book), she completed an honours degree in history, followed by an MA. Leaving her thesis on her supervisor's floor, she went to Greece for three years and taught herself to write. Her first published fiction was in the iconic English feminist magazine *Spare Rib* (1978).

Nadia's first book, *Five Times Dizzy* (1982), was hailed as Australia's first multicultural book for children. Other social and political issues explored in her work have included conservation, unemployment and refugees. Her biography, *The Life and Myth of Charmian Clift*, was the *Age* Non-Fiction Book of the Year, 2001, and is the only biography to have won the Australian History Prize in the NSW Premier's History Awards.

Nadia's political activism has continued alongside her writing. Her silliest charge was for Malicious Damage to Salmon *Vol au Vents*, after an incident in an Unemployed People's Union demonstration against Malcolm Fraser. Nadia's barrister argued that you simply can't be malicious to a *vol au vent*, but she ended up spending twelve days in Mulawa women's prison – luckily coinciding with a strike by her fellow prisoners.

Her commitment to Aboriginal social justice led her to work for five years as a consultant at Papunya School in the Northern Territory, where she supported Anangu staff and students in the development of their own curriculum model, and in the publication of the multi-award-winning *Papunya School Book of Country and History* (2001).

An active member of the Australian Society of Authors, Nadia was deputy chair for a number of years and is a member of the ASA Council. In 2014 she was awarded the ASA Medal.

In 2014, Sydney University awarded Nadia an honorary Doctorate of Letters, in recognition of 'her exceptional creative achievements in the field of children's and adult literature, her work as an historian and her contribution to our understanding of Indigenous issues, cultural diversity, equity and social justice and the environment through story'.

Nadia's most recent publication is the memoir, *Her Mother's Daughter* (2018).

Gary Williams

Gary Williams is a Gumbaynggirr Elder and community activist. He has spent the last twenty-five years bringing his language back home to the Nambucca region in northern New South Wales.

Following his participation in the 1965 Freedom Ride through country New South Wales and his involvement in setting up the Aboriginal Legal Service and the Aboriginal Health Service in Redfern, Gary has spent his time committed to the betterment of Indigenous life in its many iterations.

During 1973 and 1974, he used his community experience and legal understanding working as a field officer for the Aboriginal Legal Service in Redfern.

In 1976, Gary travelled to the Northern Territory, where he first worked as a driver in the Indigenous community of Papunya. Later, in 1977 and 1978, at the Central Land Council in Alice Springs, he worked closely with the redoubtable chairman, Wenten Rubuntja, who was fighting hard for meaningful land rights and also for the viability of the 'outstation movement'.

In 1997, Gary returned permanently to his Country at Nambucca. Here he has become a vital cog in the workings of the Muurrbay Aboriginal Language and Culture Co-operative (formerly the Gumbaynggirr Language and Culture Group). Muurrbay is a regional language centre providing strategic support to revitalise the languages of seven local communities. It works closely with Elders to conduct research, publish language dictionaries, run courses and produce resources. It also provides a community centre for language and cultural activities. In 2016, Gary was one of the three editors of Muurrbay's important book, *Gumbaynggirr Yuludarla Jandaygam: Gumbaynggirr Dreaming story collection*.

References

The following references are either mentioned in the text, or they directly informed our interviews and writing. They are not intended to be a comprehensive reading list for the history of the Sixties, or for the biographies of the participants.

Meredith Burgmann: That glorious time to be alive

Meredith Burgmann, *Dirty Secrets: Our ASIO files*, NewSouth Publishing, Sydney, 2014.

Nadia Wheatley: The girl who threw the tomato

Nadia Wheatley, *Her Mother's Daughter: A memoir*, Text Publishing, Melbourne, 2018.

The two interviews with 'Martin Collins' appeared in 1969 in *The Australian*, Saturday 3 May, p. 3 and Monday 5 May, p. 16. The governor's comment appeared in the *Sydney Morning Herald*, 3 May, p. 1. Other coverage of this event can be found in the *Mirror*, 2 May, p. 2; the *Daily Telegraph*, 3 May, pp. 1, 3 and 7 May, p. 2; the *Sun Herald*, 4 May, pp. 1, 2; the *Sydney Morning Herald*, 5 May, Letters and 7 May, p. 1; *The Australian*,

3 May, p. 1, also 6 May, pp. 3, 4 and 14 June, p. 2; *Honi Soit*, 11 September and 25 September.

Correspondence: William O'Neill, Deputy Vice-Chancellor University of Sydney to NW, 23 May 1969; H McCredie, Registrar to NW, 8 July 1969 and 22 August 1969.

Gary Foley: Fighting for truth, justice and the Aboriginal way

The Koori History Website, <kooriweb.org>.

Geoffrey Robertson: The right side of history

Geoffrey Robertson, *Rather His Own Man: In court with tyrants, tarts and troublemakers*, Penguin Random House, Sydney, 2019.

Margret RoadKnight: Troubadour

Margret RoadKnight, program notes for *Deep Bells Ring: The life and songs of Paul Robeson* (musical play by Nancy Wills), ACTU production, Melbourne, March–April 1988.

Albert Langer (Arthur Dent): Hardened apparatchik

Michael Hyde, *It Is Right to Rebel*, Diplomat, Canberra, 1972; improved epub edition <https://archive.org/details/it-is-right-to-rebel-1972>.

——, *All Along the Watchtower: Memoir of a sixties revolutionary*, Vulgar Press, Melbourne, 2010.

Ken Mansell, 'The Yeast Is Red: A history of The Bakery, off-campus centre of the Monash Labor Club, 1968–1971', in Emily Floyd, *Disobedience: The university as a site of political potential*, Monash University, Museum of Art, Melbourne, 2013.

References

Philip Mendes, *The New Left, the Jews and the Vietnam War, 1965–1972*, Lazare Press, Melbourne, 1993. (This includes Langer's account of what happened after his October 1966 arrest.)

The 4 July 1968 demonstration was reported in *The Age*, 5 July 1968.

Arthur Dent posts occasionally on the blog, <C21stleft.com>.

David Marr: Taking on the rich and powerful

David Marr, *My Country: Stories, essays and speeches*, Black Inc., Melbourne, 2018.

Margaret Reynolds: Born feminist

Margaret Reynolds, *Living Politics*, University of Queensland Press, Brisbane, 2007.

Brian Laver: Fighting fascism

Brian Laver, 'Behind student action', *Australian Left Review*, no. 13, June–July 1968.

Brisbane Discussion Circle, 'Remembering the University of Queensland Forum', <radicaltimes.info/PDF/Forum.pdf>.

Dan O'Neill, 'The growth of the radical movement', *Semper Floreat*, vol. 39, no. 2, 17 March 1969.

1967 Civil Liberties March, Brisbane, Australia, <player.vimeo.com/video/20105643>.

Bronwyn Penrith: Miracle child

Suzanne Ingram, 'Silent Drivers | Driving Silence – Aboriginal women's voices on domestic violence', *Social Alternatives*, vol. 35, no. 1, 2016, <socialalternatives.com/issues/silence-power>.

For information about Welfare Inspector Mrs English, see 'Farewell to Mrs I.M. English', *Dawn*, September 1957.

Ellis D Fogg (Roger Foley): I hate being bored

Roger Foley-Fogg, exhibition notes, *Spirit of the Gija: We are all friends now* (videotape), photography and film exhibition, Australia, New York and New Delhi, 2002–13.

Martin Sharp, 'The Word Flashed Round the Arms', in *Oz* 6, February 1964, p. 7.

Vivienne Binns: Searching for Truth

Catalogue list and associated material for Vivienne Binns's 1967 exhibition, Watters Gallery Archive, Art Gallery of New South Wales Archives.

Reviews for Vivienne Binns's 1967 exhibition, including those by Rodney Milgate and Helen Sweeney, are reproduced in *Refractory Girl*, no. 8, March 1975.

WOOM invitation, program notes, reviews and other ephemera are in the Watters Gallery Archive, Art Gallery of New South Wales Archives.

Gary Williams: A lot of stuff just happens

Steve Morelli, Gary Williams, Dallas Walker (eds), *Gumbaynggirr Yuludarla Jandaygam: Gumbaynggirr Dreaming Story Collection*, Muurrbay Aboriginal Language and Culture Co-operative, Nambucca Heads, 2016.

Helen Voysey: The kid from the sticks

Or Forever Hold Your Peace (1970), on *Australian Screen*, a National Film and Sound Archive (NFSA) Website, <aso.gov.au/titles/documentaries/or-forever-hold-your-peace/>.

David McKnight, *Australian Spies and their Secrets*, Allen & Unwin, Sydney, 1994, chapter 19.

Robbie Swan: Fun along the way

Robbie Swan, 'Riders on the Storm', in Paul Wilson and Robyn Lincoln (eds), *Crime on My Mind*, New Holland Publishers, Sydney, 2010.

Jozefa Sobski: Opening doors to other worlds

For the Manly pub protest, see Jozefa Sobski, 'On demonstrating and remonstrating,' *Mejane*, March 1973, p. 19.

Peter Manning: Taking a stand

Peter Manning, 'In the Middle of a Dream', in *What Did You Do in the Cold War, Daddy? Personal stories from a troubled time*, Ann Curthoys and Joy Damousi (eds), NewSouth Publishing, Sydney, 2014.

Acknowledgments

We thank all our participants who agreed to us strip-mining their lives for others' enjoyment. They were, without fail, kind and generous, both with their time and their memories. Some even helped us (unprompted) with our punctuation and spelling.

We would also like to thank those who helped us track down comrades from our Sixties past. There were many phone calls and emails before we managed to end up in front of our prey with tape recorder in hand. Thank you to Anthony Ashbolt, Verity Burgmann, Dave Nadel, Lee Walkington, Frank Watters and Larry Zetlin.

Thank you to Nadia's agent, Margaret Connolly, for overseeing the contract.

For help with the photographs we thank Janine Barrand, Jane Beattie, Mervyn Bishop, Richard Brennan, Sean Bridgeman, Andrew Chapman, Barbara Cleary, Wayne Davies, Liam Donohoe, Claudia Funder, Peter Gray, Catherine Hill, Bruce Ibsen, Josef Lebovic, Maria Manning, Adrienne Martyn, Mark Ray, Julia Robins, Karen Rogers,

Acknowledgments

and Dany Torsh. For permission to use the lyrics of 'Girls in our Town', many thanks to our comrade Bob Hudson.

Thanks also go to the wonderful folk at NewSouth: Pip McGuinness, Emma Hutchinson, Elspeth Menzies, Rosie Marson, Joumana Awad, and our meticulous copy editor Diana Hill.

Thank you to our friends who provided research, advice and support: Heather Goodall, Helen Randerson, Robin Morrow and Mariella Totaro-Genevois.

And a final thank you to our families who put up with us, particularly Ken Searle, Paddy Batchelor, Shannan Dodson and Kira Dodson.

Index

1950s xiv, 57, 280, 283, 342, 347, 352
1960s xiv–xix, 340, 347, 352

Aarons, Brian 230, 238, 332, *picture section 6*
Abbey, Brian 195, 199
Aboriginal civil rights movement xv, 43, 65, 131–33, 227–33, 235; *see also* Aboriginal Tent Embassy; racism; FCAATSI; Referendum 1967; segregation
Aboriginal deaths in custody protests xii, xviii
Aboriginal identity 160–61
Aboriginal land rights movement 33, 46–49, 80, 133, 164, 167, 198, 202, 239, 347, 350, 368, 377
Aboriginal Legal Service 44, 162, 234, 348, 361, 377
Aboriginal Medical Service 45, 162
Aboriginal Protection Act 35, 45
Aboriginal Tent Embassy xvi, 33–34, 47–48, 162, 167, 239, 361
Aborigines Progressive Association 228–29
Aborigines Protection Board *see* Aborigines Welfare Board
Aborigines Welfare Board 157, 158–59, 227
abortion 134, 136, 198, 244, 315, 321, *picture section 7*
Abschol (Aboriginal scholarship organisation) 199, 227
Ali, Tariq 152, 153
Allan, Percy 6, 13

America, influence of 10, 93, 145, 195–97, 283, 287, 349
  anti-war movement 111, 246–47, 293–94, 333, 349; *see also* anti-Vietnam movement
  art 184, 211, 219–21
  civil rights 42–43, 67, 80–81, 163, 232, 235, 239, 348
  drugs 298
  literature 163, 239, 298
  music 66–67, 73–74, 79–81, 287, 299, 301, 333
  student movement 149, 195, 197
  see also Black Panthers
anarchism 88, 138, 148, 154–55, 288
Anderson, Jim *picture section 2, 12*
Anderson, Marian 74
Anderson, Michael 47
Anglicanism *see* Protestantism
anti-apartheid movement xvi, 33–34, 45–46, 64, 85–86, 237–38, 254–55, 301, 341, 345, 347, 355, 371, *picture section 3*
anti-authoritarianism 55, 291–92
anti-Communism 73–75, 132, 141, 148, 296, 311, 317, 324–25, 328, 331
anti-Semitism 85
anti-totalitarianism 141–42, 148, 152–54, 348
anti-Vietnam movement xiii, xv, xvi, 6–7, 9, 11, 92, 111, 115, 128, 162, 181, 264, 267, 269, 282, 316–17, 333–34, 352; *see also* America, influence of, anti-war movement

Index

anti-war movement *see* anti-Vietnam movement
Antrobus, John 287–88
Apology to the Stolen Generations 2008 39, 170
Aquarius Arts Festival 1971 299–301, 344
Archdale, Betty 4
Arden, John 281, 282
Arnold, Lynn 201, *picture section 15*
arrests xv, xviii, 9–13, 23–24, 26, 68, 89, 94, 96–97, 112, 146, 150, 166, 200, 233, 238, 255, 300, 302–03, 320, 340, 356, *picture section 1, 3, 4, 6, 7, 15*
art, experimental 180, 212–13, 221
ASIO 57, 154, 235, 260, 268–69, 270
Askin, Bob 30, 181
Assimilation policy xiv, 47–49, 168, 351
Association for International Co-operation and Disarmament 337
Aunty Jack television series 275, 357
Australian Aboriginal Progressive Association 36
Australian Association for Cultural Freedom 325
Australian Women's Education Coalition 322, 372
automatic drawing 212–13

Bacon, Jim 93, 247
Baez, Joan 78, 333
Baldwin, James 239, 348
Bandler, Faith 41, 43, 133, 232
Bannon, John 196
Basically Black television series 34, 50, 361
Basten, John 233
Batchelor, Peter 242–57, 343, 345, 346, 353–54, *picture section 6*
BBB Mattress Factory 242, 249–52, 256, 257, 346, 353
Bear, Deirdre 224
Bellear, Sol 235
Bellwood (Aboriginal) Reserve 224–25, 241

Beswick, Maria 329–30, 333, 334, 336
Bielski, Joan 321
Binns, Vivienne 184–85, 205–22, 340, 341, 344, 345, 347, 351, 354, 360, *picture section 14*
Bjelke-Petersen, Joh 148
Black Lives Matter protests xi
Black Panthers 43, 131, 163, 235
Black Power 43, 131, 223, 235, *picture section 11*
Blewett, Neal 195
BLF *see* Builders Labourers' Federation
Bloch, Cathy 322
Boddy, Michael 286, *picture section 16*
Bolte, Henry 284, 285
Bonython, Kym 207
books, importance of 348–49
Bowen, Lionel 304
Boyce, Jim 238
Brindle, Ken 231
Brown, Mike 206–07, 211, 212, 215, 219, *picture section 14*
Bryant, Michael 226
Builders Labourers' Federation 238–39, 248, 254, 346
Bulletin, the 103, 114–15, 335–38, 346
Burgmann, Beverley 5, 6, 330
Burgmann, Ernest Henry 1–2
Burgmann, Meredith xi–xv, 1–15, 19–21, 62, 238, 330, 355–56, *picture section 3, 6, 15*
Burgmann, Verity 46, 84, 99
Burke, Janine 221
Burns, Ross 332

Cairns, Jim 80, 81, 89, 195, 277
Calwell, Arthur 2, 56, 127–28, 193, 311
Cameron, Alan 6, 60
Cameron, Clyde 196, 203
Campaign for Nuclear Disarmament 87, 262, 347, 349
Campbell, Martha 91

CAMP Inc 219
capital punishment 57, 59, 283–86, 358
Carmichael, Stokely 235, 348
Carr, Ken 253
Carroll, Des 141
Cassidy, Darce 90, 199, 341
Castaneda, Carlos 184, 298
Catholicism 5–6, 72, 75, 188, 236, 275–78, 309, 312–15, 323, 324, 326–31, 336, 342–43
Catholic/Protestant divide 5, 72, 121, 172, 188, 292, 342
Catley, Bob 195
Cavanagh, Jim 196
censorship 54–55, 66, 113, 178, 198, 206–07, 215, 304–05, 346, 347, 350, 373; see also obscenity
Central Court, Liverpool Street, Sydney xiii, 12, 64
Charles, Jack 289
Cherry, Wal 280–81, 283
Chifley, Ben 56, 189
Christian upbringing 2–3
climate change 273–74, 350, 354
Clint, Alf 229
Coe, Isabel 161, 237
Coe, Paul 42, 44–46, 161–62, 232, 234–38
Cohn-Bendit, Daniel 152, 195
Cold War xiv, 262, 328
Colebrook, John (Jackey) 108
Coleman, Peter 268–69, 335
Combe, David 193, 196,
Communist Party of Australia 86, 88, 120, 127, 199, 230, 254, 260, 325, 332
Communists 57, 74, 79, 87–88, 129, 139, 146, 253, 260, 270, 308, 318, 320, 332, 337
Congress for International Co-operation and Disarmament 98
conscientious objectors 14, 279, 333–34
conscription xv, xvi, 6, 21–22, 128–31, 145–46, 193, 200–01, 246, 267, 279, 281, 289, 294–95, 303, 316,

333, 347, 368; see also anti-Vietnam movement; conscientious objectors
Coorey, Tony 47, 232
Courtney, Elizabeth 244–45
Craigie, Billy 42, 46, 47, 161, 232, 238, picture section 11
Cuban Missile Crisis 262, 335
Cutler, Sir Roden 27, 30–31
Czechoslovakia, Russian invasion of 153–54, 266; see also Prague Spring

Daily Telegraph 27, 324, 327, 335
Davis, Angela 163, 239, 348
Dawn magazine 228, 234
Dawson, Paddy 230, 238
Day, Dorothy 333
Day of Rage 300–01, 341, 347
DeLisle, Jennie 113, 114, 116
demonstrations 13, 25, 83, 89, 93–94, 97, 162, 200, 236, 282, 289, 347
Dent, Arthur see Langer, Albert
Derum, Jean 276–77
Derum, John 67, 82, 275–89, 341, 343, 345, 347, 349, 357–58, picture section 16
Derum, Oliver 289
direct action 14, 203, 274
Disney, Julian 197–98
divorce 326–27
Doolan, Alana 161, 162, 166
Doolan, Susanna 161
dress 345
drugs xviii, 65, 180, 182–83, 193, 196, 213, 290, 293, 295–99, 301–03, 344–45, 347
Duncan, Graeme 195
Duncan, Peter 187–204, 341, 345, 347, 351, 358, picture section 8, 15
Dunstan, Don 193, 194, 196, 197, 198, 199–202, 358
Durbridge, Rob 194, 197
Dutschke, Rudi 152

education, importance of 312–14, 321
for women and girls 321–23
Eliot, TS 107, 293, 298
Ellis, Bob 6, 59

Index

Elsie Women's Refuge 166, 319
Ely, Marie 26, *picture section 1*
Emerald Hill Theatre 75, 280–83, 287, *picture section 16*
epiphanies xii, xix, 7, 25, 27–28, 29–32, 53, 75, 78, 103, 113–14, 124–25, 136, 141, 183, 249, 262, 283–85, 339, 345–46, 348; *see also* radical awakenings
equality of sexes 2, 135; *see also* feminism

FCAATSI 41, 65, 162, 229, 231–32
Federal Council for the Advancement of Aborigines and Torres Strait Islanders *see* FCAATSI
feminism 82, 133–36, 166–67, 198–99, 207, 214–15, 219–21, 297, 306, 314, 317–18, 321–23, 340, 348
  Aboriginal women and 166–69
  feminist art 207, 219–21
  see also Women's Liberation
Ferguson, William 229
films, experimental 176, 178–79
Fisher, John 10
Flower, Dulcie 229
Floyd, George xi
Foco, Brisbane 151, 345, 363
Fogg, Ellis D *see* Foley, Roger
Foley, Bill 34, 35
Foley, Eileen M 172–73
Foley, Gary 33–51, 161, 163, 227, 232, 234, 237–38, 240, 289, 341, 344, 347, 348, 351, 361–62, *picture section 3, 9, 11*
Foley, Hazel 173–75
Foley, Roger 171–86, 218, 341, 342, 344–45, 349, 359–60, *picture section 12*
folk music 66–67, 75–81, 85, 245, 287, 333, 345, 369–70
Foundation for Aboriginal Affairs 40–41, 161, 231–32
Fraser Island sand-mining 254
Freedom Ride 1967 xv, 67, 131, 223, 230–31, 377; *see also* Aboriginal civil rights movement

Free Love 208–11
frontier violence 126
fun xiii, 25, 58, 84, 297, 336, 352
Furnishing Trades Union 249, 251, 253, 255–56, 353, *picture section 6*

Gaines, Barbara Jane 146
George, Jennie 322
Gibbs, Pearl 229
Gilling, Jeremy 12, 26
Gilliver, Shirley 129
Ginnane, Bill 330
Gleitzman, Morris 295
global student movement 152, 195
Goodall, Heather 167, 384
Goon Show 35, 50
Gorton, John 10
Gould, Bob 265
green bans 238, 254, 346, 356
Greenland, Hall 60, 63, 332
Greer, Germaine 66, 167, 172, 317, 348, 352
Groves, Bert 229
Gumbaynggirr language and people 36, 223, 224, 225, 240–41, 351, 361, 377
Gurindji stockmen 133, 198
Guthrie, Bessie 319
Gwynne, Mary Isabel 243–44

Hack, Shelley 9
Hain, Peter 64, 370
Halfpenny, John 253
Hall, Barbara 219
Happenings 171, 178, 184–85, 186, 218, 341, 345, 359, *picture section 14*
Hardy, Frank 277–78
Hawke, Bob 119, 257
Haylen, Wayne 13
Henderson, Marian 287
Hendrix, Jimi 293, 294
Hetherington, Bob 195
Hickey-Williams (Penrith), Emma 157–61
High School Students Against the War in Vietnam 258, 265, 268, 270, 346, *picture section 9*

389

Hill, Ted 88
Holgate, Harry 123
Holland, Sekai 46, 237
Hollows, Fred 45
Holt, Harold 130–31
homosexuality 109, 116, 219, 244, 245, 289
　decriminalisation 202, 204, 351, 358
　gay rights 347
　lesbianism 209, 217, 314–15, 318–19, 340
Honi Soit student newspaper 63, 199, 329, 331
hope for the future 350
Hopgood, Alan 282
Horne, Donald 336, *picture section 8*
HSSAWV *see* High School Students Against the War in Vietnam
Hughes, Robert 66
Humanist Society 172, 264
Humphreys, Barry 66
Humphreys, Max 7, 60–61, *picture section 8*
Huxley, Aldous 183
Hyde, Mike 93, 247

Idriess, Ion 35
Indigenous struggles, international 229; *see also* Aboriginal civil rights movement; Aboriginal land rights movement
Ingram, Norma 237
Ingram, Suzanne 167
Inter-racial Citizen's Committee, Townsville 133
Iremonger, John 6, 330

Jackson, Jesse 163, 349,
Jacobs, Ken 233–34, 236
James, Clive 66, 351
James, Francis 66
Johnson, Carole 163
Johnson, Lyndon B xvi, 89–90, 287
Johnson, Phyllis 255
Jones, Mike 11–12, 26, 28, 29, *picture section 1*

Kaku, Michio 186
Kaprow, Allan 184
Kazimierska (Sobski), Maria 307–12, 323
Keefe, Jim 127, *picture section 10*
Keefe, Sheila 127
Kennedy, John F 122, 144–45
Kennedy, Robert 9
Kennedy, Father Ted 6, 330–32, 339, 342
Kennedy, Trevor 114
Kenny, Peter 214, 217
Kerr, Sir John 58, 103, 115
Kerr, Phil 58
Killoran, Pat 132, 136
King, Martin Luther 9
King, Robert 210
Kirby, Michael 6, 59, 204
Ky, Air Vice-Marshall xvi, 89

land rights *see* Aboriginal land rights movement
Langer, Albert 83–101, 247, 341, 342, 345, 349, 362–63, *picture section 13*
Laver, Brian 138–55, 342, 343, 345, 347, 363–64, *picture section 2, 7*
Laver, Janita 144, 151, 152–54 *picture section 7*
Laver, Len 139–40
Leon, Charlie 229
lesbianism 209, 217, 314–15, 318–19, 340
Lewis, Jeannie 79, 82, 286, *picture section 5*
lightshows 179, 180, 182–86, 218, 359–60
Lippard, Lucy 220
Longbottom, Fred 13
Lynn, Elwyn 180, 207

Mabo, Eddie and Bonita 132–33
MacCallum, Mungo 83
MacGregor, Peter 46
Mackinolty, Chips 267
Malcolm X 42, 67, 163, 239, 348

Index

Manning, Michael and Rosemary 325–26
Manning, Peter 6, 114, 324–39, 341, 342, 343, 351, 364–65, *picture section 8, 16*
Mannix, Archbishop Daniel 72, 276–77,
Marinetti, Filippo Tommaso 177, 179
Marks, Paul 76, 77
Marr, Andrew 104–05, 111
Marr, David 102–17, 341, 342–43, 344, 346, 347, 349, 351, 366, *picture section 8*
Marr, George Jnr 104–06
Mason, Gerry 230
Matheson, Louis 92
Matteson, Mike 13, 332
Maza, Bob 162–63, 289, 349
McCarthy, Mary 285, 292
McCarthy period (USA) 79, 261
McCarthy, Wendy 321
McClelland, Jim 233
McGuinness, Bruce 47, 48, 235
McGuinness, Joe 133
McKnight, David 268
McLean, Graham 77
McLean, Jeannie 129
McLeod, Ken 337, *picture section 1*
McMahon, Billy 46–47
McNeil, Jim 285
Mejane magazine 306, 319
Menzies era 64, 99, 103
Menzies, Robert xiv, xv, 2, 65, 103, 105, 108, 119, 140, 193, 288, 291, 311, 326, 328, 333, 343
Meyrick, Julian 280
Milgate, Rodney 206, 216
Millenials xv
Miller, Arthur 260, 283, 357
Miller (Langer), Kerry 84, 92, 247, *picture section 13*
Milligan, Spike 282, 287–89
Mindszenty, Cardinal 324
'Ming' *see* Menzies, Robert
Monash University 247
    Labor Club 83, 89–93, 96, 97, 98
    Maoists 84, 97–98, 247

Monti, Trevor 255
Moratorium 1970 xvi, 80–81, 98, 182, 195, 201, 236, 248, 258, 270–72, 336–39, *picture section 1, 5, 8, 15; see also* anti-Vietnam movement
Morrison, Jim 301
Mudgin-Gal Aboriginal Women's Centre 168–69, 351, 367–68
Muhammad, Elijah 163
Mundey, Ben 189
Mundey, Jack 254
music 71–74, 294; *see also* folk music
Myles, Julian 195

Nadel, Dave 89, 90
National Art School 208–09, 354
National Council of Women 136
National Liberation Front xiii, 91, 148, 197, 337
national service 21, 25, 236, 248; *see also* conscription
National Times, the 115–17, 346, 349, 366
Native Title 49, 132–33, 164; *see also* Aboriginal land rights movement
Neeme, Aarne 279, 286
Neilley, Warwick 234
Nettheim, Garth 233
Neville, Richard 66, 174–75, 176, 178, 373, *picture section 2*
New Left xiii, 43, 145, 153, 254, 332; *see also* Old Left
Newman Society 5, 6, 330
Nixon, Jenni 178, 359
Noffs, Ted 231
NSW Women in Education 321–22, 372
nuclear war 78, 87–88, 262, 267; *see also* Campaign for Nuclear Disarmament

Oakes, Laurie 59
O'Brien, Peter 194, 197–98
obscenity 178, 206, 215; *see also* censorship
Ochs, Phil 66–67

Radicals

Old Left xiii, 253, 332; *see also* New Left
On Dit student newspaper 197–99, 200
O'Neill, William 31
One People of Australia League *see* OPAL
OPAL 131–33
Osborne, John 282–83
Oz magazine 66, 174, 178

Page, Geoff 292
Paris protests 1968 xvi, 152
Patten, Fiona 291, 373
Patten, Jack 229
Penrith, Bronwyn 156–70, 237, 340, 345, 348, 351, 367–68, *picture section 4*
Penrith, Charlie 157–60
Penrith, Irene 157–58, 170
Percy, Jim 265
Percy, John 265
performance art 178, 184, 345, 359
Perkins, Charlie 67, 131, 228–31, 344, *picture section 10*
'Pig Iron Bob' *see* Menzies, Robert
Pinniger, Gretel 182–83
Pinter, Harold 282–83
police
  and Aboriginal people 232–33
  attitudes to 159, 162, 301–03
  harassment 43–44, 232–33
  violence 41, 42, 93–94, 146, 167, 232–33, 303
political awakenings *see* radical awakenings
Pope John XXIII 312, 328, 330
pornography 290, 292, 304–05
Prague Spring xvi, 152–54
Price, John 303, 304
Price, Peter 91
Pringle, Bob 238–39
Protestantism xiii, 1, 3, 6, 243, 292–93, 330
psychedelia 174, 180, 181, 183, 213–14
Push, Sydney 209, 210

Quadrant magazine 268
Queensland, suppression of civil liberties in 145–51

racism 2, 34, 36–40, 41, 46–47, 68, 125–26, 131, 133, 226–27, 236–37, 294, 310, 344, 348; *see also* Aboriginal civil rights movement; Aboriginal deaths in custody; anti-apartheid movement
radical awakenings xii, xvii, 24–25, 27–32, 42–43, 75, 128, 132, 141, 241, 242, 245, 262, 266, 282–85, 290, 294, 317, 331, 339, 346–49; *see also* epiphanies
radical, definition xiii–xv
Randerson, Helen 11, 384
Raynor, Joan and Betty 174
Reason Party 291
'red diaper babies' xvii, 79
Redfern, Sydney 42–45, 48, 161–65, 168–70, 232–35, 239, 241, 348, 351, 361, 367, 377, *picture section 11*
Reed, John 207, 214, 216
Referendum 1967 xv, 41, 43, 47, 133, 161
Refractory Girl magazine 219–20, 306
refuges, women's 166, 319–20
Reid, Gordon 195
Repin, Yve 217, 219, *picture section 14*
Resistance (Trotskyist organisation) 264–66, 269
Reynolds, Henry 122, 124, 125, 129
Reynolds, Malvina 78, 349, 370
Reynolds (Lyne), Margaret 118–37, 340, 343, 348, 351, 368, *picture section 7, 10*
RoadKnight, Margret 67, 70–82, 286–87, 341, 343, 345, 348, 349, 369–70, *picture section 5*
Robertson, Geoffrey 7–8, 52–69, 189, 341, 346, 347, 351, 370–71, *picture section 2, 8*

392

Index

Robeson, Paul 73–74, 81, 370
Robinson, Barry 13
Royal Commission into Aboriginal Deaths in Custody 1991 xii
Rubin, Dave 93–95
Ryan, Ronald 283–85, 347
Rylah, Arthur 285

Salmon, Gail 146
Samuels, Gordon 233
Santamaria BA 91, 139, 146, 275–76, 278, 330, 343
Save our Sons 79, 128–31
Schacht, Chris 196
schools 3–4, 30, 35–40, 53–56, 72–73, 76, 104–06, 108–10, 120–24, 136, 141, 143–44, 154–55, 160, 168, 172, 175, 189–90, 208, 225–27, 244–47, 256, 258, 263–69, 271–73, 278, 291, 293, 309–14, 318, 320–22, 324–27, 330–31, 344–46
Scribner, Bob 6, 330
Seeger, Pete 66, 78, 79, 245, 287
segregation 36, 160, 230
sexism 15, 318, 321, 340
  Ernie Awards for 356
  see also equality of sexes; feminism; Women's Liberation; women's movement
Sex Party 291, 373
sexual liberation xviii, 182, 206–07, 210–14, 217, 256, 290–91, 329, 332, 336, 344; *see also* Free Love
Sharp, Martin 66, 177, 178
Smith, Shirley (Mum Shirl) 45, 240
Sobski, Jozefa 308–23, 340, 341, 342, 343, 346, 348, 372, *picture section 12*
Sobski, Wojciech 307–09, 310–12, 317, 323
Spielman (Voysey), Eva 259–60, 262, 264, 269–70
Spielman, George 259, 261,
Spigelman, Jim 6, 67–68
Springbok rugby union team *see* anti-apartheid movement

Stackpool, Chief Inspector 11, *picture section 6*
Stolen Generations 156, 158, 170
strikes
  industrial 252–53
  school 273–74
Student Action for Aborigines 230
student power 149, 194
Student Underground newsletter 265, 267, 269
Students for Revolutionary Action 268
suburbia, middle-class 1, 8, 53–54, 208, 242–43, 258–59, 261, 163, 291
Summers, Anne 116, 319
Summy, Ralph 145, 149
Sumner, John 282
Swan, Robbie 183, 189, 290–305, 341, 343, 344, 345, 347, 373, *picture section 14*
Sweeney, Helen 215
Sydney University 5, 60, 62–63, 96, 108, 230, 306, 332
  DLP Club 328–29, 331, 333, 334, 335, 337–38
  Dramatic Society 8, 176
  Front Lawn meetings 13, 21, 28–29
  Labor Club 28–29, 60, 331
  Proctorial Board 7–8, 32, 61, *picture section 8*
  protest at increase in library fines 7, 60
  Regiment 27–29, 150, 332
St John's College 226, 228, 229
St Paul's College 109–10
Students for a Democratic Society 28–29, 145, 197, 247, 332
Students' Representative Council 6, 13, 58–59, 60, 197–98
Women's College 8, 18–19, 20, 24, 62, 110–11
Sykes, Roberta (Bobbi) 131, 132, 167, 340, 348

teachers, importance of 7, 18, 35, 108, 141, 189, 244–45, 292, 324, 343–44
tennis 138–39, 147, 155
Tent Embassy *see* Aboriginal Tent Embassy
theatre
  alternative and street 162–65, 177, 184–85, 218, 280–83, 286, 345, 357, *picture section 4, 16*
  Black 162–65
  Futurist 177
  mainstream 75, 170, 175, 260, 271, 275, 289
  university 121, 176
  see also Happenings
Third World Bookshop 265, 269
Thompson, Fred 128
Thompson, Jack 150
Thompson, Lyn (Craigie) 42, 161, 167
Thompson, Mitch 145, 146, 149, 151
Thoms, Albie 176, 177, 178–80, 182, 185, 344
Tobin, Peter 234
Tomasetti, Glen 75, 76, 77, 79, 80, 85, 341
Torsh (Humphreys), Dany 7, 318, 321, 341
Townsville 125–31, 135–37, 348, 368, *picture section 10*
trade unions 93, 127, 150–51, 188, 202, 248–49, 252–57, 270, 321, 346, 348, *picture section 6*
  Rebel Unions 253, 255
  see also Builders Labourers' Federation; Furnishing Trades Union; green bans; strikes
Tranby Co-operative College 229
transcendental meditation 303–05, 344, 373
Travers, Basil Holmes ('Jika') 106–07
Trotsky, Leon 270
Trotskyism 88, 197, 264, 287, 297, 340

True Believers television series 275
Turon, Arwed 197, 198

unions *see* trade unions
universities *see* Monash University; Sydney University; University of Adelaide; University of New South Wales; University of Queensland; University of Tasmania
University of Adelaide 192–93
University of New South Wales 13, 42, 176, 233, 316, 359
University of Queensland 125, 138, 144–50, 369, *picture section 2*
  Students for Democratic Action 145, 147
  Vietnam Action Committee 145
University of Tasmania 121
Uren, Tom 57, 80, 337–38

Vatican II 312–13, 328
Vietnam War 9, 14, 57, 66, 236, 246, 294, 304, 349
  television coverage of 6, 14, 247, 267, 349
  see also anti-Vietnam movement
Voysey, Helen 258–74, 343, 346, 347, 351, 374, *picture section 1, 9*
Voysey, Lew 259, 260, 262, 266, 269, 270
Voysey, Peter 267, 269–70

Walker, Denis 235, *picture section 11*
Wallace, Norm 248
Walsh, Richard 6, 66, 178
Warriors of the Aboriginal Resistance 49
Waterford, Jack 294, 297
Watters, Frank 205, 214, 216
Watters Gallery 184, 205–06, 218, 220–21, 354, 360, *picture section 14*
Wave Hill Station 133, 198
Webb, Rod 182
Whaley, George 280, 283, 288, *picture section 16*

Index

Wheatley, Nadia xi–xv, 9, 11, 16–32, 62, 341, 343, 348, 375–76, *picture section 1, 4, 11*
White Australia Policy xiv, xvi, 53, 56, 66, 347, 350
White, Chris 199
White, Patrick 113, 258, 366
Whitlam, Gough xii, 256, *picture section 8*
  Dismissal xvi, 103, 366
  election xvi, 14, 107, 112–15, 135, 350
  government 56, 234, 319, 368
Williams, Bert 47
Williams, Bindi 162
Williams, Clive 228–29, 344
Williams, Gary 37, 40, 42, 67, 161, 223–41, 341, 344, 348, 351, 352, 377–78, *picture section 6, 10, 11*
Williams, Jessie 224, 241
Windschuttle, Keith 63
Women's Art Movement 219–20, 222, 354

Women's Electoral Lobby 135, 297, 372
Women's Liberation 80, 166, 214, 219, 306–07, 318–19, 321, 355, 372
women's movement 166–67, 207, 321; *see also* feminism; Women's Liberation
women's refuges 166, 319–20
women workers 251–52
Wootten, Hal 44, 233–34
Wren, John 277
Wynhausen, Elizabeth 115, 116

Yellow House, the 180, 185, 360
Young Labor Association 85–86, 193, 195–96, 201
Young, Mick 196
Young, Nancy 65

Zakswiez, Kasimir 304
Zdenkowski, George 233